Japan's Security Policy and the ASEAN Regional Forum

The early 1990s witnessed a new development in the diplomatic dimension of Japan's security policy. Reversing its long resistance to any initiatives for security multilateralism in the Asia-Pacific region, Japan began to explore the possibility of forming a region-wide forum for multilateral security dialogue. Active diplomacy from Japan contributed significantly to the foundation of the ASEAN Regional Forum (ARF) in 1994, providing the only region-wide security institution in the Asia-Pacific.

Drawing on primary documentation and extensive interviews with Japanese policy makers, this book provides a comprehensive analysis of Japan's changing policy and viewpoint towards security multilateralism in the Asia-Pacific after the Cold War. Yuzawa looks at the role Japan has played in the evolution of the ARF, examining in detail a number of key areas including:

- Japan's initial motivations, expectations, and objectives for promoting security multilateralism in the Asia-Pacific region;
- Japan's diplomacy for achieving these objectives and roles in the ARF over the twelve years since its formation;
- the effectiveness and limitations of the ARF with regards to national and Asia-Pacific security; and
- the problems and difficulties that arose as a result of Japan's post-Cold War security policy of simultaneously pursuing two differing security approaches.

In using Japan's experiences in security institution-building in the region as a case study, the book not only illuminates the future direction of Japan's security policy but also questions the validity of contending theoretical perspectives in understanding the role and effectiveness of the ARF.

Japan's Security Policy and the ASEAN Regional Forum represents the first empirical study within the area to contribute to the current academic debate and as such will appeal to scholars of Japanese studies, politics, history, Asia-Pacific security and international relations.

Takeshi Yuzawa is Research Fellow at the Japan Institute of International Affairs. His research interests include Asia-Pacific security, Japan's foreign and security policy, International Relations Theory.

Sheffield Centre for Japanese Studies/Routledge Series

Series Editor: Glenn D. Hook
Professor of Japanese Studies, University of Sheffield

This series, published by Routledge in association with the Centre for Japanese Studies at the University of Sheffield, both makes available original research on a wide range of subjects dealing with Japan and provides introductory overviews of key topics in Japanese Studies.

Japan's Security Policy and the ASEAN Regional Forum

The Search for Multilateral Security in the Asia-Pacific

Takeshi Yuzawa

Routledge
Taylor & Francis Group

LONDON AND NEW YORK

First published 2007
by Routledge
2 Park Square, Milton Park, Abingdon, Oxon OX14 4RN

Simultaneously published in the USA and Canada
by Routledge
270 Madison Ave, New York, NY 10016

*Routledge is an imprint of the Taylor & Francis Group, an informa
business*

Typeset in Times New Roman by Taylor and Francis Books
Printed and bound in Great Britain by TJ International Ltd, Padstow,
Cornwall

British Library Cataloguing in Publication Data
A catalogue record for this book is available from the British Library

Library of Congress Cataloging-in-Publication Data
Yuzawa, Takeshi, 1971–
Japan's security policy and the ASEAN Regional Forum: the search
for multilateral security in the Asia-Pacific/by Takeshi Yuzawa.
p. cm.
Includes bibliographical references and index.
ISBN 0-415-40337-5 (hardback{:}alk. paper) 1. National security –
Japan. 2. ASEAN Regional Forum. 3. National security – Southeast
Asia. 4. National security – East Asia. 5. ASEAN. 6. Security,
International. I. Title.
UA845.Y89 2006
355.033552–dc22
2006019583

ISBN13: 978-0-415-40337-5 (hbk)
ISBN13: 978-0-203-96497-2 (ebk)

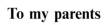

To my parents

Contents

Acknowledgements

Most of the research for this book was undertaken while I was a doctoral student at the Department of International Relations, the London School of Economics (LSE). I would like to express my deepest gratitude to my former supervisor, the late professor Michael Leifer. His guidance, keen insight and stimulation helped me to overcome the initial difficulties I had in approaching this project and the research tradition set by his work has had a significant influence on this study. It was a great pleasure and privilege to have been chosen as his student at LSE. I am also very grateful to Dr Christopher R. Hughes who became my supervisor after the unfortunate passing of Professor Leifer. It need not be said that this study could never have been completed without his guidance, encouragement and numerous valuable comments and suggestions.

For generous scholarly and friendly assistance during my field research, I would like to thank to the academic staff of the National Institute of Defence Studies (NIDS) at Tokyo, especially Kondō Shigekatsu and Ono Keishi, who invited me to the NIDS and kindly organised a workshop on my research topic and gave me many opportunities for discussions with their colleagues. I wish also to thank many Japanese scholars, among others Morimoto Satoshi, Nishihara Masashi, Soeya Yoshihide and Jinbo Ken, as well as the many government officials, both current and retired, who spared their time to discuss my research. My gratitude also goes to many academics outside Japan, among other Benjamin Self and Michael Yahuda, for providing valuable comments and suggestions.

For helpful suggestions and advice during the task of turning the PhD dissertation into the present book, I am grateful to Christopher W. Hughes, Phil Deans and anonymous reviewers at Routledge. Portions of this book have been published in *The Pacific Review* (vol.18, no.4, 2005), and parts of Chapter 4 have appeared in *Asian Survey* (vol. 46, no.5, 2006).

Finally, I would like to thank my parents, Yuzawa Katsuo and Takako, for their unfailing support in allowing me to pursue my PhD. This book is dedicated to them. I take full responsible for any factual errors and remaining shortcomings.

All Japanese names appear in this book with family name first unless they are presented in note references, in which the order is as used in English.

List of Abbreviations

ABM	Anti-Ballistic Missile
ACSA	Acquisition and Cross-Servicing Agreement
AMM	ASEAN Ministerial Meeting
APEC	Asia-Pacific Economic Cooperation
ARF	ASEAN Regional Forum
ARF-RMIC	ARF Regional Maritime Information Centre
ASDF	Air Self-Defence Force
ASEAN	Association of Southeast Asian Nations
ASEAN-ISIS	ASEAN Institutes of Strategic and International Studies
ASEAN PMC	ASEAN Post-Ministerial Conference
ASEAN+3	Association of Southeast Asian Nations, plus China, Japan and South Korea.
ASO	Annual Security Outlook
BMD	Ballistic Missile Defence
BPND	Basic Policy of National Defence
CBM	Confidence Building Measure
CSCAP	Council for Security Cooperation in the Asia-Pacific
CSCE	Conference on Security and Cooperation in Europe
CTBT	Comprehensive Test Ban Treaty
CT-TC	Counter-Terrorism and Transnational Crime
DOM	Defence Officials Meeting
DPJ	Democratic Party of Japan
EAEC	East Asia Economic Caucus
EASI	East Asia Strategic Initiative
EASR	East Asia Strategic Review
EEP	Experts and Eminent Person
EEZ	Exclusive Economic Zone
EGM on TC	Experts Group Meeting on Transnational Crime
EU	European Union
FDI	Foreign Direct Investment
GNP	gross national product
GSDF	Ground Self-Defence Force
G7	Group of seven major industrialised countries

G8	Group of seven major industrialised countries and Russia
IAEA	International Atomic Energy Agency
ICBM	intercontinental ballistic missiles
IMF	International Monetary Found
INTERFET	International Force for East Timor
IPCL	International Peace Cooperation Law
IR	international relation
ISG	Interssesional Support Group
ISM	Intersessional Meeting
JDA	Japan Defence Agency
JIIA	Japan Institute of International Affairs
KEDO	Korean Peninsula Energy Development Organization
LDP	Liberal Democratic Party
MIRV	Multiple Independently targetable Re-entry Vehicle
MITI	Ministry of International Trade and Industry
MOF	Ministry of Finance
MOFA	Ministry of Foreign Affairs
MRM	Mutual Reassurance Measure
MSA	Mutual Security Act
MSDF	Maritime Self-Defence Force
MSOM	Maritime Specialist Officials Meeting
NAM	Non-Aligned Movement
NATO	North Atlantic Treaty Organisation
NDPO	National Defence Policy Outlines
NEACD	Northeast Asian Cooperation Dialogue
NIRA	National Institute of Research Advancement
NLD	National League for Democracy
NPA	National Police Agency
NPT	Nuclear Non-Proliferation Treaty
NSF	National Safety Force
NTWD	Navy Theatre-Wide Defence
OAS	Organisation of American States
ODA	Official Development Assistance
OECD	Organisation for Economic Cooperation and Development
OSCE	Organisation for Security and Cooperation of Europe
PAC	Patriot Advanced Capability
PD	Preventative Diplomacy
PECC	Pacific Economic Cooperation Conference
PKO	Peacekeeping operations
PLA	People's Liberation Army
RIMPAC	Rim of the Pacific
SACO	Special Action Committee on Okinawa
SDF	Self-Defence Force
SDI	Strategic Defence Initiative
SDP	Social Democratic Party

SLOC	sea-lines of communication
SLORC	State Law and Order Restoration Council
SM	Standard Missile
SOM	Senior Official Meeting
TAC	Treaty of Amity and Cooperation in Southeast Asia
TBM	Trust-Building Measure
TMD	Theatre Missile Defence
UN	United Nations
UNCLS	United Nations Convention on the Law of the Sea
UNPCC	United Nations Peace Cooperation
UNRCA	United Nation Register of Conventional Arms
UNSC	United Nation Security Council
WMD	weapons of mass destruction
ZOFAN	Zone of Peace, Freedom and Neutrality

Introduction

Japan's security policy has undergone important developments in many ways since the end of the Cold War. This can be seen in the enactment of the International Peace Cooperation Law in 1992, which enabled Tokyo to dispatch Self Defence Forces (SDF) to Cambodia as part of United Nations Peace Keeping Operations (UNPKO) in 1993, marking the first overseas deployment of SDF, and subsequently to Angola, Mozambique, East Timor and elsewhere. A major turning point in Japan's international security role came again in 2003 when the National Diet passed the Iraq Reconstruction Assistance Special Measure Law, leading to the dispatch of ground troops in January 2004 for the first time since the end of World War II to a country in which fighting was still going on. While seeking to increase its military contribution to international security, since the mid-1990s, Japan also embarked on the strengthening of its defence cooperation with the USA, resulting in the issue of the Japan-US Joint Declaration on Security in 1996 and the new guidelines of the Japan-US defence cooperation in 1997. The revision of the guidelines, which explicitly expanded the scope of bilateral defence cooperation from defending Japan's home islands to dealing with regional crises not involving direct attacks on Japan, signified Japan's readiness to assume greater military responsibility for the stability of the Asia-Pacific region. The Japan-US defence cooperation has been further bolstered recently by the Japanese decision to deploy a Theatre Missile Defence (TMD) system in December 2003 and the issue of a joint statement at the meeting of the Japan-US Security Consultative Committee in February 2005, which expressed their intention to expand the scope of the bilateral security cooperation from the Asia-Pacific region to global areas.

While these moves represent the tradition of Japan's incremental approach to developing the military dimension of Japan's security policy, the beginning of the 1990s also witnessed the seeds of a new development in the diplomatic aspect. In July 1991, reversing its long resistance to any initiatives for multilateral security in the region, Japan proposed to establish a region-wide forum for multilateral security dialogue. As Paul Midford noted, 'this Japanese initiative, known as the Nakayama proposal, represents a dramatic departure from Japan's previous passive security policy because it marked the first time since World War II that Japan had taken the initiative in regional political and security affairs in the face of US opposition'.[1] This initiative and Japan's subsequent diplomacy significantly contributed to the foundation of the ASEAN Regional Forum (ARF) in 1994, the only region-wide forum for security dialogue and cooperation in the Asia-Pacific.[2] Japan's growing interest in and support for regional multilateral security in the early 1990s in part reflected the emergence of new thinking about regional security among Japanese policy makers, identifying the need to develop a new security approach to deal with the multiple threats and opportunities of the post-Cold War era. Indeed, Japan embarked on a multifaceted approach to regional security which aimed to strengthen Japan-US defence cooperation and develop a region-wide security institution simultaneously in order to cope with greater uncertainties in the regional security environment.

This book explores changes in Japan's conception of and policy toward *security multilateralism*[3] in the Asia-Pacific region after the end of the Cold War (from 1989–2005) with special reference to the ARF. Specifically, this study mainly asks the following sets of questions:

1) Why and how did Japan come to embrace regional security multilateralism in the early 1990s? What were Japan's initial expectations and objectives for promoting regional security multilateralism?
2) What problems and difficulties arise with Japan's attempt to promote a region-wide security institution in the Asia-Pacific and with its post-Cold War security policy of simultaneously pursuing two differing security approaches, the strengthening of the Japan-US alliance and the promotion of regional security institutions, most notably the ARF?
3) What are the effectiveness and limitations of the ARF with regards to Japan's national and regional security?
4) What are the effects of Japan's experiences in the ARF on its initial view of regional security multilateralism and the implications of this for the direction of its overall security policy?

In the interest of pursuing the above questions, this book aims to contribute to the scholarship on Japanese security, the international relations of the Asia-Pacific, and International Relations (IR) theory. For scholarship on Japan's security policy, the empirical analysis of Japan's policy toward regional security multilateralism over the decade furthers our understanding of this new aspect of its post-Cold War security policy. As discussed more fully below, Japan's diplomacy in the ARF has been neither well documented nor sufficiently analysed in the literature while the attention of recent studies on Japan's security policy has been given overwhelmingly to the Japan-US alliance.[4] Moreover, although there has been an impressive amount of scholarship on Japan's role in multilateralism, these studies have tended to focus on either Japan's policy towards the UN or its role in promoting Asia-Pacific regional multilateralism in the realm of political economy centring on APEC.[5] Given that many scholars of Japan's international relations have suggested that its active involvement in the ARF is an important feature of its post-Cold War security policy, this is somewhat surprising.

For scholarship of both the Asia-Pacific and IR, as discussed in more detail below, the case study of Japan's experiences in the ARF over twelve years serves not only as an empirical basis for the understanding of the roles and efficacies of international institutions in the realm of security affairs, which has been the subject of intense debate between differing theoretical paradigms of IR, but also as a vehicle for the comparative study of security institutions in different regions. It also promotes our knowledge of problems that arise with the process of security institution building in the Asia-Pacific region.

Japan, the ARF and multilateral security in the Asia-Pacific

Japan's growing interest in promoting security multilateralism in the Asia-Pacific region in the early 1990s, represented by its active contribution to the formation of the ARF, was a significant development in its regional security policy. Until that time Japan had intentionally avoided getting directly involved in regional security outside the framework of the Japan-US alliance and thus any Japanese initiatives for regional security in the face of the US opposition had been unthinkable. Notwithstanding this significance, however, there have been only a small number of studies that have examined this development.[6] One of the distinctive studies among these has been Kawasaki Tsuyoshi's work. Kawasaki's approach that attempted to illuminate and conceptualise Japan's perspective on regional security multilateralism in the inception years of the ARF (1991–95) from three IR theories provides this study with a useful starting point.[7] Yet, it is clear that more detailed research is necessary to comprehend the complex process of changes in Japan's conception of and policy towards regional security multilateralism in that period. In particular, there is a need to provide an adequate account of the connection between the conceptions of policy makers and Japan's actual policy, which preceding studies do not fully deal with. The questions must be addressed, for instance, of how and why Japan came to embrace regional security multilateralism, why such an idea spread rapidly within the mainstream of Japan's policy makers, and how it was actually translated into Japan's official policy. Consequently, the existing studies have not fully captured the evolution of the Japanese conception of regional security multilateralism during that period. This study will fill these gaps by conducting an empirical analysis of Japan's ARF policy that allows us to comprehend the evolving character of Japan's conceptions and provide insights into the policy making process.

This book is also the first major study to conduct a detailed examination of Japan's actual diplomacy in the ARF covering the period from the mid 1990s to the early twenty-first century. The implementation phase of Japan's ARF policy is largely neglected by the existing studies, which are more concerned to focus on the stage of formulation from the early 1990s to the mid-1990s, when the multilateral impulse grew in Japan's policy thinking, as mentioned above. Some of these studies have depicted Japan as an unfailing supporter for the ARF in spite of widespread criticisms of its ineffectiveness based on the assumption that the idea of 'cooperative security' or a 'multifaceted approach to regional security', has begun to take hold in Japan's policy thinking since the early 1990s. However, it seems that such arguments overemphasise the continuity of one specific norm or idea over time and lack an empirical basis because their studies only look at the stage of policy making and the open expressions of Japan's policies. In other words, the whole process of Japan's policy towards regional security multilateralism cannot be considered without taking account of the implementation stage, from which various problems and difficulties arise. As Christopher Hill notes, 'implementation is integral to the whole policy making cycle because, at the least, implementation feeds back into the original decision and often also begets new problems'.[8] In order to achieve comprehensive understanding of Japan's ARF policy, this study conducts a detailed analysis of its implementation stage, namely Japan's diplomacy in the ARF, revealing how Japanese policy makers have actually implemented their decisions and policies, what problems have arisen out of implementation, and how the outcomes of implementation have fed back to them and influenced their original views or ideas of regional security multilateralism. As will be stated more fully below, Japan's disappointing experiences in the ARF over twelve years since its formation considerably diluted Japan's enthusiasm for regional security multilateralism, which once intensified in the early 1990s.

The same sorts of problems stemming from the inadequacy of the empirical analysis of the implementation phase can also be applied to the wider field of Japanese security studies. While many scholars of Japanese security have embraced the idea of the multifaceted approach, arguing that a bilateral (the strengthening of the Japan-US defence cooperation) and multilateral security approach (developing a cooperative security framework like the ARF) can function complementarily and that the combination of the two approaches can more effectively ensure Japan's national as well as regional security, again, no serious attempt has been made to empirically examine whether Japanese policy makers have been able to enmesh the two differing approaches into its security policy in practice. It is theoretically possible to boost two approaches at the same time, but in practice the implementation of the multifaceted approach is extremely difficult.

Japan's security policy in competing analytical frameworks

The analysis of Japan's diplomacy and experience in the ARF has important implications not only for research on one dimension of Japan's security
policy but also for the wider debate on the direction of its overall security
policy. This is because the success or failure of Japan's ARF policy, which
represents the country's effort to promote security multilateralism in the
Asia-Pacific, would inevitably affect policy makers' beliefs about the utilities
of a multilateral security approach that has been one of the major pillars of
the nation's regional security policy since the early 1990s. As will be discussed in more detail in Chapter 1 and 2, Japan's growing expectations for
regional security multilateralism in the early 1990s generated a new way of
thinking about Japan's approach to Asia-Pacific security and thus gave
influences over the course of its regional security policy during this period.
In this regard, it may be said that changes in Japan's beliefs about the efficacies of regional security multilateralism as a result of its experiences in the
ARF may have important ramifications for new trends in Japan's security
policy.

In the literature, Japanese security policy is often characterised as passive
and reactive. This description is mainly a reflection of Japan's post-war
policy of using military force only in response to direct attacks on Japanese
territories, underpinned by Article 9 of the Constitution as well as its long
tradition of utilising economic power as a major instrument of contributing
to regional stability in East Asia. The new developments in the military
dimension of Japan's security policy after the end of the Cold War described
at the beginning of this chapter, however, have raised the question of whether
Japanese security policy has begun to move in a new direction. Some
analysts have regarded these developments as evidence of Japan's changing
policy thinking that increasingly realises the need to explicitly utilise military power as an instrument for contributing to regional as well as international stability and is thus leading Japan to pursue a 'normal' security
policy.[9] Others have claimed that the traditional political forces of anti-
militarism have persisted and will continuously lead Japan to focus on
economic and diplomatic means of security.[10]

The latter position is represented by constructivist scholars, such as Peter
Katzenstein and Thomas Berger. Their arguments begin with the rejection
of neorealist accounts of Japan's security policy, which assume that structural
forces will lead Japan to build massive military capabilities to countervail
other major powers because the increase of its economic capabilities to the
great power level places it at the centre of regional and global affairs.[11] By
rejecting structural approaches, Katzenstein and Berger focus on the roles
of domestic cultural and institutional factors in shaping Japan's security
policy. They argue that the Japanese culture of anti-militarism, which
became institutionalised in the Japanese political system in the immediate
post-war period, have made Japanese policy makers highly reluctant to

greatly expand the nation's military capabilities and use military power as an instrument of addressing Japan's security interests.[12] The findings of their studies lead them to contend that significant shifts in Japan's culture of anti-militarism and in its security policy are unlikely unless major shocks, such as the dissolution of the Japan-US Security Treaty, seriously damage the credibility of Japan's current security policy. However, they also add that even in the face of such an event, domestic political forces will still constrain their choices of new policy options.[13] Consequently, Katzenstein concludes that 'Japan's security policy will continue to be largely shaped by the domestic factors rather than the international forces, such as balance of power' and thus 'Japan is likely to maintain comprehensive security policy even if the US military presence should weaken'.[14]

Some analysts, however, have drawn a somewhat different conclusion from Japan's new security policies, suggesting that Japan's strategic culture is gradually shifting toward greater realism.[15] For example, Michael Green argues that Japan's foreign policy thinking has been increasingly influenced by strategic consideration of balance of power and growing sensibilities regarding external security threats. According to Green, the emerging strategic culture of realism in Japan is a result of changes in the domestic political environment, such as the growing aspirations of new generations and political realignment, as well as material changes, including the decline of Japan's economic power and growing insecurity about China and North Korea, all of which have shaken Japan's pacifist culture. Whilst arguing that the important elements of Japan's post-war security policy still remain, such as domestic normative constraints on the use of force and the tendency to rely on economic tools for influence, Green concludes that the above changes will continue to force Japanese policy makers to pursue a more 'normal' national security policy, 'but ever increasing speed', and eventually to revise the Japanese Constitution, which enables the country to exercise the right of collective self-defence.[16]

The academic debate on the course of Japan's security policy is thus divided. In spite of looking at the same trends, scholars reach different conclusions. This is because 'there is evidence of both change and non-change' in Japan's security policy'.[17] Perhaps more importantly is that interpretation of new developments in Japan's security policy depends on the analytical framework that they use. While bearing these propensities in mind, this study takes part in the debate by providing new empirical findings drawn from the examinations of Japan's changing beliefs about the utilities of regional security multilateralism and its implications for new trends in Japan's security policy.

The ARF in three major theoretical perspectives

Finally, the empirical examinations of Japan's experience in the ARF would also contribute to the academic debate on the role of the ARF. In recent years, the question of whether regional institutions do matter in Asia-Pacific security order has been subject to an intense debate among specialists in the Asia-Pacific as well as scholars in IR as the interest, both empirical and theoretical, in the role of regional institutions has dramatically increased since the formation of the ARF. The debate is roughly split into two sides with those who argue that the ARF will play a significant role in reshaping the behaviour of regional major powers on the one hand and those who claim that it will remain 'adjuncts' to the region's balance of power dynamics on the other. The following section briefly examines competing theoretical perspectives on the role on international institutions, focusing on neoliberal institutionalism, realism and constructivism, and looks at extant studies on the ARF, each of which proceed from a different theoretical starting point and thus end with differing assessments and conclusions. This undertaking is necessary not only for realising this study's potential contribution to the debate on the role of the ARF but also for presenting a theoretical framework for analysing the complex nature of Japan's conception of regional security multilateralism that underlies its actual ARF policy. These theoretical perspectives offer important insights into how Japanese policy makers conceive and approach the ARF because policy makers themselves have appropriated a variety of paradigms.

Neoliberal institutionalists claim that security institutions can play a useful role in cultivating cooperative security relationships between states. They argue that security issues often create incentives for states to take cooperative efforts, but actual cooperation between states is often difficult to achieve because of concerns about being exploited and the dilemma of relative gains in the anarchic nature of the international system. Yet, the probability of security cooperation, according to them, can be increased if states can solve uncertainties regarding information about intentions, interests and actions of other states since a state's choice of policy does not merely depend on what it wants but also on what it believes other states seek. This is why states often attempt to form security institutions, according to institutionalists. By facilitating exchange of information, reducing transaction costs and developing norms and rules that regularise the behaviour of states, security institutions can help to solve those uncertainties, thus enhancing the predictability of their member states' actions and increasing the chance of long-term security cooperation.[18] Scholars examining the ARF through an institutionalist perspective stress the significance of the evolution of the multilateral security dialogue process and of the Confidence Building Measures (CBMs) in the ARF for enhancing mutual trust and military transparency between the participating countries. They argue that promoting greater transparency in military programmes and intention in the ARF can help reduce mutual suspicion and misperception among regional countries, thus ameliorating the security dilemma.[19]

Contrary to neoliberal institutionalists and constructivists, realists are highly suspicious of the roles of multilateral security institutions in managing international order. Realists claim that in the anarchic nature of the international environment, in which states must rely on self-help strategies, states often fail to engage in cooperative actions even in the face of common interest because they are motivated primarily by relative gains concerns when considering cooperation.[20] Realists admit that states sometimes act through institutions, but this largely reflects calculations of self-interest based on the international distribution of power. In this line of thought, states only cooperate with one another when facing a significant security threat since balance of power logic often causes states to create alliances to deter aggressors.[21] Because of these reasons, realists claim that institutions can affect the prospects for cooperation only marginally. They basically have no effect on either state behaviour or the prospects for international stability since, as Mearsheimer notes, 'the cause of war and peace are a function of the balance of power and institutions largely reflect the distribution of power'.[22] In this regard, security institutions only serve as a venue for power politics and are used by states as mere tools for maintaining or expanding their own national interests.

Realist oriented scholars studying Asia-Pacific security are thus highly sceptical of the ARF's capacity to shape regional order.[23] Among others, Michael Leifer represents this line of perspective on the ARF. While it may be not appropriate to describe him as a realist, as his analytical framework incorporates non-power factors, such as norms, identities, culture and historical legacies, Leifer's final assessment of the utilities of the ARF clearly shares many common points with a realist pessimistic balance of power interpretation of the role of security institutions:

> Indeed, the prerequisite for a successful ARF may well be the prior existence of a stable balance of power. The central issue in the case of the ARF is whether, in addition to diplomatic encouragement for a culture of cooperation driven partly by economic interdependence, the region shows the makings of a stable, supporting balance or distribution of power that would allow the multilateral venture to proceed in circumstances of some predictability. The ARF's structural problem is that its viability seems to depend on the prior existence of a stable balance, but it is not really in a position to create it.[24]

Leifer hence asserts that it is a 'categorical mistake' to assume that the ARF can actually solve regional problems and conflict. The maximum value of the ARF, according to him, is to make 'a modest contribution to a viable balance of power in the Asia-Pacific' by providing an additional point of diplomatic contact for regional major powers.[25]

Finally, from a constructivist perspective, security institutions can do more than facilitate the exchange of information. They can provide cooperation by helping redefine or alter state identities and interests. Constructivists argue that the interests and preferences of states are defined or redefined through social interactions among them. According to constructivists, through systematic interactions over time, for instance in international institutions, states are socialised into a specific set of norms and expectations, which define acceptable and legitimate state behaviour, and this may lead them to form collective identities and interests.[26] In the long-term, such collective identities in turn lead them to create a security community, composed of shared knowledge in which states trust one another to resolve disputes without war.[27]

In recent years, more scholars have examined the ARF through the lens of constructivism.[28] Constructivist oriented scholars evaluate the potential roles of the ARF for regional security by exploring the possible application of the ASEAN model of security cooperation to the wider Asia-Pacific regional forum. At the forefront of this movement stands Amitav Acharya. Acharya argues that ASEAN is moving toward a nascent security community as ASEAN countries are forming a sort of collective identity by their social interactions through adherence to a set of norms called the 'ASEAN Way', among which are non-use of force, non-interference in internal affairs of other states, and a decision-making process based on informal consultation and consensus-building.[29] While acknowledging the difficulties of adopting the ASEAN Way in a wider Asia-Pacific security arena, Acharya contends that in the long-term, the ARF, which embraces the ASEAN norms, may be able to generate a collective identity among the participating countries. Acharya, for instance, claims that:

> The usefulness of the ARF will be partly determined by structural conditions which constrain the traditional balancing options by the Great Powers, limit their ability to ensure stability and predictability, and thereby create an opportunity for lesser actors to seek a role in the management of international order. Through the ARF, ASEAN may be able to exercise a degree of influence over Great Power geopolitics. In the final analysis, therefore, the ARF may be a useful tool of regional order in more ways than as a mere adjunct approach to balance of power mechanisms. In the short-term, the ARF may help shape the balance of power by providing norms of restraint and avenues of confidence building among the major powers. In the long-term, the ARF may even enable states to transcend the balance of power approach.[30]

Alastair Iain Johnston demonstrates the possibility of identity transformation in the ARF. Johnston observes that China, which was traditionally sceptical about security multilateralism, increasingly adopted a positive and proactive attitude toward the ARF. It is asserted that such changes occurred in part because the ARF socialised Chinese officials through its dialogue process and thus altered their beliefs about their own national interests.[31]

The paradigmatic debates in the field of Asia-Pacific security have intensified in recent years as realists' materialist explanations have been challenged by constructivist approaches. Sorpong Peou, for instance, argues that 'a constructivist approach is closer to the truth than balance of power realism since it seeks to explain regional security by looking at a wide range of ideational, inter-subjective as well as material factors'.[32] However, whereas it is true that a material presentation of realism is alone not sufficient to explain and understand the evolution and role of regional institutions as well as the nature of states' approach towards them, a parsimonious constructivist explanation is not without its problems. Many constructivist studies of the ARF, for instance, seem to overemphasise the significance of security dialogues or the 'ASEAN Way' for changing the preferences and identities of regional countries without providing substantial empirical evidences that can support their claims.

These observations suggest that it is necessary to examine the evolution and efficacy of the ARF based not on a narrow theory driven analysis that sticks with a single perspective even in the face of anomalous evidence for the need to maintain theoretical parsimony but a problem driven analysis underpinned by extensive empirical research. In this regard, the detailed empirical analysis of Japan's experience in the ARF over twelve years would not only further our understanding of the problem of security institution-building in the Asia-Pacific region but also serve as an empirical basis for testing the validity of the three major theoretical perspectives on the role of the ARF and on the nature of state approach to it. As almost twelve years have passed since the foundation of the ARF, the time is ripe for providing a meaningful assessment of the utilities and limitations of the ARF for regional security.

Research method

As stated at the beginning of this chapter, one of the main objects of this study is to explore changes in Japan's conception of regional security multilateralism underlying actual policy after the end of the Cold War. While perception has become important for constructivist approaches to IR, it has in fact been acknowledged as an important factor in the sub-discipline of Foreign Policy Analysis (FPA) for a somewhat longer time. Psychological approaches to the scholarship of FPA have long suggested that beliefs, image, and perceptions held by the policy makers have a significant impact on decision-making since they influence the process of the policy maker's diagnosis and cognition of phenomenon, thus significantly affecting their foreign policy choices.[33]

This book makes extensive use of the term 'conception', a psychological term that I take to refer to complex attitudinal states giving rise to dispositions. This term encompasses but is not exhaustively defined by 'views', 'beliefs', 'perceptions' and 'expectations'. Thus, for the purposes of this book, 'Japan's conception of regional security multilateralism' refers to a range of psychological states including views, beliefs, perceptions and expectations pertaining to the form, roles and efficacies of regional security institutions (in this case, the ARF), shared by the mainstream of Japan's policy makers in charge of security policy. This book examines how such conceptions changed over the course of this study and guided actual policy. Particular focus is given to conceptions held within MOFA since it is this organisation that is largely responsible for the formulation and implementation of Japan's ARF policy. MOFA's dominant role reflects not only the nature of the ARF, in which the main participants are members of the foreign ministries rather than the defence ministries, but also its overall responsibility for devising Japan's security policy, including both diplomatic and military aspects.[34] In the light of the rigid civilian control system in Japan, MOFA holds far greater power in overall security policy making than the Japan Defence Agency (JDA) let alone the SDF (Self Defence Force), though the JDA's policy making role has increased dramatically since the mid-1990s when JDA officials played critical roles in redefining the Japan-US alliance.[35]

In contrast with the focus on the role of MOFA in policy making, this study gives little attention to the role played by politicians. In general, Japanese politicians do not exert direct control or even significant influence over the formulation of ARF policy. As will be discussed in more detail in Chapter 7, Japanese politicians, including the prime minister, play a much less important role in the formulation of security policy than the bureaucracy due to a number of factors including the bureaucrats' control of information needed for policy formulation, a shortage of staff, and even a lack of interest in security policy issues. Although an increasing number of Diet members in the two major political parties, namely the ruling Liberal Democratic Party (LDP) and the opposing Democratic Party of Japan (DPJ), have become willing to take the initiative in security policy making in recent years, their attention has mainly been devoted to the normalisation of Japan's security policy through the enhancement of Japan-US defence cooperation. As will be discussed in more detail in Chapters 2 and 7, whereas the idea of Asia-Pacific security multilateralism actually attracted great attention from some influential politicians in the early 1990s, it has been outside the mainstream of Japanese political debate since the late 1990s. The low level of interest shown by Japanese politicians has thus allowed MOFA to dominate Japan's ARF policy.

As mentioned already, however, the examination of policy makers' conceptions of regional security multilateralism is alone not adequate for understanding the complex nature of Japan's policy towards it. Policy makers' conceptions as well as policy making are influenced by many variables lying at the international, domestic and individual levels of analysis, such as the balance between state capabilities, the external threats and opportunities that the material environment provides, domestic political conditions, policy makers' experiences and shared ideas. For instance, external environmental factors must be taken into consideration since changes in the strategic environment of the Asia-Pacific region, such as shifts in the balance of material capabilities and the amelioration of diplomatic relations, have had significant impacts on policy makers' perceptions of external threats and opportunities, which are closely associated with their conceptions of regional security multilateralism. Moreover, as stated above, it is particularly important to investigate Japan's actual diplomacy and experience in the ARF. The interactions between Japan and other countries in the ARF over regional security issues as well as the outcomes of Japan's policy in terms of actual development of the ARF functions certainly influence the changes or continuity of the initial views of regional security multilateralism. In addition, an examination of Japan's domestic policy making agents is also necessary. The limitations of organisational capabilities at the disposal of foreign policy and inter-bureau rivalries within the domestic institution often prevent policy makers from smoothly implementing decisions and policies, as scholars of FPA suggest.[36] This investigation illuminates the domestic causes of the problems and difficulties complicating Japan's ARF policy, which again influence policy makers' conceptions of regional security multilateralism. In this regard, this study develops an eclectic analysis, which draws on the insights and strengths of various theoretical models in IR and thus does not solely focus on either ideational or material, domestic or international level factors.[37] Consequently, this study takes into account three levels of analysis – international, domestic and individual – and adopts appropriate theoretical models for each. An eclectic analysis is important since, as we will see in the following chapters, no single factor can fully explain changes in Japan's changing conceptions of and policy toward regional security multilateralism.

In the context of the nature of this study, a historical narrative approach should be adopted as its methodological approach. A historical narrative, which is often equated with what Alexander George termed 'a process tracing', fits well the study that implicitly or explicitly uses theories on several levels of analysis to attempt comprehensive understanding or explanations of the complex nature of international events.[38] The historical narrative approach is also useful for identifying the causal importance of different types of factors in the case of this study, because it allows us to trace empirically the temporal and potentially causal sequences of events, decisions, actions, within a specific case. Consequently, it permits a greater understanding of the origin, evolutions, and outcome of Japan's policy towards Asia-Pacific security multilateralism.

Sources

As for evidence, this book attempts to rely on primary sources as much as possible, including MOFA's internal documents, internal reports on the ARF activities produced by foreign ministries in other ARF countries, document materials distributed in the ARF meetings, policy papers written by practitioners and extensive interviews with them. This study has benefited from Japan's new freedom of information law, which has provided public access to internal documents at government ministries and agencies since May 1999. Although this new governmental procedure has not allowed the author to gain access to all of MOFA's internal documents about ARF policy, information gleaned from obtained materials has helped enable the author to discern how Japanese policy makers conceive the ARF at different periods and what policies they proposed or intended. MOFA's internal reports, as well as those of other foreign ministries, have also provided insights into the inner workings of ARF meetings, in which interactions between the participating countries take place.

This book has also conducted extensive interviews with both retired and current Japanese officials, security analysts and academics who have been either directly or indirectly involved in the formulation of Japan's security policies, as well as scholars outside Japan who have frequently participated in the ARF's Track Two meetings. The use of interviews is extremely important for this study since it provides information that document materials cannot cover and reveals insights into the decision-making process. Moreover, extensive interviews with policy makers offer important insights into the actual intentions and motivations behind Japan's ARF policy as well as real conceptions of the ARF, which have been seldom expressed in public statements.

Structure

This book is organised into three sections. The first section clarifies the origin and objectives of Japan's ARF policy by analysing shifts in Japan's policy toward regional security multilateralism during the period from the cusp of the end of the Cold War to the formation of the ARF (1989–93). This section combines the study of decision-making with a narrative that explores the effects of other causal levels of analysis. It is split into two chapters according to the following time phrase: from 1989 to 1991 and from 1992 to 1994, since in each phase Japan's interest in regional security multilateralism was sparked by different factors, thus constituting differing conceptions of regional security multilateralism at different periods. Chapter 1 explores the origin of the multilateral impulse in Japan's regional security policy. It scrutinises the policy making process for the Nakayama proposal and ponders major factors, such as changes in the regional security environment brought about by the end of the Cold War and the emergence of new ideas about regional security in MOFA, influencing Japan's initial motivation to embrace regional security multilateralism. Chapter 2 looks at further changes in Japan's conception of regional security multilateralism after the Nakayama proposal (1992–93). Whereas the Nakayama proposal proved to be abortive, Japan's initial enthusiasm for regional security multilateralism did not dwindle, rather it grew considerably during this period. Japan also continued to take the lead in the formation of a region-wide forum, but this time from 'behind'. In this context, this chapter examines Japan's behind-the-scenes diplomacy in the formation of the ARF and then considers the main factors affecting the surge of Japan's enthusiasm. This analysis is followed by a clarification of the objectives of Japan's ARF policy, looking at how the combination of these factors constituted Japan's initial conceptions of the ARF. The final part of this chapter considers the positions of Japan's ARF policy in the wider framework of Japan's overall regional security policy with special reference to its association with the Japan-US alliance.

The second section of this book looks into Japan's actual diplomacy in the ARF from 1994 to 2005. This section is essentially descriptive and looks at the following two differing dimensions of Japan's ARF policy: (1) diplomacy concerned with the promotion of cooperative security measures, namely CBMs and Preventive Diplomacy (PD) measures, and (2) diplomacy in multilateral dialogues on regional security issues through which Japan has tried to address its security concerns and interests. This section is split into two parts according to these two differing dimensions of Japan's policy, and each chapter carefully examines how Japan actually attempted to develop or utilise the ARF process along with its original expectations discussed in Chapter 2 and the extent to which the Forum could meet them. These examinations also illuminate the problems that arise with the process of security institution-building in the Asia-Pacific region. Chapter 3 focuses on Japan's endeavours to promote multilateral CBMs in the ARF. Enhancing military transparency and trust among regional countries through CBMs is one of the prime goals of Japan's ARF policy. The success of cooperation in this area is a prerequisite for further steps of security cooperation and is an important yardstick for the validity of neoliberal institutionalism. Japan's attempt to promote PD in the ARF is the focus of Chapter 4. The detailed analysis of Japan's experience in this area is critically important for assessing the ARF's potential to move beyond a talking shop to a credible security institution in the future. Chapter 5 looks at Japan's diplomacy in the process of multilateral security dialogue in the ARF during the first four years of its meetings (First to Fourth ARF meetings) with special reference to Japan's security relations with China. Rising tensions in bilateral security relations serve as a test of whether a cooperative security forum like the ARF can meet Japanese expectations for multilateral security diplomacy as a means of addressing its security interests, as specified in Chapter 2. Chapter 6 deals with Japan's diplomacy in the security dialogue process during the period from 1998 to 2005 (Fifth to Twelfth ARF meetings). Again this chapter looks at Japan's attempts to utilise the ARF to address its security concerns stemming from these events and examines the extent to which the Forum contributes to Japanese as well as regional security. Chapter 7 highlights the achievements and limitations of the ARF from the viewpoint of Japanese policy makers in order to see how their experiences in the Forum over the twelve years since its formation have influenced their conceptions of and policy towards regional security multilateralism. It argues that Japan's enthusiasm for regional security multilateralism, which intensified in the early 1990s, has begun to dwindle noticeably from the late 1990s, due mainly to its disappointing experience in the ARF, evinced by abortive efforts to promote cooperative security measures and the failings of the multilateral security approach to address its security interests. This chapter also explores other factors accounting for Japan's waning enthusiasm for regional security multilateralism, namely the frictions and difficulties at both the international and domestic levels, that Japanese policy makers have encountered in implementing ARF policy.

The final section of this book, consisting of the concluding chapter, returns to and addresses three main issues raised at the beginning; Japan's changing conceptions of and policy towards regional security multi-lateralism, the future direction of Japan's security policy, and the validity and limitations of three theoretical approaches to understanding the role of the ARF.

1 Japan's growing interest in Asia-Pacific security multilateralism

The road to the Nakayama proposal (1989–91)

Introduction

The main object of this chapter is to examine Japan's changing conception of and policy towards Asia-Pacific security multilateralism in the period from the cusp of the end of the Cold War up to the Nakayama proposal (1989–91). Specifically, it asks the following questions:

1) Why did Japan suddenly change its position on regional security multilateralism and propose to establish a region-wide forum for security dialogue in 1991?
2) What were the main objectives of Japan's multilateral security policy in this period?
3) What factors explain the rapid shift in Japan's conceptions of and policy toward regional security multilateralism?

This chapter first briefly reviews the evolution of Japan's security policy and its position on regional security multilateralism during the Cold War period. The second section of the chapter conducts a detailed analysis of the policy making process behind the Nakayama proposal. The analysis of this section begins with an individual level analysis, focusing on the role of Satō Yukio, a senior MOFA official, in the formation of the Nakayama proposal. Satō played a significant role in motivating the Japanese government to take the lead in promoting a region-wide security forum by advocating a new approach to the post-Cold War regional security, which became the intellectual underpinning of the Nakayama proposal. It then moves on to examine the underlying factors that influenced the Japan's decision to take the initiative in promoting a region-wide security forum. The focus of this section includes factors at the international level, including the opportunities and uncertainties presented by changes in the regional strategic environment with the end of the Cold War. The remainder of this chapter rethinks the relationship between the individual and international levels to explain the motivations behind the Nakayama proposal.

The evolution of Japan's security policy during the Cold War

It has been argued that Japan's foreign and security policy during the Cold War era was 'passive' and 'reactive'. While successfully ascending to great economic power status, Tokyo intentionally kept itself as far removed as possible from involvement in the Cold War contest. As a result, Japan was often criticised for eschewing international responsibilities commensurate with its economic power and pursuing a policy of 'one nation pacifism'. Japan's passivity in part reflected a well-defined strategy, which aimed to concentrate on the reconstruction of its economy while eschewing major military build-up by relying on the US for its national security. The strategy, which was developed by Prime Minister Yoshida Shigeru and thus came to be known as the 'Yoshida doctrine', has served as the basic framework for Japan's foreign and security policy ever since, though Yoshida himself admitted that Japan should not continue to rely on its security on the US.[1]

In September 1951, Yoshida signed the Japan-US Security Treaty in order to keep the US forces on Japanese soil while simultaneously concluding the San Francisco Peace Treaty, which restored Japan's sovereignty. The 1951 security treaty only granted bases to the US forces and did not oblige it to defend Japan, but the treaty was revised in 1960. The revised treaty provided that 'the US is granted the use of bases and facilities in Japan for the purpose of contributing to the security of Japan and the maintenance of international peace and security in the Far East' (Article VI).[2]

The build-up of Japanese military forces was also intentionally limited in line with the Yoshida doctrine. The intensification of the Cold War, marked by the outbreak of the Korean War in 1950, led Washington to press Tokyo to initiate a major build-up of its own military force. Despite significant pressure, the Japanese government made only minimal concessions, agreeing to set up the National Safety Force (NSF) with 110,000 personnel. In 1954, Japan passed the Two Defence Laws that formed the Japan Defence Agency (JDA) and the Self Defence Force (SDF), including the ground, maritime and air forces, out of the NSF. However, Japan's defence capability was still limited to those necessary for only minimum defence. For instance, the total number of SDF personnel was limited to 152,000, which was less than half of what Washington had demanded.[3] At the same time, the Japanese government formally articulated its defence policy along the lines of the Yoshida doctrine. In 1957, the Japanese government adopted the Basic Policy of National Defence (BPND), which established general principles that not only codified Japan's dependence on the US in dealing with external aggression against Japan but also guided the gradual development of the SDF pertinent to the nation's power and situation.[4]

The overwhelming influence of the 'Yoshida doctrine' over Japan's security policy making during 1950s and 60s also rested on the existence of a number of legal and normative constraints on Japan's security policy. One of the major domestic constraints was the Constitution, which was promulgated in 1946. Article 9 of the Constitution, which was originally imposed by the US occupation authorities with the aim of demilitarising Japan, stated that 'Japanese people will forever renounce use of force as a means of settling international disputes and thus not maintain land, sea and air forces as well as other war potential'. Although this peace clause caused serious disputes about the legitimacy of Japanese rearmament between the ruling and opposition parties especially in the early post-war years, since then most of the Japanese public has supported the government interpretation of the Constitution that Japan as a sovereign state has the right of both individual and collective self-defence and thus can possess the SDF as long as it is maintained strictly for self-defence purposes.[5] However, the Japanese government has proclaimed that actual exercise of the right of collective self-defence is unconstitutional since this would exceed the minimum forces levels for self-defence.[6] These legal constraints also generated the notion of 'exclusive defensive defence policy' (*senshu bōei*), which would legitimise the use of military forces only in the case of an attack on Japanese territories and would limit defensive forces to the minimum required for self-defence.[7]

The Constitution alone, however, could not place significant limits on the conduct of Japan's security policy. This legal constraint was buttressed by anti-militarist sentiments in broad segments of the Japanese public, which grew out of the traumatic experience of total defeat in World War II, including the atomic bombings on Hiroshima and Nagasaki. The Japanese public was, as a result of these experiences, highly sensitive to any policy to revise Article 9 of the Constitution and develop a more active security policy.[8] This anti-militarism surfaced when Prime Minister Kishi Nobusuke attempted to revise the Japan-US Security Treaty in order to make Japan an equal partner of the US. Kishi's initiative was seen by a majority of the Japanese public as a move to expand Japan's military role and return to pre-war militarism. The move provoked the mass demonstrations that forced the cancellation of a planned visit by President Eisenhower, the largest demonstrations ever in Japanese history. In July 1960, the Diet eventually passed the ratification of the new security treaty, but Kishi was forced to pay the price by tendering his resignation.[9] The crisis over the revision of the security treaty had a major influence on the government's subsequent treatment of security policy, as policy makers realised that rapid changes would not be possible without a political backlash.

The Yoshida strategy was further institutionalised in Japan's security policy in the 1960s under the administrations of Ikeda Hayato and Satō Eisaku. The US involvement in the Vietnam War posed serious concerns to Japan over the possibility of its entanglement in the US led War as Washington put enormous pressure on Tokyo to provide full-scale support for the US forces. However, the Japanese military contribution to the US war effort was limited to the provision of bases. Japan even implemented a number of new constraints on its security policy in order to ease public concerns about its entrapment in the Vietnam War. For instance, in 1967, the Satō administration introduced a ban on the export of arms, which prohibited the export of weapons to communist countries, to countries covered by UN Security Council's resolutions on arms embargoes and to countries involving conflicts (in 1976, Prime Minister Miki Takeo administration further strengthened the restriction, extending the ban to all countries and forbidding the export of arms production-related technologies). In 1968, Satō also enunciated the three non-nuclear principles, which declared that Japan would not produce, possess or bring nuclear weapons into Japan.[10]

Hence, under the Pax Americana, Japan could achieve unprecedented economic growth while avoiding direct involvement in Cold War military entanglements. Indeed, by the end of the 1960s Japan took a seat in the Organisation for Economic Cooperation and Development (OECD) and its economic power was even approaching that of the US.

Japan's inactive security policy, however, began gradually to change after the late 1960s with the relative decline of American hegemony in both military and economic spheres. The weakening of US power was demonstrated by President Nixon's announcement of the Guam Doctrine in 1969, which sought to reduce US forces overseas while demanding that its allies share more of the burden of their own defence, and the removal of the US dollar from the gold standard, which collapsed the Bretton Woods system. Nixon's unilateral decision to open relations with China (called 'Nixon shocks' in Japan) also exposed the relative decline of US power, thus altering the strategic environment and generating a more fluid international system. These events gave Japan a real sense of insecurity since they threatened the basic conditions for Japan's post-war economic success; the US commitment to the defence of Japan, which enabled Japan to pursue almost exclusively its own economic interest, and the stable international currency system, which allowed Japan to gain access to international markets.[11] Japan's concerns about the weakening of the US military presence in Asia were further amplified in the mid 1970s by a number of factors, including the intensification of bilateral trade frictions, the US withdrawal from Vietnam and the inauguration of the Carter administration, which publicly pledged to remove the US forces from South Korea. Added to this, the threat to reliable oil supplies during the 1973 oil crisis was for Japan a potent reminder of its economic vulnerability. These shocks forced Japan to seek a more independent foreign and security policy within the context of the Yoshida strategy.

The first step was the adoption of the National Defence Programme Outline (NDPO) in 1976, which provided a policy framework for weapons procurement and the improvement of defence capabilities for the first time in the post-war era. The NDPO stressed the need to enhance the quality of the SDF based on the 'Standard Defence Force Concept', which stated that Japan should possess an adequate defence capability that could repel 'limited and small scale aggression' without US assistance while large-scale attack directly against Japan, which was considered beyond its capacity, should be dealt in cooperation with US forces. Whilst reaffirming Japan's reliance on the US security guarantee, the NDPO signalled a departure from total dependence on the US and its intention to take greater responsibility for its own national defence. At the same time, however, the Japanese government adopted a limit of one percent of gross national product (GNP) on defence spending as a compensation for opposition parties' support for the NDPO.[12]

Heightened concerns about US strategic intentions in Asia also persuaded Japanese policy makers to take the initiative in securing its commitment to defending Japan. In 1975, the Japanese government proposed a bilateral dialogue on coordinating military operations under the provision of the Japan-US Security Treaty. This eventually led to the two countries concluding the Guidelines for Japan-US Defence Cooperation in 1978, which called for joint studies of operational issues in the three contingencies, including deterrence of aggression against Japan, response to an armed attack on Japan and bilateral cooperation in case of conflicts in the Far East, which would have an important influence on Japan's national security. The establishment of the guidelines stipulated greater military cooperation between Japan and the US, including joint military planning and exercises, operational preparations and intelligence exchanges.[13] In short, the guidelines elevated the Japan-US security relationship to that of military allies and provided Japan with a framework through which it could make a military contribution to regional security, albeit indirectly.

The US withdrawal from Indo-China in 1975 following the end of the Vietnam War also provoked Japan to take the diplomatic initiative for the first time in its post-war history with a view to contributing to the stability of Southeast Asia. In 1977, Prime Minister Fukuda Takeo took a tour of Southeast Asian countries and announced the 'Fukuda Doctrine', which demonstrated Japan's willingness to share in efforts to maintain regional peace and security through economic and diplomatic means.[14] The Japanese government hence began to utilise its economic aid to bridge the gap between ASEAN countries and Vietnam with the purpose of achieving greater stability in Southeast Asia. It also established a number of dialogue processes with ASEAN to develop greater political and economic cooperation.[15] These initiatives can be seen as indicative of Japan's aspiration to fill the vacuum left by the US withdrawal from Southeast Asia.

The Japanese concept of security was also redefined in response to changes in the international strategic environment. In 1979, Prime Minister Ōhira Masayoshi initiated a research group to formulate a new national security strategy. The result was the emergence of the concept of 'comprehensive security', (*sōgō anzen hoshō*) which called for Japan to employ comprehensive measures to maintain its national security, including not only military means but also political and economic instruments.[16] The pursuit of comprehensive security was motivated primarily by Japan's awareness of the need to contribute to the maintenance of international peace and security, as necessitated by the end of Pax Americana. The report of the Ōhira research group recommended that Japan should make greater efforts towards self-reliance and contribute to the maintenance and strengthening of the international system, particularly through non-military measures, such as diplomacy, economic and technological cooperation. The special emphasis given to the use of non-military instruments in addressing its international obligations in part reflected Japan's intention to resist US pressure to assume a larger military role.[17] It is important to note, however, that the concept of comprehensive security did not entirely disregard the military dimension of Japan's security policy. For instance, the report strongly suggested that 'Japan strengthen its self-reliance efforts for defending its national security'.[18] Although the concept was not adopted as an official guideline for Japan's security policy, it has nevertheless had a significant impact on Japan's policy making since then.

The 1980s witnessed new developments in Japan's security policy. The outbreak of 'the Second Cold War', marked by the Soviet invasion of Afghanistan in 1979 and the massive increase in its naval and air deployment in the Pacific, once again prompted the Japanese government to undertake more responsibility with regards to its defence, not only because the actions of the Soviet Union were perceived as a direct threat to Japan but also because of heightened American pressure on Japan to shoulder more of the security burden. In 1981, the Suzuki administration, for example, announced that Japan would assume responsibility for the defence of the sea-lines of communication (SLOC) up to 1,000 nautical miles from Japan. This instigated a study on the joint operational requirements of the sea-lane's defence.[19]

Japan's defence cooperation with the US was further expanded under the Premiership of Nakasone Yasuhiro, a nationalist politician enthusiastic about boosting Japan's international profile. Nakasone took a number of initiatives that weakened the constraints on Japan's security policy including a decision to ease the ban on the defence technology exports to the US in 1983, to increase host nation support for the US military base in Okinawa and to participate in research on the US Strategic Defence Initiative (SDI). Finally, Nakasone abandoned the one percent GNP ceiling on defence spending in 1987 and Japan's defence budget was increased by six percent per year with the aim of upgrading air defence and sea control capabilities to support the US security strategy.[20] At the same time, the Nakasone administration also initiated the political use of foreign aid, attempting to support US strategic objectives as exemplified by the substantial increase of Japan's Official Development Assistance (ODA) to countries deemed to be of strategic importance to the West, such as Turkey, Pakistan and Egypt. As a result, by the end of 1980s, Japan became the world's largest donor of foreign aid.[21]

Overall, although external factors during the Cold War period, including the intensification of superpower confrontations and US pressures, provided constant pressure on Japan to expand its military capabilities and its defence cooperation with the US, these two aspects of Japan's security policy developed only incrementally. Indeed, the existence of firm domestic legal and normative constraints prevented Japanese policy makers from seeking the enlargement of the nation's military capabilities and its roles in the bilateral alliance beyond the minimum level required for its national defence. The result was that Japan's military role in the Asia-Pacific region was almost invisible as its military contribution to regional security was primarily confined to providing rear bases for US military forces. Japan's regional political role was also relatively passive due mainly to strategic limitations set by the Cold War bipolar structure and Asian suspicions of its diplomatic initiatives stemming from the history of Japanese aggression in Asia. It was thus inevitable that Japan sought to make a direct contribution to regional security by using its economic power in the form of ODA and economic cooperation.

However, this does not mean that Japan was shying away from assuming active political roles, if not military roles, in the region during the Cold War period. As the Fukuda Doctrine demonstrates, Japan's aspirations for a more active and independent political role in the maintenance of regional security and stability had already begun to surface in 1970s. As we will see later in this chapter, Japan's search for greater regional political roles was accelerated dramatically by the collapse of the bipolar structure, which freed it from strategic constraints and gave fresh impetus to the search for new means to play such roles. This had significant ramifications for Japan's sudden tilt towards regional security multilateralism at the beginning of 1990s.

Japan's view of regional security multilateralism during the Cold War

Considering Japan's passive and indirect involvement in regional security during the Cold War period, it is not surprising that Tokyo was not enthusiastic about proposals for security multilateralism in the Asia-Pacific region. Security multilateralism in the region was first proposed by the Soviet Union when, in 1969, Soviet President Leonid Brezhnev proposed an Asian Community on Security. Although this initiative was dismissed as propaganda by regional countries, including Japan, the Soviet Union continued to float similar proposals. In a major speech at Vladivostok in July 1986, President Mikhail Gorbachev proposed to establish a Pacific Ocean Conference along the lines of the Helsinki Conference on Security and Cooperation in Europe (CSCE). This was followed by his proposal for promoting a region-wide consultative community in Krasnoyarsk in 1998.[22] These proposals drew strong opposition from the US due to its suspicion of the Soviet intention behind them. Because the Soviet initiatives stressed the promotion of CBMs in naval areas, such as the reduction and limitations of naval forces in the Western Pacific, the US policy makers were concerned that the proposals may lead to naval arms control talks designed to weaken the US military superiority in the Asia-Pacific region.[23] They also feared that establishing a CSCE type of regional security institution would harm the credibility of the US-centred bilateral security arrangements in the region. Needless to say, Japan followed the US in taking a negative stance towards the Soviet proposal, claiming that it would damage the Japan-US alliance.[24]

With the gradual winding down of Cold War tensions, initiatives for regional security multilateralism were revived by medium-sized powers, including Australia and Canada. In July 1990, the Australian Foreign Minister, Gareth Evans, advocated convening an Asia-Pacific security conference modelled on the CSCE for addressing and resolving regional security problems. Following this, in the same month, the Canadian Foreign Minister, Joe Clark, proposed a similar idea, suggesting that 'we might consider an adaptation of the CSCE in the Pacific'.[25] Both the Australian and Canadian proposals were influenced by the strategic philosophy of 'common security', emerging from the liberal European tradition of security and the evolution of the CSCE.

However, these proposals were, again, not warmly received by major powers, including the US and Japan. In the month following their proposals, US Secretary of State, James Baker, expressed strong reservations, arguing that 'bilateral security arrangements were sufficient to meet regional security needs'.[26] Japan also rejected them on the grounds that the CSCE developed in Europe was not applicable to security conditions in the Asia-Pacific region, which were completely different from those of Europe.[27] Moreover, Japanese policy makers believed that a CSCE type of security forum was impractical in the Asia-Pacific region since, in their view, 'conflicts in the Asia-Pacific region, such as the Korean Peninsula and Cambodia, would be better settled through meetings of the concerned parties rather than a region-wide security forum'.[28] Like Japan, ASEAN countries also rebuffed the idea of an Asian version of CSCE, being concerned that establishing such a formal regional security institution might undermine ASEAN's identity and authority in handling security problems in its own way. Traditionally, ASEAN used informal consultation and dialogue to address security and develop intramural solidarity. This method was broadly referred to as the 'ASEAN Way', which was very much to be contrasted with the more legalistic, rule-bound and institution building European approach.[29] Finally, the proposal for a region-wide security forum was opposed by China, which feared that such a forum would be used by other states to intervene in what it considered to be its internal affairs, such as the issues of Taiwan and the South China Sea.[30]

The formation of the Nakayama proposal of 1991

Although publicly rejecting a series of proposals for an Asian version of CSCE floated by Canada and Australia, Tokyo did not entirely rule out the possibility of regional security multilateralism. Indeed, Japan's view of regional security multilateralism began to change from the beginning of 1990 as it became clear that the Cold War was coming to an end. Japan's reconsideration of the idea of regional security multilateralism began when Satō Yukio assumed the position of Director General of the Information Analysis, Research and Planning Bureau at MOFA in January 1990. The first main task for Satō in his new position was to consider how to respond to the Soviet proposal to convene bilateral talks on Asia-Pacific security issues, including the promotion of regional CBMs, disarmament and arms control, and to its long-standing proposal for the Asian version of CSCE.[31]

As noted above, Japan had initially rebuffed the Soviet proposal but President Gorbachev's planned visit to Japan in 1991, which had first been announced by the Soviet Union in September 1989, pushed Japan to reconsider. The Japanese government could no longer simply ignore proposals that would certainly be major issues in the Japan-Soviet Foreign Ministers Conference scheduled for March 1990 as well as the planned Japan-Soviet summit.[32] In fact, Moscow put continuous pressure on Tokyo to accept bilateral talks on CBMs and, informally, even pressed it for a number of bilateral CBMs on the grounds that this would help create favourable conditions between the two countries in advance of Gorbachev's visit to Tokyo.[33] After extensive consultations within the Japanese government, it was decided to accept some of the Soviet proposals in the expectation that a positive response to the Soviet initiative for CBMs might produce a breakthrough for the deadlocked Northern Territorial issue.[34] Thus, in July 1990, Japan formally accepted the Soviet proposal for initiating a discussion on regional security issues at the Japan-Soviet Foreign Minister Conference scheduled for September 1990. Moreover, at the bilateral conference, in response to Soviet Foreign Minister Eduard Shevardnadze's 10-point proposal on CBMs, Japanese Foreign Minister Nakayama Tarō proposed to establish policy planning talks to discuss the proposal. The first policy planning talks were held in Moscow in December 1990. By this time, the Japanese government was ready to accept a number of Soviet's CBM proposals, including exchanges between military personnel, exchanges of military information and the conclusion of arrangements to prevent accidental clashes.[35]

These positive developments in the two countries' security relations helped MOFA officials to see regional security multilateralism in a more favourable light since they not only mitigated the perceived threat posed by the Soviet Union but also helped to allay Japanese suspicions of Soviet intentions to use a regional security arrangement to undermine the Japan-US alliance.[36] The Soviet's official position on the Japan-US alliance had begun to alter ever since the bilateral foreign minister meeting in May 1989, at which Shevardnadze told his Japanese counterpart Uno Sōsuke that 'it would be possible to conclude a Soviet-Japanese peace treaty whether the bilateral alliance existed or not'.[37]

The rapid improvement of Japan-Soviet relations was, however, not the only important factor in Japan's changing view of regional security multilateralism.

Japanese concerns about the uncertain future prospects of the regional security environment also played a major part. Anticipating that the winding down of US-Soviet confrontations and the rapid transformation in Eastern Europe would inevitably bring changes in the Asia-Pacific region, MOFA officials came to hold the view that there was an immediate need for Asian countries to discuss how to ensure long-term regional security and stability.[38] This in turn brought about an important change in Japan's position on regional security multilateralism. At the Foreign Minister Conference between Japan and South Korea in May 1990, Japan's Foreign Minister Nakayama proposed convening the Asia-Pacific Foreign Minister Conference on the sidelines of the 45th UN General Assembly held in September 1990.[39] Japan made vigorous efforts to gather regional support for its proposal and successfully co-hosted the conference with Indonesia. At the conference, foreign ministers from 15 countries, including Japan, Indonesia, the USA, the Soviet Union, South Korea, China, Canada, Australia, New Zealand, Mongolia, Laos, Vietnam, Thailand, Singapore and the Philippines, discussed a number of security issues, such as the Cambodian problem, the Korean Peninsula and the Gulf crisis.[40] Signs of Japan's changing conceptions of regional security multilateralism were also evident in Foreign Minister Nakayama's speech at the 1990 General Assembly of the UN. Nakayama stated that 'peace and stability in the Asia-Pacific region has a direct bearing on Japan's stability, and I feel it is essential to work together to eliminate the political distrust and resolve other regional problems. Accordingly, it is Japan's policy, as part of its diplomatic efforts, to encourage more vigorous and constructive dialogue among all countries concerned'.[41]

The success of Japan's initiative for the Asia-Pacific Foreign Minister Conference, accompanied by the rapid improvement of Japan-Soviet security relations, further ameliorated Japan's prospect of regional security multilateralism. In this context, MOFA officials, most notably Satō Yukio, concluded that the time was ripe for regional countries to establish a region-wide forum for multilateral political and security dialogue and that Japan should seize the initiative in promoting it rather than just rejecting a number of impractical and unrealistic proposals for the Asian version of CSCE. Hence, in the task of considering possible counter-measures to the Soviet CSCA proposal, Satō began to articulate a new concept of regional security that would enable Japan to take the initiative in promoting a region-wide security forum.[42]

The concept of a multifaceted approach to Asia-Pacific security and stability

Satō's idea on how to establish a region-wide security forum reflected his own perspective on the post-Cold War regional security order. As noted above, Satō as well as other MOFA officials believed that a European model of security cooperation, notably the CSCE, would not suit the Asia-Pacific region on the grounds that the security environment in the Asia-Pacific region was too complex and different from that in Europe. According to Satō, there were four main differences between the two regions. First, unlike Europe, where the major policy concern was the reduction of military tension, the first policy priority for many East Asian countries was economic development. Secondly, the effect of the collapse of bipolar structures on Asia-Pacific security was limited compared with Europe. China's independence of the East-West dichotomy meant that bipolar structures were not the main dividing lines in the Asia-Pacific region, unlike in Europe where Cold War confrontation between the North Atlantic Treaty Organisation (NATO) and the Warsaw Pact had been of primary importance. Thirdly, military conditions in the Asia-Pacific region were far more complex than those in Europe as the threat perceptions held by East Asian countries were diverse and the form of alliance was bilateral rather than multilateral. Finally, in contrast to Europe, in which cross-border issues had been resolved before the CSCE was established, the Asia Pacific region still had a number of unresolved territorial conflicts and disputes.[43] Hence, Satō contended that the countries of the Asia-Pacific region would need different approaches to address regional security and that the best approach to enhance it would be to comprehensively utilise existing frameworks or arrangements for cooperation in the region rather than creating a new CSCE-type institution.

According to Satō, the existing frameworks and arrangements were:

1) Regional economic forums and organisations, such as ASEAN, ASEAN-PMC, APEC and PECC.
2) Emerging frameworks for the management of ongoing disputes, such as Cambodia, the Korean Peninsula and the South China Sea.
3) Networks and arrangements of security cooperation, such as bilateral alliances centring on the US, in particular the Japan-US alliance, the growing cooperation within ASEAN and Soviet-Chinese military cooperation.

Yet Satō did not think that strengthening regional economic and security cooperation on these bases was enough for enhancing regional security and stability in the post-Cold War era. A worrying feature of the Asia-Pacific region, according to Satō, was the absence of any arrangements for enhancing the level of 'mutual reassurance' among regional countries. In his view, given that relations among regional countries were still affected by sentiments of scepticism and guardedness, mainly stemming from bitter memories of past Japan's militarism and a deep rooted scepticism vis-à-vis the dominating influence of major powers, enhancing the level of mutual reassurance among regional countries was particularly important since it was a prerequisite of promoting deeper political and security cooperation among them. Satō thus argued that in addition to advancing cooperation in the above three fields, regional countries should promote a new arrangement, namely 'the process of political dialogue on matters of mutual concern, such as questions related to the future direction of American and Japanese policy in the region'. Satō suggested that regional countries employ ASEAN-PMC as a forum for a political dialogue process among regional countries.[44] Regarding the enhancement of mutual reassurance among regional countries, Satō in particular emphasised the importance for Japan to remove Asian concerns about the future direction of Japan's policy. Satō argued that:

> In the coming years, Japan will engage herself more positively in the process to enhance political stability and security in the Asia and Pacific region ... Yet, as noted earlier, anxiety on the part of many Asian countries about the possibility of Japan becoming a 'military power' will persist. It might grow as Asians come to hear of the Japanese preparedness to play a larger political role in this region. It is important in this context for Japan to continue to explicitly commit herself to the policy of not becoming a 'military power'. It is equally important for Japan to place herself in multilateral venues, wherein the countries which are worried about the future direction of Japanese defence policy can express their concerns. This must be an important part of Japanese participation in the process for political stability and security in the Asia and Pacific region.[45]

Satō's comments represented both Japan's intention to play a greater role in regional political and security affairs and its realisation of the need to reassure neighbouring countries if Japan wanted to play such a role. Satō believed that a region-wide security forum facilitating political dialogue on a multilateral basis would allow other Asian countries to express concerns about Japan's security policy and intentions more openly than on the existing bilateral basis, under which most Asian neighbours were hesitant to air such concerns because of their dependence on Japan's ODA.[46] In short, establishing a region-wide forum for multilateral security dialogue was for Tokyo a necessary vehicle not only for enhancing the level of mutual reassurance among regional countries but also for assisting Japan's aspirations to play a larger political role in the region.

Satō conceptualised the idea of advancing the four different approaches through the arrangements and frameworks as 'a multiplex mechanism for stability and security' or 'a multifaceted approach to stability and security' and suggested that 'regional countries share this concept in order to effectively run the multiplex mechanism thus achieving their common purpose of maintaining regional security and stability'.[47] Satō's concept of a multifaceted approach quickly gained broad support from other senior MOFA officials, and by the beginning of 1991 part of the concept had already been presented to the general public. In an address to the National Diet in January 1991, Foreign Minister Nakayama Tarō stated that:

I believe that the time has come to give serious consideration to how to ensure long-term stability in the Asia-Pacific region. The approaches to achieving long-term stability in this region would inevitably differ from those applied in Europe, as the geopolitical conditions and the security environments in this region are considerably different from Europe. ... I think the most appropriate approach for this region is to expand dialogue and cooperation on various political and economic questions in the region, making full use of the existing fora such as ASEAN, ASEAN Post-Ministerial Conference, Asian Pacific Economic Cooperation (APEC) Ministerial Meeting, Pacific Economic Cooperation Council. Based on this position, Japan proposes to promote dialogue with interlocutors of the Asia-Pacific region for the purpose of forming an international consensus on how to achieve long-term stability in this region.[48]

Seeking a regional consensus on Japan's idea

Japan's contention that the CSCE process was not applicable to the security conditions of the Asia-Pacific region seemed to gradually influence other countries' thinking of regional security multilateralism. Indeed, during his visit to Japan in April 1991, President Gorbachev no longer referred to the long-standing Soviet proposal for an Asian version of CSCE. By that time, Canada and Australia had also withdrawn their CSCE proposals and instead had begun to seek an approach more specifically suited to the Asia-Pacific region.[49] After Gorbachev's visit to Japan, MOFA hence began to make serious efforts to push for its idea of promoting regional multilateral dialogue and cooperation, namely the concept of the 'multifaceted approach to Asia-Pacific stability and security'.

An opportunity for gauging the regional interest in this concept came soon after Gorbachev's visit to Japan. Satō was invited to attend two conferences, involving officials and security analysts from major Asia-Pacific countries; the sixth annual meeting of the directors of the ASEAN Institutes of Strategic and International Studies (ISIS), held in Jakarta on June 2–3, 1991 and another ASEAN related conference sponsored by the Philippine and Thai governments (named ASEAN and the Asia-Pacific region: Prospects for Security Cooperation in the 1990s) held in Manila on June 5, 1991. At these conferences, Satō discovered considerable interest in multilateral political dialogue. At the Jakarta meeting, Satō's vision of regional security multilateralism as articulated in the concept of the multifaceted approach successfully drew support from ASEAN participants. By this time, like MOFA, intellectuals in ASEAN-ISIS also reached a consensus on the need to establish a region-wide forum for multilateral security dialogue.[50] At the end of the conference, ASEAN-ISIS submitted a recommendation to ASEAN which urged ASEAN to take the initiative in promoting a forum for Asia-Pacific political dialogue at the forthcoming fourth ASEAN summit and proposed to set up such a forum as an extension of the ASEAN-PMC. The ASEAN-ISIS also suggested setting up a Senior Officials Meeting (SOM) between ASEAN and its dialogue partners in order to prepare an agenda for a new conference.[51] At the Manila conference too, where officials from Asia-Pacific countries were present, Satō's concept made a significant contribution to the emergence of a consensus on the merits of promoting a process of multilateral political dialogue in the region.[52]

Satō's concept was able to gather broad support from the officials and intellectuals of regional countries primarily for the following reasons. First, Satō's concept carefully avoided devaluing existing bilateral security arrangements, in particular the Japan-US alliance. As noted above, US policy makers remained cautious about any proposal regarding regional security multilateralism, fearing that it would undermine the rationale for bilateral security arrangements in the region. Satō removed these concerns by explaining that the process of multilateral security dialogue was neither a NATO type collective security system nor a CSCE like security institution, rather it was a loose consultative forum that would not affect the utility of the existing bilateral alliances. He added that the process of multilateral security dialogue and the bilateral alliance system would exist independently in separate arrangements in the region, but would complement one another since they could provide different functions. Moreover, Satō's paper, which was presented to the Manila conference, deliberately emphasised that the Japan-US Alliance, which sustained the US military presence, was the most important stabilising factor for regional security, thus easing concerns of a US State Department official participating in the conference over the negative impact of a multilateral security arrangement on the US-centred bilateral alliances.[53]

Secondly, Satō's proposal deliberately avoided using the term 'confidence building'. He well recognised that one of main reasons for the US as well as ASEAN rejections of the CSCA proposal was their concern about the introduction of CSCE type CBMs to the region. As noted above, while the US feared that the application of European type CBMs to the Asia-Pacific region would lead to naval arms control, ASEAN was reluctant to accept any legalistic measure that would conflict with its own approach to security. Therefore, instead of merely borrowing the concept of confidence building, which was associated with CSCE type CBMs such as arms control, Satō elaborated a new concept of 'mutual reassurance', a loose consultative form of political dialogue, which focused on foreign policy aspects of security rather than the military dimension. This new concept was successful in allaying US and ASEAN's concerns about CBMs.[54]

Thirdly, Satō's idea of utilising the ASEAN-PMC as a forum for multilateral security dialogue assuaged ASEAN's concern that the development of a region-wide security forum might weaken its identity and autonomy in addressing its own security issues. This was because an ASEAN related conference could ensure its diplomatic centrality and managerial role. The idea of using the PMC was also attractive from a Japanese perspective. While many Asian countries remained suspicious of Japan's larger political role, Satō worried that Japan's strong leadership in establishing a new security forum would prevent the garnering of regional support to its initiative. Satō believed that the use of an ASEAN sponsored forum would allow Japan to eradicate such regional suspicions. Overall, in the eyes of Japan, utilising the ASEAN-PMC was far less costly than creating an entirely new regional security forum. It was expected that an ASEAN-PMC based forum would provide Japan with a framework in which Tokyo could influence the regional security agenda without provoking suspicions of Japan's intentions.[55]

The success of Satō's presentation at both the Jakarta and Manila conferences gave high impetus to MOFA to formulate Satō's idea into a practical proposal, eventually leading to MOFA's decision to float a formal proposal at the forthcoming ASEAN-PMC held in Kuala Lumpur in July 1991. Thus, Satō revised the draft of Nakayama's statement for the 1991 ASEAN-PMC, which had been prepared by the MOFA's Asian Bureau, based on his paper submitted to the conferences.[56]

The Nakayama proposal

In July 1991, at the ASEAN-PMC held in Kuala Lumpur, Japan's Foreign Minister, Nakayama Tarō, formally launched a proposal for establishing a region-wide forum for multilateral political dialogue. After arguing that the use of the existing arrangements and frameworks for cooperation was the most effective approach to ensure long-term stability in the Asia-Pacific region, Nakayama stated that:

> If there is anything to add to the mechanisms and frameworks for cooperation in the three fields of economic cooperation, diplomacy and security, the first would be a forum for political dialogue where friendly countries in this region could engage in frank exchanges of opinion on matters of mutual interest. ... I believe it would be meaningful and timely to use the ASEAN Post Ministerial Conference as a process for mutual reassurance among us. In order for such dialogue to be effective, it might be advisable to organise senior official's meeting, which would then report its deliberations to the ASEAN Post Ministerial Conference for further discussion.[57]

As noted above, the Nakayama proposal was formulated based on Satō's idea of how to promote regional multilateral security dialogue, but there was one major difference between the Nakayama proposal and Satō's concept, namely the proposal for establishing a SOM. The proposal to establish the SOM was the most important but controversial point of the Nakayama proposal. This idea was not contained in Satō's concept presented at the Jakarta and Manila conferences, which only suggested using the PMC as a venue for multilateral security dialogue. (However, it was included in the ASEAN ISIS's proposal as described above.) There had been a serious debate in MOFA as to whether to insert the SOM proposal into the Nakayama proposal. Satō opposed the inclusion, worrying that ASEAN observers might suspect that Japan stole ASEAN's idea. However, as a result of a strong suggestion from the Asian Bureau, MOFA decided to put forward the SOM proposal.[58]

Negative reactions to the Nakayama proposal

The Nakayama proposal, however, failed to muster substantive support from foreign ministers in those countries whereas Satō's tentative proposal received positive reactions from ASEAN and the US officials at the Manila and Jakarta conferences. One of the main reasons for their cool response was the lack of prior consultation between MOFA and its counterparts in ASEAN and the US before the Nakayama proposal. Although Satō introduced his idea of promoting multilateral security dialogue to them in those conferences, Satō's presentation did not signify Tokyo's intention to actually float the proposal. The US and ASEAN officials, therefore, did not anticipate that Satō's concept would appear as Japan's official proposal just one month after those conferences.[59] As for the US side, although the increasing number of senior US officials, including Dennis Ross, Director of Policy Planning in the State Department, came to endorse Satō's idea and thus changed their suspicious view of regional security multilateralism, such emerging consensus at the official level had not completely reached to the top level of the State Department, namely Secretary of State James Baker, by the time of the Nakayama proposal. Hence, Baker ignored the Nakayama proposal, regarding it as a threat to the US bilateral alliances.[60]

As for the ASEAN side, its reluctance to endorse the Nakayama proposal mainly derived from its fear of any initiative from Japan. Like Japan, by the time of the July 1991 ASEAN-PMC, some ASEAN countries, particularly Singapore, had also sought the possibility of ASEAN's initiative in promoting multilateral security dialogue as a part of the ASEAN-PMC although ASEAN as a whole was not totally ready to take such an initiative. Though unintended, Japan's pre-emptive proposal aroused ASEAN's suspicions that Tokyo was aiming to seize a leadership role in a new security dialogue process from ASEAN.[61] Some ASEAN officials even complained that 'Tokyo stole the ASEAN's idea and initiative for promoting a multilateral security dialogue'.[62] ASEAN's negative response also stemmed from their opposition to Japan's SOM proposal. Whereas basically supporting the idea of multilateral security dialogue, most ASEAN countries were concerned that creating the SOM focusing exclusively on security issues would change the nature of the ASEAN-PMC, which they basically regarded as a forum for political and economic dialogue. Indonesian Foreign Minister, Ali Alatas, voiced this view, saying that 'we cannot set up a working group on security. People will have the impression that the PMC is becoming a security forum'.[63]

Japanese policy makers clearly recognised that ASEAN's hostile response to the Nakayama proposal reflected its doubts about Japan's intentions, not the content of the proposal. Nakayama, for instance, told the reporters after the PMC that 'it was apparent that negative response stemmed from misunderstanding of Japan's real intentions' and added that 'Japan hopes to hold the first SOM before the next ASEAN-PMC held at Manila 1992'.[64] Yet, due to unpredictable negative reactions to the Nakayama proposal, MOFA realised that Japan should refrain from taking such a lead in establishing a new regional security forum so as not to inflame suspicions of Japanese intent, thus deciding to encourage and back up ASEAN initiative to achieve its goal.

Underlying factors for the Nakayama proposal

This section will examine underlying factors influencing Japan's decision to formulate the Nakayama proposal. It argues that at the initial stage, Japan's intention to establish a region-wide forum for multilateral security dialogue was mainly influenced by political rather than security reasons. More specifically, the Nakayama proposal was driven by a perceived change in the regional security environment following the end of the Cold War, which not only aroused Japan's hidden aspiration to play a larger political role in the region but also presented both a necessary condition and a common interest to regional countries to seek a new approach to enhance regional security.

Growing aspiration for a larger political role in international affairs

As discussed previously, throughout the Cold War era, Japan was criticised for its refusal to accept international responsibilities commensurate with its economic power. However, over a long period Japanese leaders as well as the general public simultaneously developed awareness that Japan could not for much longer continue to act as a passive player in international affairs. By the beginning of the 1990s, many Japanese leaders had become increasingly dissatisfied with the lack of symmetry between its economic power and various constraints on its political and security roles in international affairs. Particularly, the new generation of politicians and bureaucrats who had grown up with Japan's economic success became less patient with passive policy and believed that in the emerging world order, Japan had to play an important role in shaping it.[65] In this regard, the termination of bipolar structure with the end of the Cold War was seen by Japanese leaders as a major opportunity to remove the image of 'economic animal' since the decrease of Washington and Moscow's influence in the region created room for Tokyo to adopt a more expansive and independent foreign and security policy. Japan's greater assertiveness was evident in a series of major speeches and publications made by Japanese leaders. Prime Minister Kaifu Toshiki, for instance, stated in the general policy speech to the National Diet in March 1990 that:

> International relations are undergoing major changes in both the political realm and the economic realm. ... Looking ahead from this perspective, even though the 1990s is the start of a new age, the blueprint for progress is yet incomplete and this is an era of both hope and anxiety intermixed. It is precisely at such a time that it is important that Japan take part in the building of an international order conductive to the creation of an international community full of hope and embark upon what might be called 'a foreign policy of aspirations'.[66]

Following this, in May 1990, Kuriyama Takakazu, the then Administrative Vice Minister of Foreign Affairs, also wrote in *Gaikō Forum* (a MOFA affiliated journal), that 'in post-war history, like other minor states, Japan maintained peace and prosperity by fully depending on the world order that the United States sustained. ... However, today Japan is an important member of the club of industrialised democracies. Japan should maintain prosperity and security by actively involving itself in the construction of a new world order'.[67] It was clear that by the beginning of 1990s, as a result of massive economic development, Japanese leaders increasingly identified the country as one of the world's major powers, which in turn increased its national pride. This led them to seek international roles and responsibility appropriate to the country's status. That is to say, Japan's greater political and possibly security roles in international affairs were necessary not only for ensuring its future prosperity but also for raising its political profile and thus satisfying its growing national pride.

The Asia-Pacific region as the main field of Japan's larger political role

In the search for a larger political role in international affairs, Japanese leaders increasingly saw the need for an active contribution to the creation of a new Asia-Pacific regional order. In January 1991, Prime Minister Kaifu, for instance, stated that 'in the Asia-Pacific region, the important issues are those of promoting the reduction of tensions and working for the region's further economic development. We must play an active role for the resolution of conflicts and confrontations in the region and in bringing peace and prosperity to the region as a whole'.[68] Japan's growing policy focus on the Asia-Pacific region was in part accompanied by the rise of 'Asianism' in Japan. The end of the Cold War, which freed Japan from ideological and strategic constraints, gave a new impetus for Japan to refocus on Asia. By the end of 1980's, Tokyo had already established economic leadership in East Asia by using an impressive array of economic tools, including ODA, Foreign Direct Investment (FDI) and technology transfer. The success of Japan's economic role in East Asia naturally helped generate new confidence and motivation to assume a greater role in regional political and security affairs, thus leading Japanese policy makers to look more carefully at Asia with regard to foreign policy making.[69]

A growing spirit of independence from the US also motivated Japan's growing interest in Asia. The rising tensions between Tokyo and Washington, stemming from the bilateral economic conflicts in the late 1980s, had stoked anti-American sentiment in Japan. Some Japanese political and opinion leaders criticised their country's subordination to the US and even suggested that Japan should shift its diplomatic focus from the US to Asia. One representative of such extreme Asianism was Ishihara Shintarō, the author of the bestseller *Japan That Can Say No*, in which he argued that Japan should become more independent from the US and should articulate its position of being a member of the Asia bloc.[70] Voices calling for more independent policy regarding Asia were not only coming from inside Japan but also from other Asian countries. With Japan's growing economic influence in the region, some ASEAN countries, particularly Thailand and Malaysia, began to demand that Japan take a leading role as a regional political and economic hub. In 1990, Malaysia's Prime Minister, Mahathir Mohamad, floated a proposal for the East Asia Economic Caucus (EAEC), which called for a greater role for Japan in creating an Asian economic group. This attracted huge media attention in Japan and further evoked such Asianist sentiment. Whereas the EAEC was defined to exclude non-Asian countries, notably the US, New Zealand and Australia, there was a certain degree of sympathy for the EAEC proposal with Japanese officials, such as pro-Asia bureaucrats who had obtained senior posts in MOFA, Ministry of Finance (MOF) and Ministry of International Trade and Industry (MITI).[71]

This radical vision of Asian regionalism, however, had lost ground to Japanese political and opinion leaders as well as public. Despite Japan's growing self-confidence and interest in Asia, the mainstream of Japanese policy makers did not downgrade the nation's relationship with the US. Given that Japan depended on the US for security and access to the global economy, Japanese policy makers had no choice but sought to expand its regional role in the pursuit of maintaining its bilateral link with the US. Yanai Shunji, a senior MOFA official, argued that 'for Japan there is no such thing as a choice between Asia and the US. Cooperation between the US and Asian countries is indispensable for the peace and stability of Asia-Pacific region'.[72] Japan's leading role in the creation of the APEC instead of supporting the EAEC proposal reflected its recognition that making a division between East Asia and North America was likely to weaken not only the US security commitment to East Asia but also the growth of the East Asian economy.

Hence, with the end of the Cold War, the expectations for Japan's greater political and even possibly security roles in the Asia-Pacific region had been dramatically heightened in both the international and domestic contexts. Yet there was also an awareness among Japanese policy makers that such an aspiration would not be entirely acceptable to all Asian countries, particularly those that had suffered as a result of Japanese aggression, arousing as it would, deep-rooted scepticism and concern about the direction of Japan's new diplomacy. In short, Japanese policy makers were confronted by a dilemma. On the one hand, there were growing calls, from both domestic and international voices, demanding that Japan make a more active contribution to regional security. On the other, there were fears of Japan's new assertiveness. Indeed, as Soeya Yoshihide put it 'the challenge that Tokyo faced (at the beginning of 1990s) was to seek possible roles Japan should or could play in the construction of a new regional order while simultaneously dealing with regional concerns for the future direction of Japan's foreign and security policy'.[73] In this regard, as discussed below, the idea of developing a region-wide security forum appealed to Japanese policy makers as an effective and convenient instrument for overcoming this policy challenge.

Japan's changing perception of the regional security environment

In the eyes of Japanese policy makers, the end of the US-Soviet rivalry, which had become conspicuous since 1989, certainly ameliorated the conditions of the Asia-Pacific regional security environment. Its positive impacts on regional affairs were evident in the rapid improvement of diplomatic relations among regional countries from the late 1980s to the beginning of 1990. Most significantly, Sino-Soviet relations, which had been under serious strain since the 1960s, were normalised in April 1990. China's relations with Vietnam and a number of ASEAN countries, including Indonesia and Singapore, were also normalised by the end of 1990. Moreover, the relationship between the Soviet Union and both Japan and South Korea underwent rapid improvement, and regional tensions were significantly mitigated by the reduction of the Soviet military presence in East Asia, evinced by its withdrawal from Mongolia and Cam Ranh Bay.[74] In sum, the end of the Cold War made the strategic situation in East Asia more favourable to Japan than at any time in the last century. In the view of Japanese policy makers, these positive developments finally provided regional countries with great opportunities to undertake collective efforts to promote regional political and security cooperation.[75] As Satō Yukio wrote in 1991 that:

A number of developments to reduce tension have begun to take place also in the Asia and Pacific region. Soviet military disengagements have taken place in South East Asia, along the Sino-Soviet border. ... Changes in diplomatic dimensions (in the Asia-Pacific region) are more remarkable than the progress in force reduction and military disengagement. ... All these developments point to the maturing of such conditions that would make it possible for countries in the Asia-Pacific region to settle the on-going conflicts and disputes, expand regional cooperation (political as well as economic) and further force reduction and arms control.[76]

However, regardless of the positive developments regarding diplomatic relations between regional countries, as Japan perceived it, the post-Cold War regional security environment was still prevailed upon by a variety of uncertainties and security risks. Firstly, there remained various unresolved disputes and conflicts in the region, such as the confrontation in the Taiwan Straits, the Korean Peninsula, the Cambodian problem, the South China Sea territorial issue and the issue of the Northern Territories of Japan. Second, the relations between regional countries were still penetrated by deep distrust and suspicion, deriving mainly from the history of Japanese aggression and a sense of rivalry among them. Thirdly, there were emerging regional concerns that the decline of Soviet and the US military influences over the region would change the regional balance of military power, and this might generate dangerous competition for regional hegemony, thus producing geopolitical uncertainty in the region.[77] Finally, Japanese policy makers also identified new security risks arising from a variety of political, economic and social issues, such as ethnic conflicts, transnational crimes and the repression of human rights.[78]

Faced with such a fluid regional security environment, Japanese policy makers came to recognise the need to reassess the country's regional security policy. In the post-Cold War era, the major threat to Japan's security was not the Soviet Union, but a widely spread variety of uncertainties. These could not effectively be addressed by the Japan-US alliance alone, which was designed to deal particularly with the Soviet threat. To put it another way, there was emerging awareness among Japanese policy makers that Japan must expand its security policy options beyond the Japan-US security arrangements in order to effectively cope with the new regional security environment. This did not mean that Japanese policy makers downgraded the importance of the Japan-US security alliance for Japan's and regional security, as mentioned already. They still acknowledged that the alliance, which sustained American military presence in East Asia and provided a nuclear deterrent, was an indispensable stabilising factor in the post-Cold War regional security environment and thus remained the cornerstone of Japan's overall security policy.[79] Hence, while maintaining its security relationship with the US, Tokyo began to seek a new approach outside the framework of the Japan-US alliance, which could be appropriate to new regional security conditions.

The above two factors, namely the rise of Japan's aspiration for a larger political role in the Asia-Pacific region and its changing perception of regional security significantly affected Japan's motivation to formulate the Nakayama proposal. More specifically, these factors largely account for the reason why Satō's idea of promoting multilateral security dialogue was endorsed by other top level MOFA officials and thus was turned into Japan's official policy in a short period of time. Most importantly, Satō's idea of promoting a regional security forum successfully attracted Japanese policy makers because it offered a solution to Japan's dilemma. It was expected that incorporating Japan into a region-wide forum for multilateral security dialogues, which would allow Asian neighbours to express concerns about the future direction of Japan's role and intentions more openly than bilateral talks, could help Japan to play a larger political role in the region without arousing regional apprehensions about Japan's remilitarisation. In short, it was seen by MOFA as a necessary vehicle for allaying regional concerns about Japan's intention to extend its role in both political and possibly security contexts. Japan's changing perception of the regional security environment also contributed to the motivation behind the Nakayama proposal. With the end of Cold War hostilities, marked by rapid improvements in diplomatic relations among regional countries, MOFA came to think that the time was ripe for regional countries to undertake the task of expanding their political and security cooperation. Meanwhile, the emergence of a fluid security environment led MOFA to hold the view that Japan as well as other regional countries should seek a new approach to the maintenance of regional security and stability. MOFA, hence, began to conceive a region-wide security forum as an appropriate instrument for reducing uncertainties in the post-Cold War regional security environment. In MOFA's view, multilateral security dialogue on various causes of regional concern was expected not only to enhance mutual understanding among regional countries, thus reducing the likelihood of regional conflicts, but also to generate the necessary conditions for deeper political and security cooperation among them.

Alternative explanations for the Nakayama proposal

The US factor?

Existing studies of Japan's policy towards regional security multilateralism have argued that one of the major motivations behind the Nakayama proposal was the need to deal with a potential US withdrawal from East Asia. They contend that Tokyo aimed to secure a continued US military commitment in the region by entangling Washington in a multilateral security forum.[80] However, the main architects of the Nakayama proposal interviewed by the author have denied the implication of such a US factor for it. This was because in their eyes, it was not plausible that engaging the US in multilateral security dialogues would actually help to sustain its military presence in East Asia. In their view, a continued US military presence in the region exclusively depended on the preservation of the Japan-US Security Treaty.[81] Rather, as discussed earlier, MOFA intentionally avoided making any connection between the US-centred bilateral alliance arrangements and a multilateral security forum in order to allay US concerns about its potential negative impact on bilateral security alliances.

Actually, by the beginning of the 1990s, the prospects for the US military engagement in East Asia had become a matter of common concern to regional countries, including Japan, because the rationale for the continuation of US forward deployments in the region was challenged not only by the demise of communist threat but also by its huge economic problem, which constrained Washington from pursuing strategic interests at the expense of economic and domestic issues. In particular, growing domestic frustration about the economic malaise put enormous pressure on the US government to cut its defence expenditures to offset its huge fiscal deficit. Thus, in 1990, as a response to domestic pressure, the Bush administration announced plans to reduce its military budget by US$50 billion over the next five years and to decrease US military force by almost 25%.[82] Washington also showed signs of restructuring and reducing its military commitments in Asia, culminating in the issue of the report in April 1990 entitled *A Strategic Framework for the Asia-Pacific Rim: East Asia Strategic Initiatives* (EASI-I) (updated in July 1992 in the EASI-II). The report announced phased reductions in US military deployment in the region, planning to reduce 15,250 out of a total of 135,000 troops from 1990 to 1992 and further reduce US forces to around 100,000 personnel over a ten-year period.[83] Hence, the American domestic desire for deep defence cuts amplified a regional concern about the US withdrawal from Asia.

However, whereas the future of the US military presence remained somewhat clouded at the beginning of the 1990s, Japanese apprehension about US regional involvement, at least among the mainstream of Japanese policy makers, was mitigated by a series of initiatives taken by the two countries, designed to reaffirm the continuation of the bilateral security relationship on the cusp of the end of the Cold War. For instance, during his visit to Tokyo in February 1990, US Secretary of Defence Dick Cheney confirmed the importance of the Japan-US security relationship for Asia-Pacific security and of Washington's commitment to the region even after the end of the Cold War. Furthermore, on the occasion of the 30th anniversary of the conclusion of the Japan-US Security Treaty in June 1990, Prime Minister Kaifu and President Bush issued a joint statement, which identified that 'the Security Treaty would remain a vital vehicle for ensuring the freedom and security of the two countries and promoting the Asia-Pacific regional stability and peace'.[84] In response to this, in December 1990, Tokyo decided to carry more of the financial burden of the alliance by increasing the amount of host nation support for the US bases in Japan, in order to ease Washington's budgetary problem and thus strengthen its commitment to the alliance. Moreover, in January 1991, the two countries signed a special agreement, under which Tokyo would pay up to 100 percent of the utilities cost of the US bases in Japan and the basic salaries of Japanese workers in the bases.[85] In short, at the beginning of 1990, Japanese policy makers perceived no immediate threat to the Japan-US alliance and the US military presence in East Asia, and thus the US factor did not constitute an important factor for the Nakayama proposal.

Rather, serious concerns about the credibility of the alliance emerged in Japan's policy making community after the Nakayama proposal, particularly during the first years of the Clinton administration, which took a more aggressive approach to Japan's macro-economic policy than the Bush administration, thus creating serious political tension between the two countries. This raised grave concerns among defence officials in both the US and Japan that the bilateral security relationship was under serious threat, as will be discussed more detail in Chapter 7.

It can be said that the idea that a regional security forum could be used as a means to sustain continued US involvement in East Asia was held by ASEAN countries, in particular Singapore, rather than Japan. At the beginning of the 1990s, ASEAN's fears of a possible US withdrawal from East Asia were far more serious than those of Japan. As will be discussed in the next chapter, ASEAN's apprehension was dramatically heightened when the US announced in November 1991 its forthcoming withdrawal from Clark Air Base and Subic Naval Base in the Philippines. Hence, this became one of the prime motivations behind ASEAN's initiative in creating the ARF.[86]

Overall, although Japan did not expect a regional multilateral security forum to function to promote continued US involvement in the region, needless to say, Japanese officials recognised that the US participation in a regional security forum was indispensable for its success and regional stability. It was particularly important for Japan to help establish a dialogue between the US and other Asian countries so that Washington could reassure them about its military commitment to the region.

The Gulf War shock?

It has also been asserted in the previous studies that the Japanese motivation for launching the Nakayama proposal was mainly driven by its Gulf War experience. Some scholars have argued that the opposition from Asian countries to Japan's plan to dispatch SDF for non-combat operations in the Gulf served as a major motivating factor behind the Nakayama proposal on the grounds that it provided an incentive for Japanese policy makers to seek a means to reassure them.[87] Other have contended that the Nakayama proposal was driven by severe international criticism of Japan's chequebook diplomacy during the Gulf War because it created an immediate need for Japan to display a visible initiative in order to restore and increase its international political profile. However, Japanese officials, including the main architect of the Nakayama proposal, have denied the direct causal relationship between Japan's Gulf War experience and the proposal.[88]

The end of the Cold War acted as a catalyst for the debate on Japan's role in the emerging new international system. However, the impact of the Gulf crisis, the first international crisis of the post-Cold War era, on the Japanese debate was far more significant. As noted above, some Japanese leaders had already realised that in the emerging new world order, Japan must accept its share of international responsibility to preserve global security, but the Japanese government, lacking both the skill and experience to handle such a crisis, was wholly unprepared to deal with the Gulf crisis.

With the outbreak of the Gulf War, the US and its allies exerted strong pressure on the Japanese government to participate in the multinational force in the Persian Gulf. In response to calls from both nationalistic and internationalistic politicians in the ruling Liberal Democratic Party (LDP) who were willing to accept the international demand for Japan's contribution to the multinational forces, Prime Minister Kaifu Toshiki introduced the United Nation Peace Cooperation (UNPC) bill in November 1990 that would have allowed SDF to be sent to the Gulf for logistical support activities of the multilateral force. However, the bill was defeated due to resistance from opposition parties and its unpopularity amongst the general public. The Japanese government consequently made only a financial contribution, providing US$13 billion to the US led multinational forces but received no credit for its support. It was striking that Japan was not mentioned in a list of friendly countries thanked in a public letter of gratitude from the Kuwaiti government. Moreover, Japan was excluded by the US from the post-war diplomatic functions celebrating the allied victory immediately after the end of the war. Indeed, Japan's 'chequebook diplomacy' was subject to a storm of international criticism, which stunned Japanese politicians who were quite satisfied with the nation's passive role during the crisis and also the general public, most of whom were indifferent to its international role. For those working towards creating a greater international role for Japan, this diplomatic failure was a national humiliation. In sum, the Gulf shock showed to both the Japanese government and the public that 'one nation pacifism' was no longer acceptable to the international community.

This change in the domestic political mood in terms of Japan's international role enabled the Japanese government to enact the International Peace Cooperation Law (IPCL) in June 1992, promoting the dispatch of non-combat SDF personnel to Cambodia between October 1992 and September 1993 and later to Mozambique, the Golan Heights, and elsewhere.[89] Thus, the impulse for an active political and security role emerging from Japan's humiliating Gulf experience was directed into its initiatives for the UN PKO, not to the Nakayama proposal.

Neither did Asian concerns about Japan's plan to send the SDF to the UN PKO have any direct influence on MOFA's decision to formulate the Nakayama proposal. This was because MOFA was not unduly concerned about the reaction of Asian countries to Japan's participation in the UN PKO.[90] The introduction of the UNPC bill in November 1990 did initially draw criticism from some Asian countries, in particular China and South Korea.[91] However, many ASEAN countries, including Thailand and Indonesia, publicly showed understanding towards Japan's plan.[92] Since May 1991, even Beijing had gradually moderated its opposition towards the deployment of SDF for PKO activities and later even showed its acknowledgement of Japan's plan.[93] That is to say, MOFA did not regard Asian opposition as a serious obstacle to the UNPC bill. Rather, MOFA was concerned about domestic obstructions to the bill, such as the strong anti-militarist sentiment amongst the public and of opposition parties.[94] Nonetheless, it may be said that though the Nakayama proposal was not a direct result of the Gulf shock, it indirectly influenced Japanese motivation to take the lead in establishing a forum for multilateral security dialogue since it further increased the level of Japan's enthusiasm for playing a larger political role in the region.

Conclusion

This chapter has argued that at the beginning of the 1990s, Japan's motivation to establish a regional security forum was shaped by a combination of factors at the international and individual levels. Changes in regional security environment not only aroused Japan's aspirations for playing a larger political role but also led Japanese policy makers to believe that regional countries had now both better conditions for and a common interest in undertaking efforts to expand their political and security cooperation. In seeking these possibilities, they came to realise the need to dispel mutual distrust among regional countries, in particular between Japan and its Asian neighbours, who worried about Japan's future regional role due to its militarist history. At the same time, the emergence of a fluid regional security environment following the end of the Cold War convinced Japanese policy makers to seek a new approach beyond the Japan-US alliance, which by itself could not effectively cope with it.

Although these changes at the international level helped account for Japan's motivation to search for a new diplomatic instrument for overcoming the above policy challenges, Japanese inclination toward regional security multilateralism cannot be fully construed without reference to the ideational force generated at the individual level, namely the role of Satō Yukio, a senior MOFA official, in the formation of the Nakayama proposal. At the beginning of the 1990s, Satō was virtually alone in MOFA in seriously considering the possibility of Japan's initiatives in promoting a multilateral security forum in the Asia-Pacific region. In seeking counter-measures against the Soviet proposal for an Asian version of CSCE, Satō saw a chance for Japan to take the initiative and thus elaborated the concept of a 'multifaceted approach to Asia-Pacific security', suggesting the promotion of security dialogue through existing frameworks in the region, namely the ASEAN-PMC. Satō hoped that by incorporating Japan into a multilateral security arrangement, in which its neighbours could air their concerns, Japan could ameliorate such regional concerns and thus play a larger political and possibly even security role in the region. It was also expected that the enhancement of mutual reassurance among regional countries would establish strong foundations for expanding political and security cooperation among them.

Satō's idea of regional security multilateralism was stimulated by the Soviet CSCE proposal, but it was an original concept, reflecting his own perspective on the post-Cold War regional security order, which was also shared by other senior MOFA officials. The Nakayama proposal had its foundations in Satō's idea and was even drafted by Satō himself. In that sense, it can be said that without Satō's initiative, the Nakayama proposal might not have come about.

Of course, even though Satō was a high-ranking MOFA official deeply involved in Japan's foreign policy decision-making, he alone had no decision-making power. Satō's idea of regional security multilateralism attracted wide support from other senior MOFA officials, including Administrative Vice Minister for Foreign Affairs Kuriyama Takakazu who called for Japan to play an active role in building regional order in the midst of the Soviet collapse, since his concept offered a solution to various problems for Japan's diplomacy arising from changes in regional strategic environment brought about by end of the Cold War. This explains why Satō's idea came so quickly to be Japan's official policy without any serious obstacles. Thus, a sharp shift in Japan's conceptions of and policy towards regional security multilateralism at the beginning of the 1990s can be best explained by the interaction between material factors at the international level that drove Japan to seek a new approach to regional security and an ideational factor generated at the individual level, namely Satō's concept of the multifaceted approach to Asia-Pacific security, which led Japan to take the lead over multilateral security dialogue as a response to external changes. In the next chapter, we will see further changes of Japan's conception of regional security multilateralism, which continued to be influenced by both material and ideational factors.

2 The surge of Japan's enthusiasm for Asia-Pacific security multilateralism and the formation of the ASEAN Regional Forum (1992–93)

Introduction

As we have seen, the Nakayama proposal failed to muster widespread support from regional countries. It could even not attract considerable attentions from the Japanese media. In spite of this, Japan's initial enthusiasm for regional security multilateralism did not dwindle; rather it grew considerably during the early 1990s. Indeed, MOFA continued to pursue its objective of promoting a forum for multilateral security dialogues in the Asia-Pacific region although it refrained from taking the initiative and instead took the lead from behind.

The aims of this chapter are to illuminate Japan's behind-the-scenes diplomacy in the formation of the ARF and to identify main factors for Japan's burning enthusiasm for regional security multilateralism in the early 1990s. The first section of this chapter examines Japan's supporting role to Singapore's initiatives in establishing the ARF and its contribution to the rapid shift of the US position on regional security multilateralism. Japan's diplomacy in convincing the US of the importance of a region-wide forum for multilateral security dialogues in particular deserves special attention since the ARF might not have emerged if Washington did not embrace regional security multilateralism and thereby continued to resist any initiative for it. The second section investigates major factors accounting for the surge of Japan's interest in regional security multilateralism, which ensured their incessant efforts to promote it. This chapter argues that Japan's growing enthusiasm reflected mainly three factors, the wide spread of the concept of 'cooperative security' in Japan's policy making community, a growing trend towards regional cooperation in political and economic fields, and more importantly, the advent of new security challenges, including China's growing military power, the increasing military spending and arms build-up in East Asia and the perceived danger of the proliferation of weapons of mass destruction (WMD). The remainder of this chapter examines how these factors influenced Japan's conceptions of the roles of ARF and the implications of Japan's rising expectations for regional security multilateralism in relation to the course of its overall regional security policy.

Japan's behind-the-scene diplomacy in the formation of the ARF

Backing up Singapore's initiatives

ASEAN's lukewarm attitude towards the Nakayama proposal began to change shortly after the 1991 ASEAN-PMC. The context changed with the Fourth ASEAN summit held in January 1992, which countenanced multilateral political and security dialogues within the ASEAN-PMC format. By this time, most ASEAN countries had become ready to play a direct role in promoting multilateral security dialogues with the line of the Nakayama proposal. The summit mandate was taken forward by the ASEAN-PMC held in Manila in July 1992, in which the participating countries discussed security issues extensively. ASEAN also invited the foreign ministers of China, Russia, Vietnam, and Laos as guests to the ASEAN Ministerial Meeting (AMM), held in conjunction with the PMC. ASEAN's changing position on multilateral security dialogue was inspired by not only the 1991 ASEAN ISIS's recommendation and the Nakayama proposal, but also dramatic changes in the regional security environment surrounding ASEAN, most notably the US giving notice of its withdrawal from all of its military bases in the Philippines in November 1991 and the disintegration of the Soviet Union in December in the same year. The decline of the US and Soviet influences in the Asia-Pacific region raised ASEAN's apprehensions over the possibility of a greater security role for Japan and China's rising power in the region.[1] In particular, China's growing military power became a source of concern to ASEAN countries after China had passed a law on territorial water, proclaiming its sovereignty over the South China Sea and authorising the use of force to defend its claim in 1992.[2] These changes in the regional strategic environment led ASEAN states to realise the need to set up a region-wide secuity forum including all regional major powers in order to not only ensure continued US military engagement in the region, which would enable Japan not to become a military power, but also to address China's rising power. In other words, as Michael Lefier put it, 'ASEAN aimed to create the conditions for a stable balance of power among the three major states in the Asia-Pacific region, which would enable the ASEAN to maintain its operational security doctrine'.[3]

At this time, however, some ASEAN countries, in particular Indonesia, were still loath to fully support the idea of extending the existing ASEAN-PMC dialogue structure to the wider Asia-Pacific and of setting a meeting of senior officials from ASEAN-PMC countries (ASEAN-PMC SOM), which was originally proposed by Japan in July 1991. Matters were taken further after Singapore assumed the chair of ASEAN's Standing Committee for the period from July 1992 to July 1993. By taking full advantage of the chair's position, Singapore, which was the strongest supporter of multilateral security dialogue among ASEAN countries, launched a major diplomatic effort to forge a consensus on an expansion of the ASEAN-PMC dialogue structure and the establishment of an ASEAN-PMC SOM. Singapore, for instance, floated a proposal to organise the ASEAN-PMC SOM, including officials from Russia, Vietnam, and Laos before the ASEAN-PMC in July 1993. Yet, in the face of its reluctant ASEAN partners, Singapore was alone not able to take the lead without strong backing from non-ASEAN countries. Indeed, Japan and Australia played an active role in supporting Singapore's initiative.[4] In July 1992, Japan proposed to expand the agenda of the Japan-ASEAN forum, which had been established in 1977 to facilitate economic cooperation, to political and security issues. One of the main purposes of this proposal was to push ASEAN countries to move ahead with the plan for developing a region-wide multilateral security dialogue along the line of the Nakayama proposal.[5] Moreover, in January 1993, Prime Minister Miyazawa Kiichi took a tour of Southeast Asian countries and delivered a major policy speech in Bangkok. Miyazawa called for Asia-Pacific countries to 'develop a long-term vision regarding the future of regional peace and security through political and security dialogue among regional countries' and pledged Japan's active participation in such discussions.[6] This proposal was an attempt to invigorate growing momentum in ASEAN countries for regional security multilateralism and thus backing up Singapore's initiative in promoting it.

These interactions proved to be a success. At the Japan-ASEAN Forum held at Tokyo in February 1993, both sides agreed to organise the ASEAN-PMC SOM.[7] The first ASEAN-PMC SOM was held in May 1993, and in the summer of 1993, all ASEAN countries and its PMC dialogue partners agreed to create a region-wide security forum that would go beyond the ASEAN-PMC dialogue structure to include Russia and China as well as Vietnam, Laos and Papua New Guinea.[8]

Convincing the US of the importance of regional security dialogue

In parallel with shoring up Singapore's initiative, MOFA also continued its efforts to convince US policy makers of the importance of multilateral security dialogue for regional security publicly as well as informally.[9] MOFA's efforts gradually came to fruition. In November 1991, during his visit to Tokyo, Secretary of State, James Baker, softened his negative stance towards the idea of establishing a regional security forum, stating that 'multilateral process may supplant the bilateral alliances'.[10] Subsequently, in January 1992 President George Bush and Prime Minister Miyazawa Kiichi issued the Joint Declaration on the Japan-US Global Partnership, which promised that 'the two countries would promote political dialogue among Asia-Pacific regional countries through the ASEAN-PMC'.[11] However, in the eyes of MOFA officials, the level of US interest in regional security multilateralism was still considerably low. It seemed that Washington was still struggling to understand the utility of multilateral security dialogue for regional security. This drove MOFA to take further efforts to lead

Washington to hold a more positive view of it. For that purpose, in the speech of the National Press Club in Washington DC in June 1992, Prime Minister Miyazawa proposed a two track approach to Asia-Pacific security: namely: (1) the promotion of sub-regional cooperation to settle regional disputes and conflicts, such as the Korean Peninsula, Cambodia and the South China Sea; and (2) region-wide political dialogue to enhance the sense of mutual reassurance.[12] Miyazawa's proposal for the two track approach was born out of the concept of a 'multifaceted approach to Asia-Pacific security' and was actually drafted by Satō Yukio, who was then the Director-General of the North American Bureau in MOFA. It was an attempt to impress Washington of the necessity of looking beyond its traditional bilateral security arrangements and of promoting multilateral security dialogue and cooperation to deal with the new regional security context. To put it another way, the Miyazawa proposal implied that the US-centred bilateral alliance arrangement was, by itself, not sufficient to cope with an uncertain post-Cold War regional security environment in the region. In the same month in 1992, at the G-7 Summit held at Munich, Japan also took the initiative in leading the Summit's final declaration to include a statement that 'the existing regional frameworks, such as the ASEAN-PMC and APEC, would play an important role in the enhancement of regional security', in order to making a firm impression on the US observers of the importance of a regional security forum.[13]

These Japanese efforts eventually bore fruit when, at the ASEAN-PMC held in Manila in July 1992, James Baker clearly endorsed the idea of establishing a region-wide forum for security dialogues, stating that 'we are pleased that ASEAN's leaders decided last January to add regional security issues to our PMC deliberations. We may find openings for steps to bolster regional security through building trust and confidence'.[14]

With the inauguration of the Clinton administration in 1993, Washington further adjusted its regional policy to growing regional thinking about the positive value of multilateral security. Assistant Secretary of State Winston Lord, during his confirmation hearings before the Senate in April 1993, stated that the US supported the dialogue on security with the PMC and would fully participate in it.[15] Indeed, US State Department officials began to provide intensive support to Singapore's initiative in organising an ASEAN-PMC SOM.[16] Washington's positive attitude appeared more pronounced when President Clinton made a speech to the Korean National Assembly in July 1993. In the speech, Clinton called for the creation of a 'New Pacific Community', which emphasised four pillars of the new US policy for enhancing regional security: (1) a continued US military commitment to East Asia; (2) vigorous efforts to cope with the proliferation of WMD; (3) the promotion of new regional dialogues on the full range of our common security challenges; and (4) support for spread of democracy and more open societies throughout the region.[17] Clinton's speech was significant in the sense that it indicated the emergence of new thinking about regional security in Washington, explicitly identifying the need to develop new security arrangements beyond its traditional bilateral security alliances in order to cope with the multiple threats and opportunities of the post-Cold War era. This new US Asia-Pacific policy, stressing the need to practice the four major approaches through the existing arrangements and frameworks, clearly converged with Japan's idea of shaping a post-Cold War regional security order. Indeed, Clinton's doctrine of the 'New Pacific Community' was inspired by Japan's concept of the multifaceted approach to Asia-Pacific security, something which MOFA had long been suggesting to high ranking officials in both the Bush and Clinton administrations.[18] In that sense, MOFA made a significant contribution to the rapid shift of the US position on regional security multilateralism.

Of course, the shift in the US position on regional security multilateralism was not only a direct result of Japan's persuasion. US concerns about China also played a significant role. By the middle of 1993, China's growing military power was becoming a source of concern to the US as well as countries in the Asia-Pacific region. As a consequence, Washington began to acknowledge that multilateral security dialogue could potentially be a useful tool to engage and promote dialogue on security issues with Beijing.[19] President Clinton expressed this view in his 1993 speech in Seoul, stating that 'we believe China cannot become a full partner in international community if it neglects human rights and international agreements on trade and arms sales. However, we are prepared to involve China in establishing new regional security and economic frameworks. We want an engaged China, not an isolated one'.[20]

Clear shifts in ASEAN and US positions on multilateral security dialogue precipitated the process for the formation of a region-wide security forum. In May 1993 in Singapore, senior officials of ASEAN nations and their counterparts from their seven dialogue partners sat together for the first time to discuss how to shape a post-Cold War Asia-Pacific security order. Significantly, ASEAN-PMC senior officials formally agreed on the need to promote 'multilateral processes of cooperative security for achieving peaceful cooperation in the region' and to establish a region-wide forum for multilateral security dialogue beyond the existing ASEAN-PMC structure.[21] In seeking a consensus on the expanding ASEAN-PMC structure, however, there was dissent among officials over the issue of whether to include Russia and China in multilateral security dialogue. Chinese participation was endorsed by all participating countries, including Japan, since by this point there emerged a common view among them that the rapid growth of China's economic and military power could become a source of regional instability and thus that China should be involved in a multilateral security arrangement.[22] As for Russia's participation, however, there was strong opposition from Japan, which was worried that Moscow would use multilateral security dialogue to shelve the unresolved Northern territorial issue.[23] This was the main reason why the Nakayama proposal excluded socialist countries, namely the Soviet Union and China, from the member-ship of multilateral security dialogue although MOFA did not totally exclude the possibility of their participation.[24] Nonetheless, Tokyo retracted its opposition, realising that it would be harder to exclude Russia alone from multilateral security dialogue while admitting Chinese participation. In the end, it was agreed to invite China, Russia, Vietnam, Laos and Papua New Guinea to a special session of the foreign minister meeting held in conjunction with the ASEAN Ministerial Meeting in Singapore in July 1993.

In July 1993, foreign ministers from 18 countries attended the special meeting. At this point, while most regional countries were ready to partici-pate in a process of multilateral security dialogue, China still remained highly cautious about joining it, worrying that any multilateral security arrangement would be used by other countries as a means to interfere with China's sovereignty and internal matters, such as the issue of Taiwan and the territorial disputes in the South China Sea.[25] However, China eventually agreed, with obvious reluctance, to participate in a forum for multilateral security dialogue. It seemed that Beijing could not afford to ignore the political cost of not becoming a party to a new forum since political isolation would undermine its economic relations with Asian neighbours.[26] Consequently, 18 foreign ministers were able to make a landmark decision to establish a separate gathering of foreign ministers, named the ASEAN Regional Forum (ARF), and convene a first working session in Bangkok in July 1994. In the end, they declared the purpose of the ARF to develop 'a predictable and constructive pattern of relationship in the Asia-Pacific'.[27]

The upsurge of regional security multilateralism

As mentioned at the beginning of this chapter, in spite of the failing of the Nakayama proposal, Japan's enthusiasm for regional security multi-lateralism did not fade away, but rather grew considerably in the early 1990s. Indeed, during this period, the idea of regional security multi-lateralism began to attract wide attention from Japan's foreign policy com-munity, including political and academic circles. The emergence of broad support for regional security multilateralism was evident in the reports presented by a number of commissions exploring Japan's post-Cold War foreign and security policy. For instance, in May 1992, Prime Minister Miyazawa set up his own advisory panel entitled 'Committee on Asia and the Pacific and Japan in the 21st Century' whose task was to consider Japan's post-Cold War policy towards the Asia-Pacific region. In its final report, the committee strongly suggested that the Japanese government make a more concerted effort to establish a regional multilateral security forum in order to advance military transparency, disarmament and arms control issues. The committee's report served as the basis of Miyazawa's policy speech in Bangkok in January 1993.[28] In 1992, the ruling Liberal

Democratic Party (LDP) established the special commission on security affairs to explore Japan's post-Cold War security policy. In December of the same year, the LDP's commission presented a 10-point proposal. While contending that Japan should continuously make efforts to strengthen its self-defence capability and to enhance military cooperation with the US, the proposal stressed the need to establish a multilateral security framework in the Asia-Pacific region. The commission also suggested that for the time being Japan promote a political dialogue process through the ASEAN-PMC, but in the long-term it should be developed into a more formal institution, such as the CSCE.[29]

The surge of regional security multilateralism could also be found in the report presented by another Prime Minister's advisory committee. In 1994, Prime Minister Hosokawa Morihiro set up the 'Special Advisory Committee on Defence Issues', whose task was to consider the direction of Japan's security policy appropriate to a post-Cold War era and to offer input to the new NDPO. The committee's report, named *the Modality of the Security and Defence Capability of Japan: The Outlook for the 21st Century*, (also referred to as the Higuchi report since the committee was chaired by Higuchi Hirotarō, chairman of Asahi Breweries) argued that Japan should formulate a coherent and comprehensive security policy, based on three principles; (1) promoting multilateral security cooperation at both the global and regional levels, (2) enhancing the functions of the Japan-US security relation, (3) possessing highly reliable and efficient defence capabilities. While arguing that the alliance was a major pillar of Japan's security policy, the report put a special emphasis on the importance of Japan's active participation in UN PKOs and its grater efforts for strengthening the ARF and the Council for Security Cooperation in the Asia Pacific (CSCAP).[30] Though these reports did not necessarily represent Japan's official view of regional security multilateralism, they clearly indicated how it became an attractive proposition to the mainstream of Japan's policy making community.

In addition, during the early 1990s, expectations for regional security multilateralism seemed to be further intensified among the central bureaucracies, in particular MOFA. The *1994 Diplomatic Bluebook*, MOFA's official policy statement, put more emphasis on multilateral security cooperation as a major agenda for Japan's Asia-Pacific diplomacy than ever before.[31] Some MOFA officials even began to argue privately or publicly about the possibility of establishing an Asian version of CSCE in the long-term.[32] Miyamoto Yuji, a senior MOFA official, suggested in *Gaiko Forum* that Asia-Pacific countries create a multilateral security framework in the region by drawing on CSCE experiences. Miyamoto assumed that a significant decrease of the US interest in committing to Asia-Pacific regional security would be unavoidable due to the demise of the Soviet threat and that Washington would begin to remit regional security problems to international or regional institutions rather than deal with them unilaterally or directly. It was hence concluded that in order to cope with a new regional security environment, regional countries should promote regular political and security dialogues, codes of conduct, conflict resolution mechanisms and military transparency measures, all of which the CSCE had developed.[33] Finally, MOFA's increasing activism for regional security multilateralism was highlighted by its organisational reform. In 1993, MOFA established the National Security Policy Division within the Foreign Policy Bureau primarily for the purpose of handling multilateral security activities in the region at both the Track One and Two levels, thus expanding its organisational resources available for the ARF.[34]

From 1993 JDA also began to take its own initiative with regards to multilateral security dialogue, recognising that Japan's Cold War security policy, exclusively adhering to the Japan-US alliance, could not respond to regional disputes and conflict.[35] In 1994, JDA set up an Asia-Pacific security seminar, gathering middle-ranked uniformed officers from 18 regional countries, in order to enhance mutual understanding among the participating countries. Moreover, since 1996, JDA initiated an annual Forum for Defence Authorities in the Asia-Pacific Region in order to facilitate defence exchanges among ARF countries. In the Forum, senior defence officials from regional countries discussed regional security issues, defence policies of each member and CBMs. In addition, like MOFA, JDA also restructured its organisation and set up an International Policy Planning Division in the Bureau of Defence Policy to strengthen its multilateral security initiative.[36]

The factors behind avid interest in regional security multilateralism

The rise of Japan's enthusiasm for regional security multilateralism in the early 1990s was partly driven by a growing trend towards regional cooperation in both political and economic fields. This was illustrated by the rapid progress on the process of the formation of the ARF, the emergence of APEC leaders meetings in 1993, and the increasing number of multilateral security arrangements at the Track Two level. The flourishing of these multilateral arrangements naturally encouraged Japanese policy makers to be more willing to incorporate multilateralism into their Asia-Pacific policy making.[37] In particular, there was the tremendous increase of the array of Track Two efforts to promote security dialogue and cooperation in the region. The most prominent was the CSCAP, which was composed of committees made up of academics, security specialists, and former and current foreign ministry and defence officials in their private capacities drawn from a set of member countries largely identical to the ARF. It was established in 1993 as a result of a series of regional conferences on security cooperation organised by the ASEAN-ISIS, the Japan Institute of International Affairs (JIIA), the Seoul Forum for International Affairs, and the Pacific Forum from 1991 to 1992.[38]

A number of sub-regional forums for security dialogue were also established during this period. In 1993, the North East Asia Cooperation Dialogue (NEACD), which involved academics, government officials and military personnel in their private capacities from Japan, the US, South Korea, Russia and China, was initiated by the University of California's Institute on Global Conflict and Cooperation. Japan actively supported the NEACD from the beginning, initiating the study project on defence information sharing.[39] In 1994, MOFA also took the lead behind-the-scenes in establishing the Trilateral Forum on North Pacific Security issues, involving foreign and defence officials from Japan, the US, and Russia.[40] These Track Two forums have provided government officials with a useful venue to conduct informal multilateral dialogues on regional security issues and have developed policy proposals to be directed to the ARF.

Japan's growing interest in regional security multilateralism during the early 1990s also reflected how widely the notion of 'cooperative security' (kyōchō-teki anzenhoshō) had spread in Japan's policy making community. Cooperative security is basically understood as an approach to security that attempts to reduce tensions and the possibility of conflicts among states through non-military and non-coercive means, such as the promotion of international norms, codes of conduct, confidence building and preventive diplomacy measures. It works on the principle of inclusive membership and thus seeks to engage non-like-minded countries rather than isolating them.[41] In Japan, the term began to appear in policy papers, such as the Higuchi report and academic literature from the early 1990s. Many Japanese scholars saw the Organisation for Security and Cooperation of Europe (OSCE) as a practical application of the concept of cooperative security.[42] Indeed, with the growing trend towards regional cooperation in political and economic fields, many in Japan's policy making community came to be attracted by a cooperative security approach.

During the early 1990s, while positive developments regarding regional cooperation did take place in the Asia-Pacific region, the period also witnessed the emergence of new security challenges, namely the rise of China's military power, arms build-up in East Asia and a perceived danger of the proliferation of WMD. These became pronounced in the eyes of Japanese policy makers particularly after 1992. These new security problems further strengthened Japan's desire to promote a region-wide security institution because they not only increased the level of uncertainty in the regional security environment considerably but also simultaneously highlighted the absence of any security arrangements that could address the destabilising factors.

The rise of China's military power

Japan's rising interest in regional security multilateralism during the early 1990s coincided with its growing concerns over the rise of China's military power. Despite occasional flare-ups stemming from the historical issue of Japan's invasion, the relationship between Japan and China during the Cold War was a relatively stable one, particularly from 1978 when the two countries signed the Treaty of Peace and Friendship. This stability remained unshaken even by the Tiananmen incident in June 1989.[43] However, from 1992 Japan's view of China began to gradually change. Many in the Japanese security policy making community, including officials in MOFA and JDA as well as academics and politicians, began to perceive Beijing as a new challenge to regional security.[44] Japan's negative perceptions of China mainly stemmed from two notable developments regarding China's behaviour in the military security dimension after 1992: the rapid modernisation of its military capability and its assertive postures towards territorial issues.

The early 1990s saw the surge of China's military budget with the acquisition of modern military equipments, such as fighter jets, missiles and naval vessels, from the former Soviet Union.[45] In 1992, China made deals for 72 SU-27 fighter jets, SA-10s missiles, 79 MIG 31 fighters and three conventional submarines from Russia. In the same year, it was also reported that China ordered an aircraft carrier from Ukraine.[46] Beijing also engaged in modernising its entire stock of strategic missiles, including intercontinental ballistic missiles (ICBM) and intermediate-range ballistic missiles. Regional countries saw these Chinese moves as a sign of the expansion of its military capability beyond the ordinary requirement of self-defence. Although Japanese policy makers did not regard China's growing military power as security in the narrow military-strategic sense, including the possibility of impending invasion or missile attack, the rapid growth of China's defence budget and the modernisation of its military capability, in particular its air and naval assets, raised serious concerns about the direction of its security policy among them.[47] For instance, in August 1992 Vice-Foreign Minister Kakizawa Kōji criticised China's plan to purchase an aircraft carrier from Ukraine, saying that an acquisition of an aircraft carrier would destabilise the Asia-Pacific region.[48] Moreover, in the meeting with China's Foreign Minister in Qian Qichen in June 1993, Prime Minister, Miyazawa Kiichi, expressed concern about the build-up of China's military capability.[49]

Japan's concerns about China's increasing military power were also amplified by its proclamation of the Law on Territorial Waters in February 1992, which declared its sovereignty over the South China Sea and the Senkaku Islands and stipulated the right to use force to defend its claim. Indeed, the Chinese government regarded the use of force as an effective policy option as it officially admitted its willingness to attack Taiwan if Taiwan declared independence.[50] Although Japan was not a claimant state, any conflicts in the South China Sea would have significantly endangered Japan's main shipping route and therefore its access to global markets and overseas energy. Around 70% of Japan's oil imports, for example, come through the South China Sea. In sum, any conflicts in the area could well have disrupted Japan's SLOC and therefore damaged its economic prosperity. The situation in the Senkaku Islands posed a more immediate challenge to Japan. Until 1992, Japan's claim of sovereignty over the uninhabited islands in 1895 had gone largely unchallenged, as China had long shelved the Senkaku issue. The Japanese government therefore saw China's new territorial law as a significant change in its stance on the issue and thus began to worry about its territorial ambitions.[51]

Faced with China's growing military potential and assertiveness, there was an emerging view in Japanese policy makers that the expansion of China's military capability beyond the ordinary requirement of self-defence and its renewed claims over territorial disputes were evidence of its aspiration for regional hegemony and that this Chinese expansionism would be a major potential destabilising factor. For instance, in August 1992, a senior MOFA official warned that 'the rapid expansion of China's military capability and its move towards the South China Sea indicated its aspiration to fill the power vacuum created by the decline of the US and Russian influence over the region, and this would disturb military balance in the region and thus become a destabilising factor for regional stability'.[52] As we will see later, Japan's apprehensions about China further increased the value of the idea of establishing a region-wide security institution in its regional security policy making.

The growing trend toward arms build-up and the danger of the proliferation of WMD in East Asia

In the early 1990s, Japanese policy makers also perceived the rapid increase in defence spending and the arms build-up among East Asian countries as another potential destabilising factor for regional security. Despite the end of the Cold War, East Asia witnessed an unprecedented rate of increase in defence expenditure in the first half of the 1990s.[53] In particular, Southeast Asian countries sharply increased their spending on modern conventional weapons. For instance, Thailand's defence budget in 1992 was higher by 55 percent than it was in 1989 and Philippines' allocation was higher by 43 percent.[54] Moreover, defence forces in those countries had been gradually restructured from counter-insurgency capabilities to high technology and modern forces with a particular emphasis on maritime capabilities.[55] Trends in military acquisitions in Southeast Asian countries reflected mixed factors, such as their rapid economic growth, the salience of regional conflicts, mutual suspicion, rivalry among them and their growing concern about the rise of Chinese power. Among the factors that brought about this trend, the most decisive was the expansion of China's military capabilities. China's growing military power provoked serious anxiety among regional countries that Beijing would use its new military capabilities to assert supremacy over the South China Sea. By the early 1990s, ASEAN states had already been disturbed by uncertainty and suspicion of Chinese behaviour. For example, in July 1992, China seized six islands from Vietnam and consolidated its operational activities in the South China Sea. Moreover, their apprehensions about China's assertiveness were amplified by the US decision to withdraw from the Philippines, reducing the credibility of the US security umbrella. As a result, many ASEAN leaders felt a compelling need to counter China's expanding military capability by strengthening their own military.[56]

These moves rang an alarm bell for Japanese policy makers. Japanese officials and security analysts did not view their arms acquisitions as part of an 'arms race', but given the lack of trust among regional countries, the existence of various unsettled territorial disputes and the absence of effective mechanisms for arms control, they worried that the regional arms build-up might turn into an arms race, which would significantly increase the likelihood of regional conflicts.[57]

Japanese policy makers also saw the danger of nuclear and missile proliferation. The non-proliferation issue became one of Japan's major diplomatic agendas, particularly from 1993 when the North Korea nuclear issue came to a head.[58] North Korean nuclear potential had been a source of concern in the international community since 1989 when US satellites photographed a plutonium reprocessing plant under construction at Yongbyon. Pyongyang denied the existence of a nuclear weapons programme, but its attempts at concealment served only to arouse regional apprehension.[59] North Korea acceded to the Nuclear Non-Proliferation Treaty (NPT) in 1985 and had signed the Safeguards Agreement with the International Atomic Energy Agency (IAEA) in April 1992. However, IAEA inspections revealed that there were major inconsistencies in the quantity and quality of nuclear materials held by North Korea. The issue intensified in March 1993 when North Korea refused to allow an IAEA inspection and proclaimed its withdrawal from the NPT. US persuasion led North Korea to suspend its decision to withdraw from the NPT and to accept the inspections required by the IAEA. However, the situation reached a low point in spring 1994 when IAEA inspectors discovered that Pyongyang had expanded its plutonium facilities and rejected an important part of the inspection activities. Consequently, in June 1994, the US government began to seriously seek the possibility of UN economic sanctions against North Korea. Pyongyang responded to this by stating that sanctions would be regarded as a declaration of war. This crisis posed a serious threat to Japanese policy makers regarding the proliferation of WMD.[60]

Moreover, Japan's concern about the proliferation issue was amplified by the advent of the North Korea's long-range missile program. In May 1993, North Korea launched a test firing of its No-dong 1 missile that demonstrated its capability of striking most of Japan's territory. Japanese officials actually admitted that the North Korean missile system was incapable of delivering a nuclear warhead because of the immaturity of its technology. Nevertheless, the success of North Korea's test firing deepened Japanese anxiety because the North Korean missile problems were inevitably linked to the issues of a proliferation of nuclear weapons and of missile technology in the region.[61] Japan's defence white paper, for instance, stated that 'North Korea's missile development could encourage a proliferation of delivery vehicles of mass destruction weapons. Such movements could bring instability not only to Northeast Asia and Japan but also to the entire international community'.[62]

Cognisant of these new destabilising factors for regional security, there was growing awareness among Japanese policy makers that Tokyo should take the initiative in launching region-wide efforts to constrain the impact of robust arms acquisition programs and the danger of nuclear and missile proliferation since these issues were problems that could not be addressed effectively without multilateral cooperation among regional countries.

Japan's initial expectations for the ARF

As we have seen, Japan's perception of the post-Cold War regional security environment in Asia was further complicated by the emergence of the new security concerns. Although these problems were not immediate security threats for Japan, they were nonetheless potential destabilising factors for regional security, which Japan could not afford to disregard. The advent of these security challenges further highlighted the importance of regional security multilateralism for Japanese policy makers since in their view these issues were better addressed by multilateral approaches than by unilateral or bilateral approaches. In short, Japanese policy makers began to conceive a regional security institution, namely the ARF, as a means for promoting multilateral cooperation for addressing the new security concerns.[63] These security factors also significantly affected Japan's perspectives of the roles of the ARF. As discussed in Chapter 1, at the time of the Nakayama proposal of 1991, Japanese policy makers saw a region-wide forum as a vehicle for promoting security dialogues to enhance mutual reassurance among regional countries, in particular between Japan and its neighbouring countries, so that Japan could play greater political and possibly security roles in the region. Although this still had important implications for Japan's interest in regional security multilateralism, by the time of the establishment of the ARF, Japan began to expect the Forum to function beyond mere multilateral security dialogues. This was because the emergence of new security concerns generated new policy needs for more meaningful functions. The following section will analyse Japan's (MOFA) conception of the ARF in detail.

Promoting military confidence building measures among regional countries

Firstly, Japan began to envision using the ARF to promote CBMs with respect to the transparency of military programmes, the strategic objectives and intentions of regional countries. As seen in Chapter 1, at the time of the Nakayama proposal of 1991, Japan was cautious about the development of military related CBMs in the Asia-Pacific region on the grounds that such measures developed in Europe during the Cold War were not suitable to the condition of the Asia-Pacific region. Indeed, the primary aim of the Nakayama proposal was to promote a political dialogue process mainly focusing on the foreign policy aspect of security, such as the question of the reduction of the US security commitment to East Asia and the future direction of Japan's security policy rather than the military aspect of security problems. This was part of the reason why MOFA officials even avoided using the term 'confidence building' and instead presented an alternative concept, namely 'mutual reassurance'. However, increasing apprehension about China's growing military capabilities and arms build-ups in East Asian countries changed Japan's view of CBMs. Given these trends, Japanese officials increasingly came to recognise that CBMs designed to enhance military transparency were required in order to prevent the escalation of arms acquisition and the risks of misperception, thus reducing the likelihood of regional conflicts.[64] For Japan, the main focus of such confidence building efforts was China. Since 1992, there had been growing recognition among Japanese officials and security analysts of the need to clarify China's security policy regarding its defence spending, the actual size of its military forces and the strategic purpose of its new capabilities since the lack of transparency in its policy was becoming an important factor for the rapid growth in defence spending and arms acquisition in East Asia and thus a source of regional instability.[65] Reflecting these concerns, Japan began to press China for military transparency. In December 1992, Japan urged China to participate in the United Nation Register of Conventional Arms (UNRCA), which Japan in collaboration with some EU countries took the initiative to establish.[66] Moreover, in the bilateral ministerial meeting between Japan and China in May 1993, Japan's Foreign Minister, Mutō Kabun, proposed to convene a bilateral security forum with the aim of exchanging information on their own defence policies and disclosure of basic military information.[67] Japanese officials did, however, recognise that promoting CBMs between Asian countries would be an extremely difficult task since they had never before adopted and implemented such measures, unlike European nations that had recent experience of them. Moreover, most Asian countries, including ASEAN countries and China, were sceptical about the value of CBMs because in their view, military transparency would merely expose their military vulnerabilities to others and make their rivals more confident, thereby decreasing their deterrent capabilities.[68]

It was thus that Japanese policy makers began to conceive the ARF as a convenient vehicle for educating its Asian neighbours, in particular China, about the significance of military transparency for maintaining regional stability and for promoting multilateral CBMs.[69] Satō Yukio, for instance, wrote in 1994, that 'through multilateral security dialogues, regional countries should promote cooperation for enhancing transparency of defence policies, military spending, and the non-proliferation of WMD, regulating, conventional arms transfers'.[70] Although Satō and other MOFA officials had argued that the Asia-Pacific region would require a broader range of measures, including political, economic and cultural measures, and rejected the application of the concept of CBMs designed to reduce risks of military confrontation between adversaries at the time of the Nakayama proposal, by the time of the foundation of the ARF, introducing multilateral military transparency measures, if not constraining measures, became one of the top priorities of Japan's ARF policy.

A diplomatic instrument for engaging and constraining China

Tokyo also began to see the ARF as an effective instrument of engaging non-like-minded countries, most notably China. As mentioned earlier, at the time of the Nakayama proposal, Tokyo was reluctant to involve non-like-minded countries, namely China and the Soviet Union (Russia), in multilateral security dialogue at least for the time being. However, with its growing concerns regarding China's security policy, this position was reversed. Faced with China's rapidly growing military capabilities, Japan, like ASEAN countries, came to realise that involving Beijing in a multilateral security arrangement was critical for ensuring regional stability and security. Since the mid-1950s, Japan had maintained a strategy of 'constructive engagement' towards China through mainly economic tools, such as trade, investments and ODA, with the purpose of shaping China's foreign policy in directions that were favourable to Japan.[71] In this regard, the ARF offered Japan a useful vehicle for engaging China on political and on security issues. By engaging China in multilateral security discussions and in the task of building a new regional security order, Japanese policy makers expected that in the long-term, China would learn international norms of behaviour and share a feeling of responsibility for the peace and stability of the region, and thus refrain from pursuing unilateral policy. Indeed, by the mid-1990s, engaging China through regional multilateral forums became one of the top priorities of Japan's Asia Pacific diplomacy. As a senior MOFA official stated in *Nihon Keizai Shinbun*, 'keeping China in any regional multilateral forums, such as APEC or the ARF, is the common interests of all Asia-Pacific countries, including Japan'.[72]

At the same time, Japan also began to consider the ARF as a potentially useful diplomatic tool for constraining China. Japan had traditionally avoided strongly pressing sensitive security issues or criticising its neighbouring countries in bilateral talks, fearing that such actions might easily jeopardise its bilateral relations with them given its weak diplomatic position due to the historical legacy of Japanese aggression.[73] A multilateral security forum would give Japan a means to criticise a certain country without inviting direct bilateral confrontation. To put it another way, by building *ad hoc* coalitions with other countries sharing the same security concerns through a multilateral gathering, Japan would feel more able to press certain security issues than if it had had to take such action bilaterally. Kōno Masaharu, a senior MOFA official, represented this view, stating that 'by using the ARF as a venue within which to criticise the policies of certain countries, Japan can exercise wider diplomatic options'.[74] Indeed, for Japan, whose security policy conduct was restrained by various international and domestic constraints, arranging international pressure to constrain a particular target state was a useful diplomatic weapon for addressing its security interests.

Promoting policy coordination and cooperation on specific regional security issues

Finally, Tokyo hoped that in the long-term, the ARF would foster policy coordination and cooperation among regional countries for addressing unresolved regional disputes and conflicts. As the concept of the multi-faceted approach or the Miyazawa proposal of a two-track approach indicated, Japan was basically against the idea of using a region-wide security institution for the settlement of regional disputes and conflicts on the grounds that they would be better addressed separately by sub-regional frameworks, which included only concerned countries, rather than by a region-wide multilateral arrangement, involving too many unrelated countries. Yet, with the rapid progress of regional cooperation in both economic and security fields, an increasing number of Japanese officials came to believe that a region-wide security institution might be able to make a positive contribution with regards to conflict prevention. While rejecting the possibility that the ARF could play a useful role in conflict prevention and crisis management in the short-term, in the long-term Japan expected the Forum to assist sub-regional efforts for or possibly even directly address unresolved regional security disputes and conflicts, in particular the territorial disputes in the South China Sea.[75] This is not to say that Japan had a clear road map or strategy about how to develop the ARF, but at least it had some image of how Japan might utilise it. Indeed, the eventual goal of Japan regarding the development of the ARF was that it would move beyond the security dialogue stage towards policy coordination among the member states and finally collective action. One senior MOFA official argued that:

> Japan had several mid- and long-term expectations for the ARF. The first step was to promote confidence building among the participants. . . . The second step was to take the discussion further, into policy coordination among the participants. It was Japan's opinion that regional stability could be vastly improved if international public opinion could be formed, and mutual understanding, along with a certain degree of cooperation on potentially destabilising issues in Asia could be established. Some such issues included North Korea's nuclear development

and cooperation among the related parties in South China Sea. … The third step was for the participants to take common action toward certain policy goals. If this became possible, the ARF could take a substantial step forward as a multinational security framework, rather than a mere confidence-building mechanism.[76]

Under this conception of the ARF, promoting multilateral CBMs was a mere first step for further security cooperation among the participating states. Japan expected that deepening mutual understanding and policy transparency among regional countries through CBMs would lead to further stages of institutional development, in which actual policy coordination and cooperation among the participating countries would take place.

Overall, Japan's conception of the ARF indicates that Japan had became more optimistic regarding regional security multilateralism in comparison with the view it held at the beginning of the 1990s. Examining Japan's conception of the ARF in relation to the three theoretical perspectives discussed in the Introduction, especially in the light of its emphasis on the promotion of military transparency, it can be said that Japan's conception was largely coincident with the neoliberal institutionalist perspective. Realist and constructivist perspectives can also be detected in Japan's attempts to engage and constrain non-like-minded countries, in particular China. However, considering Japan's long-term expectations for the roles of the ARF discussed above, Japan's earlier conception of the ARF is best identified with an 'optimistic liberal' perspective as a large number of MOFA officials envisioned that the ARF would move beyond being merely a forum for security dialogue and transparency towards becoming a cooperative security institution that could facilitate policy coordination and cooperation for addressing regional disputes. This is not to say that Japanese policy makers saw the ARF as a replacement for the US-centred alliance system or as a promising venue for conflict resolution. As discussed already, they recognised the continued importance of the Japan-US alliance for Japan's as well as regional security in the post-Cold war era and the grave difficulties of establishing robust conflict resolution mechanisms in the region. However, at the very least they considered the ARF to be something more than a mere adjunct to the regional balance of power dynamics. As we will see below, the ARF was seen to be a potential institutional embodiment of the concept of 'cooperative security' and was for Japan a necessary instrument of increasing post-Cold War regional stability.

The implications for Japan's regional security policy

The final section of this chapter examines how Japan's avid enthusiasm for regional security multilateralism influenced its overall post-Cold War security policy towards the Asia-Pacific region. With growing interest in regional security multilateralism, Japanese policy makers began to explicitly incorporate a multilateral security approach into the country's regional security policy making. The *1994 Diplomatic Bluebook*, for example, referred to the 'multifaceted approach' as the basic guiding principles of Japan's Asia-Pacific security policy, arguing that Japan should make the following efforts in parallel in order to ensure Asia-Pacific regional security, namely '(1) maintaining the presence and engagement of the US forces based on the Japan-US Alliance, (2) promoting regional cooperation, (3) promoting the security dialogue in the entire region, and (4) encouraging economic developments'.[77]

By the mid-1990s, Japanese thinking regarding the multifaceted approach had been further refined, as evinced by Japanese policy makers integrating more explicitly a multilateral approach into the nation's regional security policy by carefully considering how it would operate alongside the Japan-US alliance. For instance, in 1995, Yanai Shunji, the then Director General of the Foreign Policy Bureau in MOFA alongside the Japan-US alliance, argued in *Gaiko Forum* that Japan's post-Cold War regional security policy would pursue the following three major approaches; (1) enhancing Japan-US security cooperation; (2) building sub-regional frameworks for security cooperation among Northeast Asian countries and for addressing the South China dispute; and (3) developing the ARF as a region-wide forum for dialogue and cooperation.[78] In the article, Yanai stressed that strengthening these three approaches, which represented a bilateral and multilateral security approach respectively, was critically important for enhancing Japan's national and regional security since the Asia-Pacific security order was gradually being shaped by 'the mutual coexistence of a bilateral and multilateral security arrangement'. Yanai, for instance, argued that:

> One of the notable developments in the post-Cold War era is a trend for constructing cooperative security relationships among regional countries, including Cold War adversaries and non-like-minded countries (this is dubbed 'cooperative security'). ... In recent years, because of the emergence of common security interests in the Asia-Pacific region, loose frameworks for dialogue and cooperation, such as the ASEAN Regional Forum, have been developing. However, though such a cooperative relationship could be developed into a regional mechanism enhancing mutual reassurance as well as preventing and settling disputes and conflicts between regional countries, it will not be able to substitute for NATO or the Japan-US alliance, which not only provides deterrence but also measures to deal with national emergencies ... we should bear in mind that the US military presence, which is indispensable for the maintenance of regional stability in the Asia-Pacific, is sustained by the bilateral security alliances in the region, most notably the Japan-US alliance, while pursuing the promotion of regional security cooperation.[79]

Yanai's remarks illustrated how the mainstream of Japanese policy makers conceived the relationship between the bilateral and multilateral security approaches in Japan's overall security policy. From a Japanese perspective, these two approaches would function in 'tandem'. Multilateral security arrangements, such as the ARF, would supplement the Japan-US alliance by providing measures to reduce the possibility of regional conflicts and aggression through confidence building and preventive diplomacy, while the bilateral alliance would provide reliable insurance should circumstances arise in which conflict could not be avoided. In short, Japan's overall regional security policy, intending to simultaneously pursue both the bilateral and multilateral security approaches, indicated Japan's long-term expectations of constructing a new regional security structure consisting of two separate security arrangements that would mutually reinforce each other by providing complementary functions; namely the Japan-US security alliance and multilateral security arrangements, most notably the ARF. One Japanese scholar has referred to this regional structure as a 'multi-layered security system'.[80] In this respect, enhancing the ARF as a mechanism for promoting confidence building, policy coordination and cooperation on regional security issues along the lines of Japanese expectations, and fusing the two different approaches into its overall regional security policy were keys to the success of Japan's long-term strategy to build the multi-layered security structure in the Asia-Pacific region.

Conclusion

This chapter has examined Japan's changing conception of regional security multilateralism in the period from after the Nakayama proposal up to the formation of the ARF. Although the Nakayama proposal proved to be abortive, Japan continued to take the lead in the formation of a region-wide forum for multilateral security dialogue, but this time from 'behind'. Japan made a significant contribution to the establishment of the ARF by not only persuading the US of the importance of promoting a region-wide forum for multilateral security dialogue and thus helping change US negative view of it but also shoring up Singapore's initiative in expanding the ASEAN-PMC structure to the wider Asia-Pacific.

Japan's continual efforts to promote regional security multilateralism, despite its futile initiative, was encouraged by a surge in enthusiasm for regional security multilateralism in the Japanese policy making community. Japan's motivation continued to be driven by both material and ideational forces, but in this period it was primarily sparked by security rather than political reasons. New security challenges, such as the rise of China's military power, the rapid growth in arms build-ups in East Asia and the danger of the proliferation of WMD, which became pronounced in the eyes of Japanese policy makers particularly after 1992, further highlighted the need to establish a regional security institution since in their view these issues were better addressed by multilateral approaches than by unilateral or bilateral approaches. Moreover, with the rapid progress on regional cooperation in both political and economic fields, such as the flourish of Track Two forums for security dialogues and cooperation, and the widespread notion of 'cooperative security' amongst Japan's policy making community, Japan's policy makers became more inclined to incorporate multilateralism into their Asia-Pacific policy making.

These factors also brought about changes in Japan's conception of a regional security institution, generating new policy needs for more meaningful functions beyond a mere process of multilateral security dialogue. Indeed, Tokyo began to perceive the ARF as a potential vehicle for promoting multilateral CBMs, policy coordination and cooperation among regional countries on specific issues and to cope with China's rising power, not merely a tool for reassuring Asian countries about its intentions and security policy. Thus, it can be argued that Japan's conception of the ARF in the early 1990s reflected primarily an optimistic 'liberal' view of a security institution while both realist and constructivist influences can be traced.

Japan's aim at enhancing the ARF's functions was also in accord with the 'multifaceted approach' to regional security, aiming to simultaneously strengthen both Japan-US defence cooperation and multilateral security arrangements, most notably the ARF. Satō's concept of the multifaceted approach was further refined as MOFA officials more explicitly incorporated regional security multilateralism into the nation's overall security policy by carefully considering its relations with the Japan-US alliance. This also signified Japan's long-term expectations of building a new regional security structure, in which two differing security arrangements, most notably the Japan-US alliance and the ARF, would mutually reinforce each other by providing complementary functions.

The next four chapters detail Japan's actual diplomacy in the ARF from 1994 to 2001. Japan's ARF policy was mainly guided by an optimistic liberal perspective while it also reflected realist and constructivist approaches in terms of dealing with China's growing military power and assertiveness, at least in its inception years. Indeed, the prevalence of the liberal impulse towards regional security multilateralism in Japan's policy thinking would prove to depend primarily on the relative success or failure of its actual ARF diplomacy. Japan's experiences in the ARF are, hence, worthy of a careful examination.

3 Japan's policy on the evolution of Confidence Building Measures in the ARF

Introduction

From this section onwards, this study conducts a detailed investigation of Japan's diplomacy in the ARF. The aim of this section is to examine how Japan attempted to develop the ARF process along with its conceptions of a regional security institution discussed in Chapter 2 and to what extent the ARF could meet its expectations. This investigation also sheds lights on the problems and difficulties that arise with the process of security institution-building in the Asia-Pacific region.

This chapter looks specifically at Japan's diplomacy regarding the CBM agenda in the ARF. As discussed in Chapter 2, promoting multilateral CBMs for enhancing military transparency and mutual reassurance among regional countries was one of the prime goals of Japan's ARF policy, and the success of cooperation in this area was seen by Japanese policy makers as the first steps for further stages of security cooperation between the participating countries, which would transform the ARF from a mere forum for security dialogue into a cooperative security institution. An examination of Japan's experiences in the CBM agenda over twelve years, however, reveals that fulfilling its aspirations was a highly problematic undertaking. Indeed, Japanese policy makers encountered serious problems and difficulties in the pursuit of security institution building in the Asia-Pacific region from the outset.

Two divergent views of CBMs

The decision to establish the ARF at the July 1993 special meeting was seen as a historical step towards Asia-Pacific security multilateralism as it paved the way for the first time for the establishment of a region-wide security forum involving all major countries in the region. However, the ARF did not run smoothly from the outset since there existed no common idea of what should, specifically, be pursued for achieving the ARF's declared objective, namely 'to develop a more predictable constructive pattern of relationships for the Asia-Pacific region'. This was particularly true for

ASEAN countries, which were more concerned with the form and composition of a new security forum than with its substance. This was because their main consideration at that time was to register ASEAN's diplomatic centrality and to promote its own model of security cooperation in the new security entity rather than to explore concrete cooperative security measures, which might arouse controversy among ASEAN countries. ASEAN Secretary-General, Dato Ajit Singh, stated immediately after the 1993 special meeting that 'the whole thing is premised on the fact that we want to have a more stable and predictable order in Southeast Asia. The ARF is not a forum, in which ASEAN countries will discuss issues which divide them'.[1] ASEAN's intentions had already been demonstrated at the 1993 ASEAN-PMC SOM. In the discussion of ways to promote political and security cooperation, ASEAN attempted to impose its own code of conduct, namely the Treaty of Amity and Cooperation (TAC)[2] on other participating countries with the aim of registering its leading position in an emerging new security entity. The meeting actually discussed various concrete proposals for CBMs, conflict management and non-proliferation, most of which were floated by non-ASEAN countries, but they were simply put off for further research. Instead, the Chairman's statement of the ASEAN-PMC SOM explicitly stated that 'TAC could complement the role of the UN by providing a regional diplomatic instrument to foster positive conditions for peace and security, and to provide measures for PD and dispute solution'.[3] However, ASEAN's resolve was not readily endorsed by a number of non-ASEAN participants, including Japan, Australia, Canada and South Korea, which were keen to place concrete cooperative security measures, such as CBMs, high on the ARF's agenda.[4]

Accordingly, the First ARF Ministerial Meeting took place in Bangkok July 1994 without any clear or common agenda. The key issue of the First ARF was whether the participating countries, having different views of the ARF, could reach a common view on appropriate measures to promote security cooperation. ARF countries acknowledged a mixture of both European and ASEAN approaches to security cooperation. The Chairman's statement of the First ARF, for instance, declared that the objective of the ARF was 'to foster constructive dialogue and consultation on political and security issues of common interest and concern' and 'to make significant contributions to efforts towards confidence building and preventive diplomacy in the Asia-Pacific region'.[5] While an emphasis on constructive dialogue and consultation indicated that the ARF inherited the ASEAN Way of addressing security, references made to confidence building and preventive diplomacy showed that the ARF had agreed to promote more practical measures for security cooperation. Meanwhile, the First ARF formally endorsed the TAC as 'a code of conduct governing relations between states and a unique diplomatic tool for regional confidence building, preventive diplomacy, and political and security cooperation'. In this regard, ASEAN's centre role, which had not been fully endorsed by a number of non-ASEAN countries, including Australia and South Korea, was formally registered in the ARF.[6]

However, even though all ARF countries ostensibly acknowledged the importance of promoting CBMs and PD for regional stability, willingness and preparedness to move towards concrete cooperation in these areas was not necessarily shared to the same degree among them. The First ARF SOM in Bangkok in May 1994, in which senior officials of 18 countries gathered to prepare for the Ministerial Meeting, witnessed some friction over the issue of the pace at which the ARF should progress. While Australia, Canada, the US and to a lesser extent South Korea suggested that ARF countries begin the examination and implementation of concrete CBMs as quickly as possible, China and ASEAN opposed this, arguing that ARF activities should be limited to security dialogues for at least the first few years before moving on to more substantial measures. At the SOM, Australia, Canada, South Korea and Japan presented concrete proposals for CBMs. Australia proposed a package of CBMs with the presentation of the concept of 'Trust-Building Measures' (TBMs), which was 'the idea of a less formal approach, built upon a base of personal political contacts and relationships'. The Australian paper introduced about 15 items relating to TBMs, such as a limited exchange of military information, observer exchanges in military exercises, notification of military deployment, and the establishment of a regional arms register.[7] Although the paper stressed the need to develop CBMs that were appropriate to the conditions of the Asia-Pacific region, most of the proposals were actually not dissimilar to those of the CSCE model. Canada also presented two papers, one on preventive diplomacy and conflict prevention and one on non-proliferation. The Canadian paper also contained ambitious proposals, such as a conflict management mechanism, prior notification of major military and naval exercises, and exchanges of observers at such exercises.[8] South Korea's proposal referred to the establishment of a framework for security dialogue and cooperation in the Northeast Asia region. It suggested that Northeast Asian countries implement some modest CBMs and explore cooperation in non-combatant activities, such as search and rescue operations as well as emergency relief.[9] Finally, both Australia and Canada advocated the foundation of an official working group on CBMs similar to those of CSCE in order to commence full discussions on their proposed CBMs.[10]

Predictably, these proposals drew negative responses from both ASEAN and China. Chinese officials, in particular, showed strong reservations about Australian and Canadian insistences on the quick implementation of proposed CBMs, fearing that this would undermine its territorial interests and security objectives in the region. Chinese representatives, for instance, stated 'there should be no attempts to use CBMs and PD to resolve internal conflicts or problems of a country. We stand for a gradual approach in finding out means for practical cooperation'.[11]

Albeit for different reasons, ASEAN countries also supported Chinese opposition since Australian and Canadian proposals were clearly opposite to the 'ASEAN Way' of addressing security, which stressed informal dialogue, consultations, and an incremental and consensus-oriented approach.[12] ASEAN countries strongly suggested that the ARF function according to the ASEAN Way, which had successfully reduced intra-ASEAN tensions and constituted intra-mural solidarity in their perceptions, believing that it would be possible to transplant ASEAN's practices into the Asia-Pacific region-wide forum. In other words, as Michael Leifer put it, 'ASEAN states conceived the ARF as the extension of ASEAN's model of regional security, extending into Northeast Asia and the Pacific their understandings and practices'.[13] ASEAN's preference for an extremely cautious approach also reflected its concerns about China's regular participation in the Forum. Having Beijing in mind, Singapore's Foreign Minister Shangmugam Jaya-kumar, for example, argued that 'forcing the pace of the ARF's development would cause discomfort to some participants and discomfort often means diminished participation'.[14] Finally, China and ASEAN's rejection of the above CBM proposals derived from their traditional suspicion of a Western notion of CBM. As discussed in Chapter 2, China and most ASEAN countries tended to see military transparency measures as destructive to national security. They thus preferred confidence building efforts mainly through informal dialogues and declaratory measures, such as TAC and the Five Principles of Peaceful Co-Existence, which stressed sovereignty and the principles of non-interference.[15]

Japan's view of CBMs

The controversy among the participating countries over the pace of the development of the ARF aroused at the First SOM was hardly a surprise to MOFA officials. MOFA had already been aware of deep divisions between the two major groupings of countries on substantive issues prior to the SOM. Two months before the First ARF SOM, MOFA organised a two day conference in Tokyo, inviting diplomats and academics from most ARF countries in order to sound out their views on the ARF as well as their reactions to the Japanese point of view.[16] Japanese thinking regarding an approach to the CBM agenda was situated between the two divergent views described above. While basically understanding the merits of ASEAN's incremental building block approach to security cooperation in the light of the need to sustain China's participation in the ARF, like Canada and Australia, MOFA officials recognised the need to set up a working group on CBMs on the grounds that only two meetings (SOM and Ministerial Meeting) during the course of a year would not be capable of either producing any concrete achievements on security cooperation or maintaining momentum.[17] MOFA officials were also concerned that extremely slow progress on security cooperation would discourage US interest in the ARF, thus leading to its natural death. Indeed, serious concern had already emerged before the first working session of the ARF that the Forum might not survive beyond a single meeting.[18] In this regard, the challenge that Japan was facing in the First ARF was to present an appropriate approach to security cooperation that could strike a middle ground between the ASEAN and the Western approach in order to put the ARF on the right track.

Japan's considerations were embodied in its paper on CBMs presented at the First ARF SOM.[19] Japan's paper outlined a number of concrete proposals for CBMs under the concept of Mutual Reassurance Measures (MRMs). It consisted of three areas of activity: (1) information sharing to enhance transparency of each country's defence policy; (2) personnel exchanges to deepen mutual understanding; and (3) cooperation towards the promotion of global activities. Proposals for information sharing, for instance, included three measures, namely the publication of defence white papers, the promotion of the UNRCA and cooperation on non-proliferation of WMD and missiles. In particular, ARF countries were urged to submit defence white papers to the chair's country on an annual basis. These papers would include information about national security policy, defence doctrine, military budgets, and future force projections in general. It was expected that they would serve to reduce the level of suspicion and misperception among regional countries uncertain about each other's strategic intention.[20] At the time of the First ARF, Japan, South Korea, Thailand and the US were the only countries that had ever issued them. The proposal for regional cooperation on non-proliferation mainly reflected Japan's concerns about North Korea's missile development and suspected nuclear programme, as mentioned in Chapter 2. Japan suggested that regional countries establish effective export control systems to prevent the diffusion of materials used for the production of such weapons and expressed its willingness to host seminars on the non-proliferation issue in order to advance regional cooperation in this field. Personal exchanges referred to high-level contacts and exchanges between defence officials. Japan had already initiated bilateral defence exchanges with China and ASEAN states as a part of confidence building efforts and thus tried to spread such activities throughout the region through the ARF. As for regional cooperation regarding global activities, Japan's paper advocated seeking cooperation in PKOs not only as a way of promoting confidence building among regional countries but also for preparing for the future challenges to the region. And finally, like Australia and Canada, the paper suggested that the ARF set up an official level-working group in order to initiate a detailed discussion on the above proposals.[21] Japan's proposals were modest compared to Australian and Canadian proposals, as they basically put emphasis on information-exchange measures and did not even touch on either notification or constraining measures, which the CSCE gave great weight to. It was clear that Japan developed the above proposals for MRMs with China and Japan very much in mind.

Indeed, as with the Nakayama proposal, Japan deliberately avoided using the term 'confidence building' and instead offered as a substitute term 'mutual reassurance' in order to mitigate concerns of Asian countries over the application of CSCE type CBMs to the ARF. Japan's paper submitted to the First ARF SOM explained the difference between the concept of MRMs and that of CBMs:

> The 'CBM' was created, against the background of East-West confrontation in Europe during the Cold War, to ease tension between the two camps and to minimise the risk of military confrontation. However, in the Asian region, there is no such bipolar structure of nations divided into two hostile camps. The most significant feature of Asia is its diversity not only in nation's security concerns, but in other areas, such as political and economic systems, culture and religion. In such circumstances, for the stability of this region, it is necessary that, in addition to minimising the risk of military confrontation, efforts be made to increase mutual assurance and openness of defence policy (transparency) through a wide variety of measures, including political, economic and cultural measures. We feel the 'CBM' is too narrow a concept to cover all the measures needed. It would be more appropriate to have such concept as 'measures to increase mutual reassurance' (Mutual Reassurance Measures: MRMs).[22]

In sum, Japan's concept of MRMs was a product of its attempt to re-conceptualise CBMs for ASEAN and China, which preferred a cautious approach to regional security cooperation. Japan believed that at the initial stage, proposals for CBMs should be less ambitious and more moderate on the grounds that pushing for the rapid promotion of CBMs might prove counter-productive, making reluctant countries more hesitant to move in the direction of achieving concrete progress. That is to say, Japan's modest proposals for CBMs aimed to balance China and ASEAN's extremely cautious approach to a multilateral process and the Western approach. In that sense, the Japanese proposal was more realistic than other countries' proposals and thus successfully led the ARF to adopt a number of CBMs in its next working session.

It is, however, important to note that Tokyo did not totally preclude CSCE type CBMs in its long-term vision of what the ARF should achieve. Although Japan's concept of MRMs stressed the need to promote non-military measures, its actual proposals for MRMs put more emphasis on military as opposed to non-military measures. As will be discussed later in this chapter, Japan even strongly urged other ARF countries to focus on military CBMs in later years when the focus of the ARF agenda was increasingly shifted from traditional military security to non-military security issues. Being a country with a relatively transparent defence policy, Japan was actually ready for more advanced CBMs, deeper defence exchanges, including notification measures and even some constraining CBMs.[23] In short, the difference between Japan's view of CBMs and that of Western countries was not the content of the measures but rather the process of promoting them. In this regard, the concept of MRMs was developed mainly for the purpose of removing the suspicions of other Asian countries regarding CBMs. In fact, the term 'MRMs' soon disappeared in Japanese security parlance as other Asian countries increasingly got used to the notion of CBMs.

CBM proposals raised by activist countries, however, were not successful in achieving any significant progress on CBMs. The First Ministerial Meeting merely agreed to enlist Brunei, the next ARF chair, 'to work in consultation with others to collate and study a number of proposals raised in the First ARF for submission to the Second ARF'. Moreover, due to Chinese opposition to the establishment of an official working group on CBMs, ARF ministers agreed only to 'convene informal meetings of officials to study all relevant papers and suggestions if necessary'.[24]Nonetheless, activist countries continued to take the initiative in promoting CBMs, organising some informal Track Two workshops on the subject.[25]

The success of Japanese proposals

In Japan's view, the First ARF was certainly not a bad start even though it did not yield any significant progress on the CBM agenda. It was a historical event, bringing together former ideological enemies and historical rivals to seek ways of enhancing peace in the post-Cold War era and to foster relations of mutual confidence for regional stability.[26] However, Japanese officials thought that the second working session of the ARF should make concrete progress on CBMs since a failure to produce concrete achievements at this stage would significantly weaken the momentum of the ARF. One senior MOFA official stated before the Second ARF that 'in the last year the ARF was sort of like a get to know each other gathering since it was the first security meeting ever in the region. But this year, we should reach an agreement on some specific CBMs in order to make qualitative progress on security cooperation'.[27] In this regard, priorities for Japan's policy in the Second ARF were straightforward: to develop a consensus on its CBM proposals, in particular the publication of defence white papers, as well as on its earlier proposal for establishing an official working group on CBMs.

At the Second ARF SOM in Brunei in May 1995, Japanese officials presented a defence white paper to put indirect pressure on other participating countries to issue their own white papers. Japan also tried to crystallise its proposal for an official working group by expressing its willingness to host a first meeting in Tokyo. With the blessings of other countries, most notably Australia, the Japanese proposals finally registered some successes. Accordingly, at the Second ARF Ministerial Meeting in Brunei in August 1995, the ministers formally agreed to promote a number of CBMs, including 'dialogues and consultations on political and security cooperation', 'the submission of an

annual statement of defence policy to the ARF or ARF-SOM on a voluntary basis', 'high-level contacts and exchanges among defence officials', and
'participation in the UNRCA'.[28] Above all, Beijing's announcement of its
intention to publish a defence white paper aroused a great deal of excite-
ment amongst Japanese observers.[29] Perhaps more importantly, the Second
ARF agreed to set up an Intersessional Support Group (ISG) on CBMs
and two Intersessional Meetings (ISM) on peacekeeping and on search and
rescue operations. The establishment of these intersessional mechanisms
finally gave the ARF a process for more detailed examination of concrete
security cooperation. The attempt to institutionalise the work of the ARF,
however, encountered some resistance from Beijing. Chinese representatives
were opposed to giving an indefinite time frame to intersessional works so
as to prevent the institutionalisation of the ARF. As a result of this, the ISG
on CBMs was allowed to convene only on an ad hoc basis and was hence
called 'group' rather than 'meeting'.[30] Meanwhile, with respect to the
arrangements for these activities, ASEAN made some concessions that each
group would be co-chaired by one ASEAN and one non-ASEAN country
to meet concerns from non-ASEAN members over ASEAN's centre role in
the ARF. In the end, Japan successfully took the position of a co-chair at
the first ISG meeting on CBMs with Indonesia. This provided Tokyo with a
golden opportunity not only to take the lead in moving its CBM proposals
toward the implementation stage, but also to show its diplomatic initiative in
the ARF to both international and domestic audiences. In addition, the US
and Singapore would co-chair the ISM on search and rescue coordination
and cooperation while Malaysia and Canada would co-chair the ISM on
peacekeeping operations. Not surprisingly, China was the only major power
not to co-chair any sessions at this time.

The Concept Paper: Controversies over the road map and ASEAN's leading role

Another highlight in the Second ARF was the presentation of a 'Concept
Paper'. The Concept Paper sought to set out the organisational principles
and future evolution of the ARF. The paper was ostensibly prepared by
Brunei, the chair of the second working session of the ARF, but in reality
Australia and Singapore played a major role in drafting it.[31] The Concept
Paper suggested that the ARF promote security cooperation in three stages:

Stage 1 Promotion of Confidence building Measures.
Stage 2 Development of Preventive Diplomacy Mechanisms.
Stage 3 Development of Conflict-Resolution Mechanisms.[32]

It presented a number of proposals for CBMs, PD measures and cooperation
in other areas, including non-proliferation, arms control and maritime
security cooperation, and divided them into two lists, annex A and B, in

each of the categories. In the case of CBMs, for instance, annex A included 'measures that can be explored and implemented by ARF participants in the immediate future', such as the publication of defence white papers, participation in UNRCA, annual seminars for defence officials and observers at military exercises on a voluntary basis. Annex B contained measures that could be explored over the 'medium and long term' by ARF countries or addressed by Track Two forums, such as 'the exploration of a regional arms register, the development of maritime information databases', 'systems of prior notification of major military deployments that have region-wide application', and 'the establishment of zones of cooperation in the South China Sea'.[33]

The Concept Paper also stipulated a number of organisational rules, which largely reflected ASEAN's norms and practices. For example, it asserted that 'decisions should be made by consensus after careful and extensive consultations' and 'the ARF should also progress at a pace comfortable to all participants'. Moreover, it excluded the possibility of further institutionalisation of the ARF, including the establishment of a permanent secretariat, by stating that 'ASEAN shall be the repository of all ARF documents and information and provide the necessary support to sustain ARF activities'.[34] In short, the specification of ASEAN norms and principles in the Concept Paper was a result of ASEAN's attempt to consolidate its leading role in the ARF.

The Concept Paper was significant in the sense that it provided the mid- and long-term objectives of the ARF about which most participating countries had had no idea. It was produced in an attempt to present an acceptable road map to all ARF countries by trying to strike a balance between activist countries and reluctant countries.[35] The idea of a three-stage development process envisioned by the Concept Paper was welcomed by Japan as it accorded largely with Japan's long-term expectations for the ARF, discussed in Chapter 2. It was also supported by other ARF countries, such as the US and Canada, which sought to develop the ARF's potential in conflict prevention and resolution. However, resistance from China obstructed consensus on the Concept Paper. At the Second ARF SOM, Chinese officials showed strong reservations about the phrase 'conflict-resolution mechanisms' specified by the paper on the grounds that the development of such mechanisms might give the ARF a mandate to interfere in China's internal problems, such as the issue of the Taiwan Strait. Assistant Chinese Foreign Minister, Wang Yingfan, stated that 'the ARF is a venue for dialogue and exchange of views. It is not a negotiating body or a body for arbitration'.[36] In the end, activist countries eventually conceded to replace the term, 'conflict-resolution mechanisms' with 'elaboration of approaches to conflict' since the changes were in wording rather than substance. In addition, ARF officials also deleted the words, 'measures' and 'mechanisms' from the Chairman's statement because the Chinese considered the word 'mechanism' too legalistic.[37]

Dissent over the Concept Paper also involved the question of ASEAN's proprietary role in the ARF. At the SOM, some activist countries criticised ASEAN for inserting a reference to 'the primary driving force of the ARF' into the Concept Paper and called for changes in wording to reflect an equal status for all ARF members.[38] By that time, frustrations over ASEAN's diplomatic centrality had grown considerably among activist countries since it limited the focus of the ARF agendas primarily to Southeast Asian issues.[39] At the Ministerial Meeting, while applauding ASEAN's contribution to the establishment of the ARF, Japan's Foreign Minister, Kōno Yōhei, implicitly expressed Japan's frustrations, stating that 'non-ASEAN countries should also actively get involved in the management of the ARF in the light of equal participation'.[40] As discussed in the previous chapter, Japan had been one of the strongest supporters of ASEAN's initiative in the formation of the ARF. However, this does not mean that Japan saw ASEAN's leading role as a permanent arrangement. Indeed, Tokyo and Washington privately held the view that the ASEAN Regional Forum should be transposed to 'Asia Regional Forum' at some point in the future.[41] China, on the other hand, ardently endorsed ASEAN's centre role of the ARF on the grounds that it would prevent either the US or Japan from dominating the Forum. In other words, Beijing saw ASEAN's diplomatic centrality as a useful counterweight to US and Japanese influence over the ARF.

Despite the existence of friction between ARF countries over ASEAN's proprietary role, the Second ARF eventually approved the substance of the Concept Paper's recommendations, and ASEAN norms and practices were explicitly written into the Chairman's statement. Activist countries, due largely to a realisation that Chinese participation in the ARF would not be ensured without maintaining it, tolerated ASEAN's leading role in the ARF. The 'ASEAN Way', which stressed consensus decision-making and a non-binding approach, was considered to be the only approach that could mitigate Beijing's strong misgivings about the ARF since it allowed China to apply a block to any proposal and thus to control the pace of the ARF's progress.[42] Indeed, as Leifer put it, 'engaging China through the ARF was ASEAN's strongest card in maintaining its proprietary role'.[43] In this regard, activist countries paid a significant price for ensuring regular Chinese participation.

Overall, the accomplishments of the Second ARF were satisfactory to Japan in the sense that ARF countries had reached agreement not only on specific CBMs and the establishment of official working groups, but also on medium and long-term objectives. MOFA's internal report on the Second ARF stated that 'in this year the ARF made qualitative progress as it was moving on to the next step of beginning to promote concrete security cooperation from the stage of security dialogue'.[44]

Challenges for moving the ARF beyond modest CBMs

Japan's initiatives for promoting CBMs in the third working session of the ARF began with its co-chair role in the ISG on CBMs, which took place in

Tokyo in January 1996 and subsequently in Jakarta in April of the same year. In the ISG, Japan set up two main objectives: (1) to deepen mutual understanding among the participants through having frank discussions on regional security issues and CBMs, and (2) to find out the basis of potential consensus on new CBMs through exchanging each participant's views of various specific CBMs.[45] Japan extended invitations to the defence officials of 18 countries to participate in the ISG in order to both foster mutual understanding among ARF countries and to make the discussion on CBMs more substantial. It was also expected that the involvement of defence officials in the ISG would facilitate the implementation of agreed CBMs, namely 'encouraging high-level contacts and exchanges among defence officials'.[46]

At the ISG, officials discussed primarily the following CBM agendas: (1) Defence Policy Publications, (2) Enhancing High-Level Defence Contacts and Exchanges among Defence Staff Colleges and Training, (3) UNRCA, and (4) Additional CBMs.[47] Against this backdrop, Tokyo's top priority was to invigorate other countries' commitments to the publication of defence white papers. By the time of the first ISG, only half of the ARF's countries had published white papers. Japanese officials reiterated the importance of defence white papers for enhancing military transparency and strongly urged other ARF countries that had not yet published them to do so.[48] Tokyo also raised another concern with regards to this measure, namely the lack of quality and quantity of information in defence white papers issued by other ARF countries. This issue became critical when Beijing first published its own white paper in November 1995. China's white paper drew severe criticism from Western observers since the information provided was far from revealing or transparent. The same sorts of observation could be made about other countries' white papers, such as Singapore, Thailand and Indonesia.[49] The information of their defence white papers was far less revealing than that of Japan. The question was therefore raised as to whether the problem caused by the lack of quality and quantity of information could be remedied if general standards or guidelines on what should be included in a white paper were established. Japanese officials supported the idea of creating minimum guidelines, expecting that this would encourage member states to reveal a certain level of detail. In the ISG meeting, Japan led the discussion on this issue by appealing to its own white paper as a possible model.[50] However, this idea was not endorsed by reluctant countries, which still regarded military transparency as a threat to their national security.

Another agreed CBM, the participation in the UNRCA, moved forward more smoothly. From the time of the First ARF onwards, ASEAN's participation in the register increased significantly. In 1993, among ASEAN members, Singapore, Malaysia and the Philippines were the only participants in the UNRCA, but by the time of the Third ARF, Brunei, Laos and Cambodia were the only ARF countries that did not submit any data to the register. The success of the UNRCA in the ARF partly reflected its flexibility and informality, as it only required the registered countries to submit information on a small number of transactions of major conventional arms. However, the contribution of the ARF should not be ignored as it was through the Forum that sufficient pressure was brought to bear on many ASEAN countries that had previously been unwilling to participate. From the perspectives of some ARF countries, however, the current conditions of the UNRCA were not sufficient to address regional concerns about the rapid growth in military spending and arms build-ups in East Asia. This is because its scope was limited to imports and exports of seven categories of conventional arms and it was left to the discretion of individual states whether to supply information on the type of armaments and systems being transferred. Reflecting the limited scope of the UNRCA, some ARF countries floated a proposal for creating a regional arms register to complement the work of the UNRCA.[51] Yet, given the fact that even moderate CBMs had not been fully implemented by participating countries, the idea of a regional arms register appeared to be premature. Beijing was loath to support the idea of a regional arms register, fearing that such a measure would force it to provide too much sensitive military information.[52]

The ISG also considered another new CBM proposal, namely the advance notification of and exchange of observers in major military exercises. As suggested earlier, Japanese officials were initially reluctant to bring CSCE-type CBMs into the Asia-Pacific region on the grounds that CBMs developed against the background of Cold War military confrontation in Europe were not applicable to the conditions of the Asia-Pacific security environment. However, by the Third ARF, Japanese officials became more willing to support some CSCE-type CBMs, thinking that confidence building among regional countries would be greatly enhanced if these measures were agreed and implemented among them.[53] Some ARF countries expected to see a quick consensus on this proposal because several regional countries outside the framework of the ARF had actually implemented this measure. However, the discussion was confounded by the row between Beijing and Washington over ways of implementing the measure. China suggested that the notification and invitation of observers should be applied only to military exercises held far from one's home territory and that involved 'more than two countries' (joint military exercises). China's proposal was clearly intended to apply to the US, which was carrying out joint military exercises with its allies, and to escape from obligations itself. US officials were therefore reluctant to accept China's proposal.[54]

The above mentioned CBM proposals were further explored at the second meeting of the ISG held in Jakarta in mid-April but little significant progress was made, primarily due to China's and ASEAN's reluctance to expand the CBM agenda. As a result, the ISG had little success in advancing the issues. For instance, the Third ARF Ministerial Meeting in Jakarta in July 1996, agreed that 'the ARF-SOM was to be opened to defence representatives and also encouraged their greater participation in intersessional activities'. It was also agreed that members would 'voluntarily exchange information concerning ongoing observer participation in and ongoing notification of military exercises among ARF participants with a view to discussing the possibilities of such measures in selected exercises'. Finally, instead of considering the establishment of a regional arms register, it was agreed to 'voluntarily circulate the same data to the ARF countries at the time of its submission to the UN'.[55]

The results of the ISG meetings showed Japanese officials that substantial progress on multilateral military CBMs was unlikely to be made in the ARF, in which regional countries having different views on CBMs sat together under the rules of consensus, at least in the short term. Considering that even moderate CBMs, such as the publication of defence white papers, were opposed by China and ASEAN countries, prospects for the promotion of more practical and meaningful CBMs, including the notification of military exercises and a regional arms register, were slender. Nonetheless, Tokyo was not totally discouraged by the result of the ISG meeting. Japanese officials were basically satisfied with the progress on the CBM agenda during the first three years.[56]

Japanese officials were also encouraged by China's increasingly active role in the ARF. By the Third ARF, the Chinese position on the ARF seemed to have become more positive and constructive. In the Third ARF meeting, for instance, Beijing surprised other ARF members by voluntarily offering to co-host the 1997 interssesional year of the ISG on CBMs with the Philippines. Whether China's proactive stance simply reflected its willingness to control the pace of the ARF's progress in accordance with its own national interest or not, it indicated China's new confidence in its ability to engage in a multilateral setting. Indeed, this was the first time that China had hosted an official multilateral conference on security issues. There were also signs that China's hostility to CBMs was softening to some degree. Although China continued to have misgivings about military CBMs within the context of the ARF, outside its framework Beijing completed a multilateral CBM treaty with Russia, Kazakhstan, Kyrgyzstan, and Tajikistan, which included a CSCE type agreement on military observers and limits on the size of military exercises within a certain distance of national borders.[57] Chinese leaders also appeared publicly sanguine about the ARF process. At the Third ARF Ministerial Meeting, for example, China's Foreign Minister stated that 'the ARF is valuable and represents a new approach to security'.[58] Japanese officials saw China's moves as a positive step, at least at this time. A senior MOFA official attending the Third ARF meeting, for instance, stated that 'I did not imagine that China's position on the ARF would change so quickly. ... This is a great success for the ARF'.[59] This does not mean, however, that Japan was totally satisfied with the achievements of the ARF. Unlike ASEAN countries, Japan did not expect that such accomplishments would be sufficient either to enhance mutual confidence between the member countries or to maintain the momentum of the ARF.

Japan's mid-term strategy for the ARF

Japan's view of the ARF at this time was expressed in a paper prepared by a MOFA official in charge of ARF policy. The paper was submitted to a series of closed workshops organised by the Japan's Institute of International Affairs (JIIA) in 1996.[60] The main purpose of the paper was to frame a mid- to long-term strategy to develop the ARF. More specifically, it considered how to move the ARF beyond a mere venue for security dialogue to a forum for security cooperation among Asia-Pacific countries without greatly changing its form and structure. It argued that the ARF had made steady progress as a forum for security dialogue in its first three years, but the process of security dialogue was by itself not adequate for either maintaining the momentum of the ARF or contributing to regional stability and security. The paper suggested that within the next five years, the ARF take the following approaches in order to achieve the above object: (1) accumulating a record of concrete achievements of regional security cooperation, (2) setting up a code of conduct for CBMs, (3) substantial works on PD measures, and (4) institutionalising the ARF to a certain degree.

The paper argued that the first priority for the ARF was to ensure the successful implementation of agreed CBMs in order to improve the quality and expand the range of security cooperation. Japan's policy priorities reflected its realisation that whether or not the ARF could actually move to the next step of implementing agreed CBMs was the key to the success of its future development. It was expected that building up concrete achievements of cooperative activities through the proper implementation of agreed CBMs would create the necessary confidence for more significant security cooperation, including more advanced CBMs and PD measures amongst participating countries, thus moving the ARF towards a forum for security cooperation.[61]

The paper also proposed to establish a code of conduct for CBMs in the ARF as a way of ensuring the effective implementation of CBMs. Whilst stressing the difficulty of setting up rule based procedures that could impose obligations on participating countries, it argued that promoting a code of conduct through an ARF chairman statement could be possible. Even though an agreement written into a chairman statement would not provide a legalistic obligation, it was expected that such an agreement would apply some psychological pressures on the ARF countries.[62]

Finally, the paper emphasised the need to institutionalise the ARF process to a certain degree. This was based on Japan's recognition that the successful implementation of CBMs would require an institutional mechanism that could collect and distribute reliable information and monitor the implementation stage. However, it also realised that establishing a permanent secretariat within the ARF would be extremely difficult due to the existence of countries opposing to the further institutionalisation of the Forum. The paper therefore suggested that the ARF first establish a research unit outside the ARF, which could function as a database for the exchange of information, such as a Regional Risk Reduction Centre, as specified in the Concept Paper.[63]

These proposed approaches to the ARF were a product of Japan's new expectations and realisations influenced by its three years experience in the ARF. Chinese and ASEAN opposition to a faster pace of ARF development led Japan to hold the view that the ARF had no choice but to maintain an incremental and building block approach to security cooperation at least for the foreseeable future. However, steady progress with its security dialogue process and agreement on some concrete CBMs during the first three years gave Japan hope that the ARF might still be able to develop itself into a valid forum for security cooperation along the lines of the Concept Paper if it could build-up concrete achievements in security cooperation through the implementation of agreed CBMs. Japanese officials thus still maintained a 'liberal' perspective on the ARF in general terms. However, in subsequent meetings, Japanese hopes began finally to dwindle. Indeed, moving the CBM process towards the implementation stage was a much more daunting task than Japanese officials had expected.

Difficult path towards the implementation stage

Whether or not the above mentioned report influenced Japan's ARF policy, it was significant that Japan's official policy for the Fourth ARF was actually matched by the mid-term strategy to develop the ARF specified in the paper. For the Fourth ARF meeting, MOFA set the following objects: (1) consolidating the ARF's commitment to agreed CBMs, (2) initiating work on PD, and (3) regularising the ISG meeting.[64] Along with its policy objectives, the Fourth Ministerial Meeting in Kuala Lumpur in July 1997, Japan's Foreign Minister Ikeda Yukihiko strongly urged other countries to properly implement agreed CBMs and suggested that the ARF conduct a periodic review of the status of the implementation. As a result of Japan's recommendations, ARF ministers agreed to direct 'the next ISG to undertake a comprehensive review of all agreed proposals that had not been implemented to date'.[65] However, these aspirations were not shared to the same degree by other ARF countries. Whilst encouraging the proper implementation of agreed CBMs, the Fourth ARF Chairman's statement declared that 'the evolutionary approach to the development of the ARF process and the practice of taking decisions by consensus shall be maintained, taking into consideration the interests of all ARF participants'.[66] This statement, which reaffirmed ASEAN's rule of the comfort level for all participants and non-binding voluntary agreement, clearly highlighted the institutional weakness of the ARF and brought home to Japan the difficulties it would face in trying to realise its aspirations.

The Fourth ARF continued to discuss a number of proposed CBMs, including a regional arms register, prior notification of and observer exchanges in military exercises. These proposals were discussed in the ISG on CBMs in Beijing in March 1997, but little progress was made. As for a regional arms register, it was found that many of ARF countries were not actually ready to go beyond the modest reporting requirements imposed by the UNRCA.[67] The idea of creating a regional arms register was also unrealistic in the eyes of Japanese officials as long as it remained an abstract concept. This is not to suggest, however, that Japan entirely lost its interest in its efforts towards military transparency through an arms register. Because of the limited possibilities of achieving consensus in this area, Japanese officials began to seek ways of utilising the existing UN register rather than establishing a new arms register in the region. This thinking stemmed from its observation that the UNRCA had not been sufficiently exploited by regional countries. The UNRCA actually encouraged participating countries to provide data on their military holdings and procurement from national production on a voluntary basis, but in the case of ARF members, only Western countries and Japan submitted such information.[68] Tokyo thus began to take the initiative for enhancing its effectiveness. In May 1997, MOFA organised a workshop on 'Transparency on Armaments' to seek an agreement on the expansion of the scope of the UNRCA to include data on military holdings and procurement through their domestic production.[69] Japan also used the ARF to garner support for its initiative. In the Ministerial Meeting, Foreign Minister Ikeda urged ARF countries to support the idea of expanding the scope of the UNRCA.[70] However, this initiative again did not receive serious consideration due to China's resistance to any obligation to provide the UNRCA with data on military holdings and domestic procurement.[71]

Meanwhile, the proposal for prior notification of and observers' participation in military exercises made little headway. The Beijing ISG failed to reach a consensus on this proposal due to continued dissension between China and the US and its allies over ways of implementing this measure. Chinese officials reiterated that it should only cover joint military exercises while the US and Japan, which actually ran such exercises, claimed that unilateral as well as bilateral exercises should be applied.[72] ARF countries also considered a proposal that suggested voluntary application of these measures to at least one of the military exercises in which that country participated, but no consensus was reached. To that end, ARF officials simply agreed to keep this proposal on the agenda.[73]

An agreement on the inclusion of defence officials in ARF activities was perhaps the only meaningful achievement on the CBM agenda in the Fourth ARF. At the ARF SOM in Malaysia in May 1997, Australia took the initiative in arranging a lunch meeting for defence officials as a way of encouraging their active involvement in the ARF. Australia, backed by Japan, had originally proposed to convene a separate meeting for defence officials in the ARF, but this was rebuffed by China and some ASEAN countries. US and Japanese officials floated an alternative proposal, suggesting to include defence officials in the Ministerial Meeting. A consensus on this proposal was eventually developed just prior to the Fourth Ministerial Meeting. Consequently, about half the ARF countries sent defence representatives to the meeting.[74]

Heightened frustration with the CBM process

In line with a mandate agreed at the Fourth ARF, the ISG on CBMs for the 1997–98 intersessional year conducted a comprehensive review of progress in the implementation of agreed CBM. The Fifth ARF Chairman's statement concluded in the results of the review that 'the ministers expressed satisfaction with the high degree of implementation'.[75] However, this was no more than diplomatic rhetoric. In actuality, the record of the implementation was desperately poor. Agreed CBMs that had been fully implemented by the Fifth ARF were of a limited kind, such as exchanges among national defence colleges and voluntary exchanges of information about ongoing observer participation in and notification of military exercises. Meanwhile, the publication of defence white papers, which Japan considered the minimal effort required to enhance the transparency of each country's defence policy, was only implemented regularly by a handful of countries, among them, Japan, South Korea, Australia and New Zealand.[76]

Recognising this, ARF officials took action to improve the situation. Accordingly, the ISG reached an agreement on the development of a set of matrices and tables showing information on the degree of implementation of agreed CBMs, which was to be updated on an annual basis. This set of matrices and tables, which would publicly reveal the status of each country's loyalty to agreed CBMs, was expected to be a means of putting psychological pressure on reluctant parties.[77] Considering the fact that the ARF was obliged to operate under the rule of non-binding voluntary agreement, this was the only possible way of encouraging their commitment to agreed CBMs.

The ISG meetings also adopted new CBMs proposals, which were divided into two baskets for consideration and implementation in the near future (Basket 1) and over the medium term (Basket 2).

First Basket

1) Encouraging ARF members to exchange visits of their naval vessels on a voluntary basis.
2) Multilateral exchanges and cooperation in military logistics and academic research in fields such as military medicine and military law.
3) Compilation of lists of publications and contact points on CBMs.
4) Multilateral communications network.
5) ARF Foreign Affairs and Defence officials training/seminar.
6) Seminar on the production of defence white papers or other defence policy documents.
7) Encouraging visits to military establishments.

8) Media support for the activities of the ARF.
9) Defence language schools conference.

Second Basket

1) ARF liaison with other regional forums.
2) A second ARF SOM.
3) Counter-narcotics project.
4) Preventing and combating illicit trafficking in conventional small arms.
5) Shoot fest among ARF riflemen.[78]

The above two lists of new CBMs were formally approved at the Fifth ARF Ministerial Meeting in Manila in July 1998. The Fifth ARF Chairman's statement lauded the increased number of agreed CBMs, expressing satisfaction regarding the progress of the work made in the ISG on CBMs. However, some ARF countries, including Japan, were not entirely happy with these developments. This was because progress on CBM in the Fifth ARF, though it appeared to be extensive, was of rather poor quality. Many of the new CBMs were even more modest than those agreed in the previous ARF meetings and clearly irrelevant to military transparency. These activities would increase transactions of foreign and defence officials among regional countries to some extent. However, Japanese officials privately held the view that it was not worthwhile for ARF countries to invest their energies in such inconsequential CBMs as China's proposed meeting on tropical military medicine and the Philippine's shoot fest for ARF riflemen, considering the limited resources available for policy implementation and the actual utility of those CBMs. Japanese officials simply did not expect that such activities would really contribute to confidence building and military transparency among regional countries.[79]

Japanese frustration with the CBM agenda was also fuelled by the growing salience of non-military or non-traditional security issues in the ARF agenda. These issues had become a part of the CBM agenda ever since the Beijing ISG on CBMs, and the subsequent 1997–98 ISG meetings discussed concrete issues including maritime safety, law and order at sea and protection and preservation of the marine environment.[80] The Fifth ARF's Chairman's statement further stressed the need to address 'non-military issues, which would have a significant impact on regional security in accordance with the ARF's comprehensive approach'.[81] The ARF's decision to include non-military security issues in the CBMs agenda mirrored a suggestion from some countries, including China and Australia. These countries proposed that non-military issues should be placed as a main focus of confidence building efforts in the ARF mainly on the grounds that they were less sensitive than traditional security issues and that they should therefore be much easier to develop consensus on.[82]

While recognising the importance of addressing non-military security issues, Japanese officials did not welcome the idea of expanding the agenda of the ARF to include them at that time mainly for two reasons. First, there was a growing concern among Japanese officials that addressing a wide range of issues in the ARF, where the agenda was already crowded, would hinder the ARF's effort to promote military CBMs, which should be the primary focus of its CBM agenda in their view.[83] These apprehensions were confirmed by the fact that military security measures increasingly lost relevance to the ARF's agenda. For instance, other ARF countries largely ignored Tokyo's earlier proposal for the enhancement of the UNRCA. The 1997–98 ISG on CBMs summary reports merely stated that 'aspects of UNRCA should continue to be discussed in the ISG on CBMs'.[84] Moreover, while the Fifth ARF Chairman's statement praised the high level of participation in the UNRCA among ARF countries, it ignored the fact that China withdrew from the UNRCA in 1998 to protest against US reporting on its arms sales to Taiwan. Beijing criticised Washington's practice as wrongly conferring legitimacy to Taiwan's independent weapons purchases.[85] In addition, there was no substantive progress on the proposal for advance notification of exercises and the invitation of observers and on the implementation of defence white paper publication. Secondly, Japanese officials were also concerned that addressing non-military security issues in the ARF would duplicate works on those issues in other regional institutions, such as APEC, ASEAN-PMC and ASEAN+3, and would thus dissipate the limited resources of the ARF. In short, it was the Japanese view that the ARF should remain as a forum for tackling traditional security issues and that non-military issues should be addressed in other regional forums.[86]

Overall, it was a source of great frustration for Japanese officials that many ARF countries, in particular China and ASEAN states, had become more inclined to push extremely moderate CBMs, on which consensus was easily developed, while proposals for more meaningful and effective CBMs were sidestepped. Japan's Foreign Minister, Kōmura Masahiko, expressed Japanese discontent in the 1998 International Forum on Asia, stating that:

> Efforts toward confidence building among Asia-Pacific regional countries are crucial in reducing uncertainty in terms of regional security. The basis for such confidence building is the awareness and confirmation of each country's intentions through frequent contact and communication among the concerned officials and people of the countries in the region, and of each country's capabilities through increasing transparency concerning military and defence strength. ... However, as for confidence building through the enhancement of transparency in each country's military policy and capabilities, though some Asian countries have begun to publish defence white papers and participate in the UN arms register, unfortunately it is not sufficient for significantly reducing many uncertainties existing in the region. Japan will continue to appeal for the importance of increasing the level of military transparency.[87]

Regardless of Japan's views on the matter, the shifting focus of the ARF agenda from traditional security to non-traditional security areas continued in the following meetings. The ISG on CBMs for the 1998–99 intersessional year put a special focus on maritime cooperation, including maritime safety, law and order at sea, and protection and preservation of the marine environment.[88] The ISG also considered the list of CBMs adopted in the Fifth ARF. The list was expanded with the adoption of a number of new modest CBMs, many of which were introduced by China. Chinese proposals included: (1) defence conversion, (2) military environmental protection exchanges, (3) mutual legal assistance coordination, and (4) cooperation against international terrorism and crime.[89] By this time, China had become the leading advocate for regional cooperation on non-military issues in the ARF and had organised some activities in this field, such as a symposium on tropical hygiene and prevention and treatment of tropical infections diseases.[90] Yet, China still remained ambivalent in its attitude towards confidence building through greater military transparency in the ARF. For instance, China issued its second defence white paper in July 1998 following the publication of the white paper in 1995, but again the Chinese paper disappointed many Western observers since it contained little reliable information about military expenditure, arms purchases and equipment.[91]

The growing trend towards the expansion of extremely modest and non-military related measures in the ARF heightened Japanese concerns about its CBM agenda. At the Sixth ARF SOM, held in Singapore in May 1999, Japanese officials finally expressed their desire that the ARF should keep the focus of its discussion and activities to traditional security areas rather than security or non-traditional security areas. However, Tokyo was forced to realise that non-traditional security issues had already attracted great attention from a growing number of the ARF countries. Japanese officials were upset when the US supported China's proposal for cooperation against transnational crime and terrorism and itself proposed to add the agenda to the next intersessional year's ISG on CBMs.[92] Consequently, Japan was forced to gradually shift its position on non-traditional security issues in the ARF. At the Sixth Ministerial Meeting in Singapore in July 1999, Japan's Foreign Minister Kōmura supported the US proposal to establish an expert group meeting on transnational crime, such as illicit trafficking of small arms. Kōmura also raised concerns about the piracy problem in Southeast Asian waters, which Japan had initially expected to address in other regional institutions, most notably ASEAN+3.[93] In the end, the Sixth ARF Chairman's statement acknowleged that 'the illegal accumulation of small arms and light weapons posed a threat to regional security' and stressed 'a need for cooperative approaches to deal with the problem of piracy and illegal migration in the region', thus pushing non-tradtional security issues more to the centre stage of the ARF's agenda.[94]

With a mandate to address transnational crime agreed at the Sixth ARF, ARF countries engaged in an extensive discussion on the issue in the ISG on CBMs for 1999–2000 and agreed to organise an Experts Group Meeting on Transnational Crime (EGM on TC). The ISG meetings, however, made almost no qualitative progress on the content of CBMs while the number of moderate CBMs continued to increase. New CBMs adopted at the Seventh ARF Ministerial Meetings in Bangkok in August 2000 were again extremely modest measures, such as the establishment of the ARF Regional Maritime Information Center (ARF-RMIC) for collecting marine weather information and a seminar on civil–military relations in peace support operations. Moreover, while the Chairman's statement expressed 'with satisfaction the successful implementation' of extremely modest CBMs, such as a meeting of heads of defence universities and seminars on a defence language school, it no longer even mentioned earlier proposals for more meaningful CBMs, such as the publication of defence white papers, the expansion of the scope of the UNRCA and the observer participation in and notification of military exercises.[95] Responding to these developments, at the Seventh Ministerial Meeting, Japan's Foreign Minister Kōno Yōhei again stressed the importance of measures to enhance the transparency of defence policy, calling for the proper implementation of agreed CBMs, in particular the publication of defence white papers.[96] However, it seemed that by this time the momentum for military transparency, which had been relatively strong in the inception years of the ARF, was already lost.

The CBM agenda after September 11

The trend towards the shift of the ARF's focus on non-traditional security issues was further reinforced by the September 11 terrorist attack in the US, which pushed counter-terrorism issues to the top of its agenda. Washington showed strong interest in using the ARF to back up its global led campaign against terrorism, leading to a series of workshops and meetings for considering possible measures on counter-terrorism. Moreover, the Ninth ARF Ministerial Meeting in Brunei in July 2002 endorsed a US proposal for setting up an ISM on Counter-Terrorism and Transnational Crime (CTTC), hence further diverting attention and resources of the ARF from traditional security to non-traditional security issues. The sudden surge of non-traditional security issues in the ARF was also evident in its paper on the 'Stock Taking of the ARF process', adopted in the Ninth ARF. The paper, which set out the future agenda of the ARF, placed 'the strengthening of measures to fight international terrorism' as the highest priority for the ARF's agenda.[97] Consequently, by the time of the Twelfth ARF Ministerial Meeting, in Vientiane in July 2005, the ARF adopted a number of cooperative measures on counter-terrorism, such as blocking the financing of terrorism, beefing up border controls against the cross-border movement of terrorists, and the strengthening of information sharing and intelligence exchange, as will be discussed more fully in Chapter 6. In addition, the growing momentum for multilateral cooperation on counter-terrorism in the ARF has given impetus for cooperation on another non-traditional security issue, namely piracy. As a result, the Tenth ARF Ministerial Meeting in Phnom Penhv in June 2003, issued the 'statement on cooperation against piracy and other threats to maritime security'.[98]

As will be discussed in more details in Chapter 6, September 11 also had an impact on Japan's position on non-traditional security issues in the ARF. The immediate need for promoting regional cooperation on counter-terrorism arising from the September 11 incident has inevitably led Japanese policy makers to become more willing to take the initiative in promoting such cooperation. Since then, Japan has floated a number of concrete proposals in this field, such as the idea of promoting the ARF dossier on counter-terrorism measures. This indicated Japan's intention to increase the relevance of the ARF as well as other regional institutions in the global campaign against terrorism. However, although Japan has become more proactive in promoting multilateral cooperation on non-traditional security issues in the ARF since September 11, this does not mean that Japanese frustration with its CBM agenda have evaporated. While recognising the need to develop regional cooperation on the issues, Japanese officials have been concerned that the ARF has narrowed its focus to these issues at the expense of the CBM agenda. In their eyes, there is still a need for promoting more meaningful CBMs in the Asia-Pacific region, which has not only contained a large number of potential military flash points but also witnessed a growing trend among many regional states towards military build-up and modernisation.[99] Reflecting this apprehension, at the Ninth ARF Ministerial Meeting, Japan's Foreign Minister Kawaguchi Yoriko called for other ARF countries to make further efforts to consolidate the CBM process.[100]

Latest ARF meetings, however, have given no signs that truly remarkable progress will be made on its CBM agenda in the foreseeable future. At the Ninth ARF, it was agreed to set up a separate meeting for defence officials in order to increase their involvement in the ARF's activities and to facilitate discussions on legal and law enforcement matters for fighting terrorism.[101] Moreover, the Eleventh ARF agreed to establish an ASEAN Regional Forum Security Policy Conference (ASPC) in order to intensify the participation of defence representatives (vice-minister level) in the ARF and to strengthen 'the cooperation of CBMs in military sphere'.[102] Although the formation of these defence official meetings can certainly be regarded as a significant development, to what extent they can actually contribute to the enhancement of military transparency and confidence building among ARF countries has still remained in question. This is because their content have been largely limited to the brief exchange of views on regional security issues like that taking place in the ARF's SOM and Ministerial Meeting.[103] An examination of CBM proposals agreed in the latest ISG meetings has also suggested that the CBM agenda has not made any qualitative progress. The Twelfth ARF's Chairman statement again recorded the implementation of only modest measures, almost irrelevant to the transparency of participating country's defence policies. Among them are such measures as the meetings of heads of national defence colleges, workshops on alternative development, and evolving changes in the security perceptions of ARF countries.[104] It seems that the ARF is still a long way from achieving the first stage of regional security cooperation.

Conclusion

The main task that Japan had faced in the CBM agenda in the ARF in its inception years was to play a mediating role between activist countries, including the US, Australia, and Canada, which emphasised the need to enhance confidence building through the implementation of concrete CBMs aiming for greater military transparency, and reluctant countries, notably China and ASEAN countries, which supported confidence building efforts through informal dialogues and declaratory measures because of deep scepticism about military transparency. Tensions between the two parties over ways of promoting the first stage of security cooperation identified in the Concept Paper overshadowed the future prospects of the ARF from the outset. In order to overcome this, Japan performed an active mediating role between the two parties by floating concrete proposals for CBMs. Tokyo's CBM proposals were modest compared to those of other countries, but it struck middle ground between the two parties, thus successfully putting CBMs high on the ARF agenda and leading the Forum to reach an agreement on a number of concrete CBMs. The progress on the CBM agenda in its first three years gave Japanese policy makers the impression that the ARF was beginning to make progress towards security cooperation along the lines of the Concept Paper.

However, in the late 1990s, Japan's hopes dwindled as momentum towards the CBM agenda began to slow. Indeed, mainly due to resistance from reluctant countries, the ARF failed in both materialising earlier proposals for more advanced military CBMs, and in ensuring the proper implementation of agreed CBMs, including the publication of defence white papers, which Japan regarded as the minimum required effort towards the transparency of each country's defence policy. Japanese frustrations with the CBM process were exacerbated further by the shift of the ARF's focus from traditional security to non-traditional security issues in particular after September 11, which also hindered the ARF's efforts to promote meaningful military CBMs.

Overall, though the ARF has adopted a modest set of CBMs which may help to increase the frequency of interactions between member countries and thus may contribute to a minimal level of confidence building between participating countries, it has contributed little to facilitating the exchange of reliable information about each country's defence policy, and has thus failed to reduce mutual suspicion among them stemming from uncertainties about their intentions. The lack of trust among ARF countries has made considerably more difficult Japan's objective of moving the ARF process towards a higher level of security cooperation, namely the development of preventive diplomacy, which will be discussed in the next chapter.

4 Japan's challenges for promoting preventive diplomacy in the ARF

Introduction

This chapter explores Japan's ARF policy with reference to the process of preventive diplomacy (PD). This chapter begins by providing a brief review of regional discussion on the concept and measures of PD at the Track Two level in the first years after the establishment of the ARF in order to explain the origin and meaning of PD. The second section examines both Japan's and China's views of the concept and measures of PD and contrasts them with each other. The third section looks at Japan's actual diplomacy in the PD agenda in the ARF. Japan's experience in this area has demonstrated that the Forum has encountered grave difficulties in developing practical PD mechanisms and that its potential to play a meaningful PD role has so far remained highly limited.

Debate on the concept and measures of PD

The concept and measures of PD

The concept of PD was first introduced by former Secretary-General of the UN, Boutros Boutros-Ghali. His 1992 publication, *An Agenda for Peace*, defined PD as 'action to prevent disputes from arising between the parties, to prevent existing disputes from escalating into conflicts and to limit the spread of the latter when they occur'.[1] The concept soon drew considerable attention from a number of ASEAN countries. In 1993, the Thai Ministry of Foreign Affairs and the Institute of Policy Studies in Singapore began a joint initiative to organise a series of meetings on 'ASEAN-UN Cooperation on Peace and Preventive Diplomacy'.[2] PD was discussed extensively at these meetings and various ideas were generated. In 1994, for instance, Amitav Acharya presented a broad definition of PD, which became the basis of subsequent regional discussions on PD. In his paper, PD was conceptualised as diplomatic, political, military, economic and humanitarian action taken by governments, multilateral organisations and international agencies for the purpose of:

1) Preventing severe disputes and conflicts from arising between and within states.
2) Preventing such disputes and conflicts from escalating into armed confrontation.
3) Limiting the intensity of violence resulting from such conflict and preventing it from spreading geographically.
4) Preventing and managing acute humanitarian crises associated with (either as the cause or the effect) such conflicts.
5) As part of the immediate response to a crisis or pre-crisis situation, initiating measures that might contribute to the eventual resolution of the dispute.[3]

The formation of the ARF in 1994 helped move regional discussions on PD from the academic up to the Track Two level, which involved both academics and officials in a private capacity. Under the auspices of the ARF, three Track Two seminars on PD, the first in Seoul in 1995, the second in Paris in 1996 and the third in Singapore in 1997, were organised. In the second meeting, a consensus emerged that the ARF seminar would explore the concept and principles of PD appropriate for the Asia-Pacific regional context based on Boutros-Ghali's 1992 definition. The meeting also agreed that the scope of the PD agenda in the ARF would include not only traditional security issues, such as territorial disputes, proliferation of conventional weapons and WMD, but also non-traditional security issues, such as drug trafficking, terrorism, resource problems, environmental degradation, and maritime safety.[4]

Along with definitional issues, intellectuals in the Asia-Pacific region also gave serious consideration to specific means and tools for the exercise of PD. They presented a number of proposals, many of which were incorporated into the ARF Concept Paper adopted in the Second ARF Ministerial Meeting. The paper identified the promotion of PD as the second stage of its security cooperation and listed a number of concrete PD measures, divided into Annexes A and B. Annex A included 'measures that can be explored and implemented by ARF participants in the immediate future'. These were: (1) 'developing a set of guidelines for the peaceful settlement of disputes, taking into account the principles of the UN Charter and the TAC', (2) 'promoting the principles of the TAC and its provision for the settlement of disputes in the Pacific', and (3) 'seeking the endorsement of other countries for the ASEAN Declaration on the South China Sea in order to strengthen its political and moral effect'. Annex B contained more intrusive PD measures, which would be explored over the medium and long-term by the ARF, such as: (1) 'exploring and devising ways and means to prevent conflict', (2) 'exploring the idea of appointing Special Representatives to undertake fact-finding missions at the request of the parties involved in an issue and to offer their good offices', and (3) 'exploring the idea of establishing Regional Risk Reduction Centres which could serve as a database for the exchange of information'.[5] These ideas were further refined in the ARF Track Two seminars on PD. The Second ARF seminar, for instance, agreed to recommend the following proposals to the ARF SOM for their consideration: (1) 'an annual security outlook and the gathering of relevant information and analyses', (2) 'creating a regional research and information centre', (3) 'establishing an early warning system to act as a repository of information on preventive diplomacy, including monitoring outcomes of specific cases', (4) 'expanding the Chair's role to include a good offices role', (5) 'establishing a register of experts on preventive diplomacy', and (6) 'considering the idea of an ARF risk-reduction centre as a long-term measure'.[6]

However, whereas numerous ideas about the concept and measures of PD had been presented in these Track Two seminars, they did not successfully bring about common understanding on definitions. Somewhat surprisingly, there was less consensus on the concept and measures of PD among regional countries in 1997 than there was in 1995.[7]

Two divergent views of PD: Japan and China

The increasing difficulty in building consensus on the concept and measures of PD among regional countries during the early years of the ARF derived not from uncertainties about the meaning of PD, but rather growing disagreements among regional countries about specific concepts, principles and measures of PD. Indeed, greater clarification of the concept and measures of PD through Track Two seminars generated a very different set of attitudes towards the idea of PD as well as varying degrees of readiness to move the ARF towards the PD stage among participating countries, promoting their understanding of how exactly PD would affect their own security interests. As with CBMs, ARF countries were again split roughly into two groups according to their views of PD with activist countries, most notably Australia, Canada, the US, and Japan on the one hand and reluctant countries, including China and most ASEAN countries on the other. Before entering into a detailed investigation of Japan's actual diplomacy in the PD agenda, the following section examines both Japan's and China's views of the concept and measures of PD and contrasts them with each other. Each state represented the attitude of the group to which it belonged.

Japan's view of and approach to PD (activist countries)

Japan was one of the most active supporters of the idea of developing PD mechanisms in the ARF, along with the US, Canada and Australia. Japan was attracted by the idea of PD soon after the introduction of the concept to the Asia-Pacific region. This was due mainly to three reasons. First, Japan's interest in PD was prompted by their growing concerns about the regional security environment. As discussed in Chapter 2, in the view of Japanese policy makers, the likelihood of regional conflicts had somewhat increased in the early 1990s because of the intensification of some regional disputes, such as the South China Sea, Cambodia, and the Korean Peninsula, and a growing trend among many regional states towards military build-up and modernisation. This led Japanese policy makers to hold the view that regional countries should make collective efforts to create mechanisms for conflict prevention in order to avoid the outbreak of any armed conflict, which would impede the steady progress on regional economy.[8]

Secondly, the activities of PD, which mainly relied on non-military instruments, were ideally suited to Japan whose military roles in regional security affairs were subject to a number of domestic and international constraints.[9] It was expected that PD would provide Tokyo with a great opportunity and means to make an actual contribution to regional security in non-military ways, something which Japan had been trying to achieve since the end of the Cold War.

Last but not least, the promotion of PD was also seen by Japan as the key to the success of Japan's long-term policy of building a multi-layered structure in the region, consisting of two separate security arrangements that would mutually reinforce each other by providing different functions; namely the Japan-US alliance and multilateral security arrangements, notably the ARF. The development of PD measures would enable the ARF to truly complement the Japan-US alliance in the way that it could help prevent regional disputes from escalating into armed confrontation while the bilateral alliance would provide reliable insurance should circumstances arise in which aggression actually occurred.

Japan's view of the concept and measures of PD rested on what measures it thought necessary for the ARF to perform active PD roles. In the early years of the ARF, for instance, Japan envisioned that in the future the ARF should be able to implement PD measures, such as early warning, fact-finding missions, convening ad hoc meetings, dispatching special representatives, and a good offices role for the ARF chair, which would include offering practical solutions to regional disputes.[10] Based on these expectations, Japanese officials held the view that the concept and principles of PD in the ARF should be defined as broadly as possible so that the Forum could have greater discretion to implement various PD measures in response to regional crises since narrow and specific definitions of PD would considerably restrict their options. In other words, Japan wished to not only expand the scope of PD to cover intra-state issues but also to leave largely undefined the implications of PD for the principles of non-interference and state sovereignty since rigid adherence to these principles would be sure to exclude many potential regional conflicts from even being considered. Obviously in the Asia-Pacific region, PD that was unable to cover intra-state issues was pointless because most potential regional conflicts were intra-state in nature, as the crises in Cambodia and East Timor issues had shown. Yet,

Japan recognised that it was highly unrealistic to expect that the ARF would be able to intervene in any regional dispute and conflict without the consent of states involved, given China's and ASEAN's obsession with that principle. However, this does not mean that Japan dismissed all possibilities of making the ARF useful in intra-state issues. From Japan's perspective, the ARF should have been allowed to play PD roles in intra-state conflicts so long as such roles were carried out with the request or consent of the states involved in the conflicts. Japan believed that the use of PD in intra-state issues would not violate either state sovereignty or the principle of non-interference in internal affairs as long as it was authorised by the states involved. This was not an unrealistic idea at that time given the fact that some ASEAN countries, namely Thailand and Philippines, began to seek ways of mitigating the traditional principles of non-interference of internal affairs, as will be discussed in more detail in Chapter 6. Overall, in Japan's thinking, intra-state conflicts in the region should be applicable to PD if such conflicts influence the security of other regional countries and involve humanitarian contingencies and emergency situations.[11]

In addition, Japan's disinclination to seek precise and narrow definitions of PD also reflected the fact that attempting to build consensus on the concept and principles of PD in the ARF was likely to be a fruitless exercise and cause further stagnation. This concern was part of the reason why Japan took the initiative in promoting concrete PD measures, namely the enhanced roles for the ARF chair, rather than trying to define PD, as will be discussed more fully below. Japan believed that this was a practical and productive approach to the PD agenda in the ARF.[12] Western countries, including Canada, Australia and the US, basically shared Japan's view of PD.

China's view of and approach to PD (reluctant countries)

China and most ASEAN states were generally, but with varying degrees of reluctance, unwilling to move the ARF toward the PD stage, at least as fast as activist states would have wished. For instance, while China, Vietnam and Myanmar basically preferred that the ARF remain merely a venue for security dialogue, some ASEAN countries, including Singapore, Thailand and the Philippines, were much more sympathetic to the forum's work on PD. Nonetheless, the activist states' view of PD was not palatable to these countries because of their adherence to the principle of non-interference. Indeed, China and most ASEAN states were opposed to the idea of applying PD to intra-state conflicts since this might have allowed outsiders to intervene in security problems involving their sovereignty and internal affairs, such as the South China Sea disputes and the Taiwan Strait in the case of China.[13] This cautious view of PD was demonstrated by Chinese Ambassador, Shi Chunlai, secretary general of the

CSCAP China. In his paper, Shi outlined seven principles for the operations of PD:

1) To handle State-to-State relations and carry out cooperation in CBMs and PD in accordance with the fundamental principles enshrined in the UN charter, TAC in Southeast Asia, the Five Principles of Peaceful Coexistence, and other universally recognised international laws;
2) Mutual respect for sovereignty, independence and territorial integrity;
3) To refrain from interfering in other countries' internal affairs or directing security cooperation against a third country;
4) Take the 'mutual consent by parties directly relevant to an issue' as one of the most important prerequisites for preventive diplomacy;
5) To settle international disputes through peaceful means and refrain from the use of force;
6) To implement and maintain national defense polices of a defensive nature and not to threaten or undermine the security and stability of other countries with one's military forces;
7) To promote mutually beneficial cooperation among countries and friendly exchanges among peoples.[14]

Under these principles, which put a particular emphasis on sovereignty and non-interference, PD measures, such as early warning, good offices and third party mediation, were perceived as intrusive since these measures had the potential to infringe on the principle of non-interference in the internal affairs of states. This view of PD was shared by many ASEAN countries, in particular Vietnam and Myanmar, which repeatedly expressed reservations against accelerating the pace of the discussion of PD.

The difference between Japanese and Chinese views of PD was also demonstrated by their differing approaches towards the ARF's PD agenda. As will be discussed more fully below, contrary to Japan's wish to focus on the examinations of PD measures rather than definitions of its concept and principles, China stressed the need to fully discuss the definitions of PD before examining specific measures.[15] China's preference for the extensive consultations on the concept and principles of PD was an indication of its intention to constrain the ARF's room for developing various concrete PD measures. More specifically, by carefully defining concept and principles, stressing the importance of the principle of non-interference, and excluding all intra-state matters from the purview of PD, Beijing sought to eliminate any possibility that the ARF would develop PD measures that might amount to interference in the internal affairs of states.

Initiating the work for PD

By the end of 1996, Japan's interest had matured to the extent that it was considering the possibility of Japanese initiatives in PD in the ARF. Signs of

Japan's growing interest in PD can be found in a report prepared by the MOFA official in charge of Japan's ARF policy submitted to a JIIA's workshop in August 1996. The paper, whose aim was to consider Japan's mid- and long-term strategy, suggested that the time was ripe for the ARF to initiate work on PD and that within five years the Forum should achieve two objectives: (1) examining concrete PD measures that could be useful in situations in which a crisis is likely to become an actual conflict and creating the broadest possible range of PD options, and (2) developing a mechanism for convening an emergency meeting in the event of a crisis so that ARF countries can discuss ways of responding to it. Finally, as a short-term objective, the paper recommended that the ARF should initiate an official working group on PD within one or two years in order to commence detailed discussion.[16]

Accordingly, in the Fourth ARF SOM in Malaysia in May 1997, Japanese officials proposed to establish an official working group on PD.[17] Some observers saw this proposal as an ambitious undertaking because of the ARF's very limited progress on CBM at that time. Yet they believed that the time was ripe for the ARF to commence a discussion on PD at the Track One level since, by the time of the Fourth ARF, two Track Two seminars on PD had been already organised as noted above.[18] The proposal also reflected Japanese apprehensions about the stagnation of the ARF process. As discussed in Chapter 3, progress towards CBM began to show signs of stagnation from the Third ARF onwards, due mainly to the difficulty of ensuring the proper implementation of agreed CBMs. This fuelled concern among Japanese officials that the ARF would not be able to sustain its momentum without setting a new agenda, and they thus began to seek new possibilities for concrete security cooperation. It was therefore expected that initiating discussion on PD in the ARF would help revitalise its momentum.[19]

However, the Japanese proposal proved to be highly controversial, exposing ideological differences between activist and reluctant countries. While the Japanese proposal received support from many countries, in particular Australia and Singapore, it attracted sharp criticism from China. Chinese officials agreed that PD could become a subject for consideration in the ARF but rebuffed the proposal on the grounds that the definitions of PD were still too diverse and it was therefore too early to launch a discussion at the Track One level.[20] The main reason for Beijing's opposition to PD, however, derived mainly from what it saw as PD's potential for interfering in internal affairs of states. By this time, China had begun to play an increasingly proactive role in the CBM process, but it was still far from supporting cooperative security measures that would tread on the delicate area of non-interference in the internal affairs of states. To that end, Chinese officials claimed that the ARF should maintain its focus on CBMs, arguing that they had the best prospects of success in the immediate future.[21] The serious dissent between the two camps on the

Japanese proposal was eventually overcome by an alternative proposal offered by Malaysia, the chair of the Fourth ARF, which suggested placing PD on the agenda of the ISG on CBMs so the two issues could be discussed in tandem. This compromise was acceptable to China, and an agreement was reached at the Fourth ARF Ministerial Meeting in Malaysia in July 1997 that 'the next ISG would discuss an overlapping area between the first stage of CBMs and the second stage of PD'.[22] Japan's original proposal for establishing an official working group on PD did not come to fruition, but Tokyo was successful in leading the ARF to take a first step towards the PD stage.

Uncertainty over the overlap between CBM and PD

In accordance with the mandate of the Fourth ARF, the ISG on CBMs in the 1997–98 intersessional year initiated the first discussions on PD, exploring the matter of the overlap between CBMs and PD measures. However, the discussion faltered from the outset. One of major causes for this was the Chinese veto on moving forward into substantive work on PD. While activist countries endeavoured to move the PD process forward, Beijing remained extremely reluctant to bring PD into the ARF's agenda. The PD agenda was also stymied by definitional confusion about the matter of the overlap between CBMs and PD. The distinction between these two concepts was a much more complicated matter than the ARF Concept Paper had indicated. The lack of productive discussion was a source of great irritation for activist countries, in particular the US. At the Fifth Ministerial Meeting, the US Secretary of State Madeleine Albright expressed these frustrations, stating that 'we should take the next steps in this process by exploring the overlap between CBMs and PD. While the confidence building foundations must be solid, the ARF must also move forward if it is to remain vital and relevant'.[23] Whether or not it was as a result of pressure brought to bear by the US, reluctant countries eventually made some concessions, enabling the ARF to make modest progress on PD. The Fifth ARF Ministerial Meeting in Manila in July 1998 agreed to approve the recommendation by the ISG that the ISG for the next intersessional year (1998–99) would hold two meetings and dedicate one of its meetings to discussion on PD. It was also agreed that the ARF would discuss the following concrete proposals in addressing the area of overlap between CBMs and PD:

1) An enhanced role for the ARF Chair, particularly the idea of a good office role.
2) The development of a Register of Experts or Eminent Persons (EEPs) among ARF participants.
3) Production of an Annual Security Outlook (ASO).
4) Voluntary background briefing on regional security issues.[24]

These proposals were generated at the Third ARF Track Two Conference on Preventive Diplomacy held in Singapore in September 1997, in which participants made a great effort to find ways of addressing the issue of conceptual overlap. The proposals successfully served as a basis of compromise between activist and reluctant countries regarding PD.[25] While the first two proposals could be regarded as authentic PD measures that activist countries wished to promote, the other two proposals were more like CBMs, and thus more acceptable to reluctant countries.

The four proposals were addressed at the ISG on CBMs held in Bangkok in March 1999. The first ever extensive discussion of PD produced some modest progress. Endorsing the recommendation of the ISG meetings, the Sixth ARF Ministerial Meeting in Singapore in July 1999 agreed to expand the chair's role to include liaison with other institutions, such as the OAS and OSCE, and with track two forums, most notably CSCAP, to exchange information and share experience on an informal and case-by-case basis. There was also broad agreement that the coordinating role of the ARF chair should include the ability to convene special sessions and to issue statements on particular issues after prior consultation with all ARF participants and with their consent. Moreover, the Sixth ARF formally agreed to develop a register of EEPs, which would offer professional advice and recommendations as well as undertake research on matters of PD. As for other PD related proposals, the production of an ASO on a voluntary basis was endorsed by all of the ARF ministers without disagreement.[26] In the end, the Sixth ARF Chairman's statement concluded that 'common understandings reached on the four tabled proposals relating to the overlap between CBMs and PD'.[27] However, in actuality, the common understanding was of a highly limited nature. While ARF countries reached general agreement on modest PD related measures, there was no consensus on the most contentious issue, namely the concept of a good offices role for the ARF chair. There was serious dissension among ARF countries over whether the chair's enhanced role should include good offices or mediation roles in regional conflicts. China and many ASEAN representatives objected to the idea of empowering the ARF chair to actually get involved in regional disputes and conflicts because of its potential for interference in their internal affairs while officials from activist countries supported it.[28] Disagreement regarding the good offices role for the ARF chair further stymied the ARF's discussion on PD.

In addition, the Sixth ARF Ministerial Meeting also agreed that the ISG on CBMs for the 1999–2000 intersessional year would carry out an examination on the concept and principles of PD and accepted ASEAN's offer to prepare a relevant paper for consideration by the Seventh ARF SOM. This decision was made because at the Sixth ARF meeting Chinese representatives strongly suggested that the ARF define the concept and principles of PD before examining concrete PD measures, reversing Beijing's long opposition to fully discussing PD at the Track One level.

Debate on the structural reform of the ARF

The discussion on PD at the Sixth ARF meetings was also complicated by the contentious issues of ASEAN's diplomatic centrality in the ARF and the institutionalisation of it. As discussed in Chapter 3, these issues had been salient in the inception years of the ARF. With a heated discussion on PD, those issues again attracted widespread attention amongst activist countries. They worried that the present arrangements of the ARF, namely ASEAN's exclusive chairmanship and its embryonic institutional structure, would not be adequate for the development of PD mechanisms in the light of the equality of ARF members as well as of available resources. One Japanese official in charge of ARF policy, for instance, wrote in 1999 that:

> in order to move the ARF toward a credible regional security institution, there is a need to discuss the possibility of abolishing or diluting ASEAN's leadership role. ... For example, in the future, if the ARF chair plays good offices and mediator roles, we must address questions as to whether preventive diplomacy is to be initiated only by ASEAN states and whether ASEAN countries can be responsive to the concerns of non-ASEAN countries.[29]

It was also apparent that a certain degree of institutionalisation of the ARF is prerequisite for promoting practical PD measures. For instance, the practice of early warning, which is regarded as one of crucial measures to the success of PD efforts, requires a mechanism that can collect and analyse reliable information on a potential conflict situation. To fulfil these tasks, the establishment of either the permanent secretariat in the ARF or a special unit, such as a Regional Risk Reduction Center, is necessary.[30] Voices calling for the structural reform of the ARF for the success of its PD agenda even came from within ASEAN. Jusuf Wanandi, a prominent scholar in Jakarta contended that:

> The past few years have seen an emergence of real worries about ARF and ASEAN's leadership of it... For these efforts to become practical, two other improvements have to be made by ARF. One is a minimum degree of institutionalization. The ASEAN tradition of a revolving leadership and its institutional support will not be adequate to implement concrete programs... The other improvement is for ASEAN to agree on having a co-chair from a non-member in leading ARF.[31]

The Sixth ARF witnessed disagreement over the issues of ASEAN's centre role and the institutionalisation of the ARF. At the Sixth ARF SOM, US officials, backed by other activist countries, called for the promotion of co-chairmanship held by one ASEAN and one non-ASEAN country and the creation of a permanent secretariat within the Forum for coordinating and recording its work.[32] Tokyo also strongly supported the structural reform of the ARF. MOFA officials, in an interview with Kyodo News Agency just before the Sixth ARF Ministerial Meeting, stated that 'Japan may call for allowing non-ASEAN members to co-chair ARF annual meetings'. They also stated that 'if a permanent secretariat is necessary to assist the chair nation, Japan intends to actively contribute to its establishment and operations'.[33]

However, ASEAN was neither ready to relinquish its leadership role nor support further institutionalisation of the ARF. The joint communiqué issued in the AMM, held just before the Sixth ARF Ministerial Meeting, stated that 'we are committed to strengthening ASEAN's role as the primary driving force of the ARF process'.[34] Malaysian Foreign Minister, Syed Hamid Albar, dismissed the proposal for the establishment of the ARF secretariat, saying that 'we feel the ARF should not be institutionalised ... it should be allowed to continue in its current form where issues are decided on the basis of discussions and consensus'.[35] China also ardently supported the continuation of ASEAN's leadership role in the ARF since Beijing saw it as a useful counterweight to US and Japanese influence over the Forum. Hence, Beijing rejected the US proposal by reiterating its conventional argument that 'the ARF should progress at a pace comfortable to all participants'. Staunch opposition from both ASEAN and China to any proposal for reforming the ARF structure generated a sense of grievance among Japanese officials which in turn served to dilute their expectations of the ARF. MOFA's internal report on the Sixth ARF SOM concluded that 'it is not to be expected that the ARF will make any significant progress on its institutional building in the near future'.[36]

Launching a mediating role

Japan's paper on an enhanced role for the ARF chair

The ARF's discussion on PD regained its momentum shortly after the Sixth ARF Ministerial Meeting. The context changed with the ISG on CBMs for 1999–2000, in Tokyo in November 1999 and in Singapore in April 2000. At the Singapore ISG, Japan presented concrete proposals for the enhanced role for the chair. As a leading supporter of PD and a co-chair of the 1999–2000 ISG on CBMs, Japan sought to bridge the divide between activist and reluctant states over the issue of the chair's enhanced role in order to push the PD agenda forward. Japan's paper outlined seven main roles for the ARF chair regarding good offices and coordination between ARF meetings: (1) providing early warning by taking up and drawing attention to potential regional disputes and conflicts that may have a negative impact on regional stability, (2) convening an emergency meeting, (3) issuing statements at the chair's discretion (without the consent of ARF members), (4) facilitating discussion on norms building in the ARF, (5) enhancing liaison with external parties, such as international organisations and Track Two forums, (6) promoting confidence building among ARF members by facilitating information exchange and dialogue, and (7) fostering cooperation between ARF members by facilitating discussion on potential areas of cooperation.[37]

Japan's proposals were in part formulated through its case studies, including Germany's active good offices roles during the Kosovo conflict. As the chair of G8, Germany took the initiative to convene an emergency meeting and offered concrete proposals for a political resolution of the conflict. This gave Japan the hope that the ARF chair might be able to play a similar role in the event of regional crises.[38]

Japan's paper also contained the idea of creating a mechanism to support the ARF chair. The proposed mechanism intended to provide the ARF chair with greater assistance in implementing PD measures by enabling the chair to draw on resources and expertise from all ARF countries and Track Two forums, such as CSCAP. There was another motivation behind this proposal, however. Japanese officials also expected that the establishment of the supporting mechanism, which would allow non-ASEAN countries to get involved in the chair's activities, would help dilute ASEAN's diplomatic centrality in the ARF. In short, realising the difficulties of reforming the ARF structure, Japan had sought a way of expanding the power and influence of non-ASEAN members within the ARF without changing ASEAN's chairmanship role.[39]

Overall, Japan's proposal for the enhanced role of the ARF chair was modest and cautious, far from what Japanese officials had envisioned in earlier years. The modesty of Tokyo's proposal clearly demonstrated how the deep reservations of reluctant countries about the chair's active PD roles had influenced its policy making. Japan worried that presenting ambitious proposals would be counter-productive, provoking negative reactions and thus further complicating the ARF's work on PD.[40]

Within these limitations, Japan tried to present proposals acceptable to both activist and reluctant countries and to empower the ARF chair to play a meaningful PD role. However, finding a middle point between the two parties proved to be extremely difficult. Unfortunately, the aversion of reluctant countries to the chair's PD roles was stronger than Japan had presumed. They contended that there was no need to examine the chair's PD roles in detail because CBMs should be the centre of the ARF's activities. Some reluctant countries even criticised Japan for drafting the paper for the enhanced role of the ARF chair without the prior consent of all other ARF countries. Criticism was also levelled at the Japanese paper in terms of its contents. While all ARF countries were basically in agreement that the chair played a useful role as a conduit for information sharing between ARF meetings, some Japanese proposals, including the proposals to extend the

chair's authority to provide early warnings, to convene emergency meetings, and to issue statements at its own discretion, were rebuffed by reluctant countries on the grounds that these measures would amount to
interference in the internal affairs of states.[41] In the end, the ISG requested
that Japan revise the paper by the next ISG meeting, taking into account
written comments from other countries.[42] In addition, regarding the
enhanced role of the ARF chair, at the Seventh Ministerial Meeting in
Bangkok in July 2000, Australia floated a proposal for setting up the ARF
Troika, whereby the ARF chair would be supported in its activities by the
previous chair, along with a non-ASEAN ARF member, based on a rota-
tional system.[43] However, this proposal drew only cautious responses from
reluctant countries.

The Seventh working session nonetheless produced some small developments
on PD. Thailand, the chair of the Seventh ARF meetings, established an
informal link with the UN, the OAS and the OSCE. It was expected that
these links would be utilised for the exchange of information and sharing of
experiences with these organisations.[44] The Seventh ARF also reached a
formal agreement on the establishment of EEPs. A discussion on a paper on
EEPs prepared by Japan was held at the Singapore ISG, and it was agreed
that the register would be available to ARF countries to be used on a
voluntary basis and that the next ISG meetings would discuss the terms of
reference for the use of the register. In addition, the Seventh ARF published
the first volume of the ASO.[45]

ASEAN's paper on the concept and principles of PD

Another highlight of the ISG on CBMs for 1999–2000 was ASEAN's
draft paper on the concept and principles of PD, submitted to the Tokyo
ISG. ASEAN's ideas of the concept and principles of PD were developed
based on those agreed upon at the CSCAP workshop on PD held in Bangkok in March 1999.[46] Along with the ARF sponsored Track Two seminars
on PD, CSCAP had also attempted to define the concept and principles of
PD appropriate to the Asia-Pacific region in order to help move the PD
process forward. The Bangkok CSCAP meeting, which many ARF officials
attended in their private capacities, eventually agreed on a working definition of PD. During the drafting exercise, there was considerable debate
on whether the objects of PD should cover intra-state disputes and conflicts.
A US participant suggested that PD could involve both intra- and inter-state
conflicts, but this was opposed by a Chinese participant.[47] Consequently,
the CSCAP paper limited the scope of PD to inter-state issues. The
paper defined PD as consensual diplomatic and political action with the
aim of:

1) Preventing severe disputes and conflicts from arising between states
   which pose a serious threat to regional peace and stability;

2) Preventing such disputes and conflicts from escalating into armed confrontation; and
3) Limiting the intensity of violence and humanitarian problems resulting from such conflicts and preventing them from spreading geographically.

The paper also identified the following principles of PD:

1) It is about diplomacy. It relies on diplomatic and peaceful methods such as persuasion, negotiation, enquiry, mediation, and conciliation.
2) It is voluntary. Preventive diplomacy practices are employed at the request of the parties or with their consent.
3) It is a non-coercive activity. Acts that require military action or use of force, or other coercive practices, such as sanctions, are outside the scope of preventive diplomacy.
4) It requires trust and confidence. The facilitator or mediator in the dispute must be seen as trustworthy and as an impartial honest broker by all involved parties.
5) It rests upon international law. Any preventive diplomacy action should be in accordance with the basic principles of international law.
6) It is based on respect for sovereignty and non-interference in the internal affairs of a state. This includes the principles of sovereign equality and territorial integrity.
7) It requires timeliness. Action is to be preventive, rather than curative. Preventive diplomacy methods are most effectively employed at an early stage of a dispute or crisis.[48]

Although the CSCAP paper had already accommodated many of China's and ASEAN's suggestions, as evinced by the hedged language of the paper, ASEAN's draft paper tilted further in that direction. For instance, it focused on pre-crisis PD measures rather than those taken at the onset of a crisis. In the paper, pre-crisis PD measures were identified as 'confidence building efforts', 'norms building', 'enhancing channels of communication', and there was no consideration for more authentic pre-crisis PD measures, such as a fact-finding missions and early warning. The paper presented eight principles of PD, including the CSCAP's above mentioned seven principles. However, the language of the CSCAP's principles was modified drastically in order to more explicitly specify the exclusion of intra-state disputes from the scope of PD. ASEAN's draft principles, for instance, stated that 'PD applies only to problems between and among states'. Moreover, the ASEAN paper excluded the limitation of the intensity of violence and humanitarian problems from the objectives of PD, which the CSCAP paper included.[49] ASEAN countries believed that humanitarian intervention had the potential to subvert the principle of non-interference since it would not only weaken political solidarity but also allow Western countries to challenge the legitimacy of governments.[50]

In spite of the presentation of a watered down version of the original CSCAP concept and principles of PD, the ISG yielded no significant progress because some reluctant countries were still not satisfied with the contents of the paper. There were also strong reservations on the part of activist countries. The US and Australia were apparently not satisfied with the contents of the ASEAN draft paper, in particular the applicability of PD only to inter-state issues.[51] Canada also complained that the ASEAN paper neglected the concepts of human rights and the rule of law while overemphasising the principles of non-interference in internal affairs.[52] In the end, it was agreed that Singapore would revise the draft paper by the ISG on CBMs in the next intersessional year, taking into account written comments submitted by ARF countries.[53]

The Seventh ARF exposed the profound difficulties of building consensus on PD in the Forum. Deep divisions between activist and reluctant countries over PD proved difficult to overcome, thereby posing concerns among Japanese officials that this would further damage the momentum of the ARF.

The adoption of three papers on PD: Progressing or posturing?

The ISG on CBMs held in Seoul in November 2000 and Kuala Lumpur in April 2001 continued the discussion on three papers on PD; Singapore's paper on the concept and principles of PD, Japan's paper on the enhanced role of the ARF chair and South Korea's paper on EEPs. However, despite revisions, disagreements were not easily overcome. Consensus on Singapore's paper was finally achieved at the Kuala Lumpur ISG.[54] However, as a result of extensive revisions, the content of the paper was further watered down. For instance, while the original ASEAN draft paper simply referred to 'the basic principles of international law' as a guide to PD, the adopted paper specifically included 'the UN Charter, ASEAN's Treaty of Amity and Co-operation and the Five Principles of Peaceful Co-Existence as the principles of international law, thereby further stressing the adherence to states' sovereignty and non-interference in internal affairs.[55] In the end, the principles and concept of PD adopted by the ARF became very similar to those specified in the Chinese paper, a clear indication of how Chinese preferences and suggestions had influenced Singapore's revisions.

Reaching consensus on Japan's paper on the enhanced role of the ARF chair was more time consuming. Discussion of the Japanese paper did not progress smoothly because of continued resistance from China and a number of ASEAN countries. Chinese officials were opposed to substantial discussions on enhanced roles of the ARF chair before the ARF had finalised the concept and principles of PD. Detailed discussion finally took place in the Kuala Lumpur ISG on CBMs. However, consensus on the paper was not reached, and Japan was requested to further revise its paper based on the suggestions of ARF countries. Japan continued to make vigorous efforts to steer a middle path between activist and reluctant countries through informal consultations. MOFA officials even visited Beijing to discuss the Japanese paper with Chinese counterparts and to reconcile their differing views.[56]

As a result of these efforts, the Eighth ARF SOM in Hanoi in May 2001 finally reached agreement on the Japanese paper, but some important proposals were modified or simply eliminated. For example, proposals to give the chair's authority to issue a chairman statement 'at its discretion' and to provide early warning were excluded from the final paper. The only chair's role on which agreement was reached and which was potentially useful in the event of a regional crisis was the power to convene an emergency meeting of ARF members. However, contrary to the wishes of Japan, the implementation of this measure became subject to the 'consent of states involved in disputes and the consensus of all ARF members'.[57] Overall, enhanced measures approved at the SOM were limited to the chair's role as discussion facilitator and as liaison officer with external parties. There were almost no practical measures that the ARF could actually exercise in response to regional crises. The adopted paper even noted that 'the paper is mainly focusing on the role of the ARF chair in CBM stage rather than PD'.[58]

In addition, though the Seoul ISG meeting reached a general consensus on the terms of reference for the use of EEPs, like other PD papers, its content was watered down. The consensus paper stated, for example, that 'EEPs may only provide non-binding and professional recommendations to the ARF countries when they undertake in-depth studies and researches or serve as resource persons in ARF meetings on issues of relevance to their expertise'. Moreover, the use of EEPs became subject to the consensus of all ARF members.[59]

The Eighth Ministerial Meeting in Hanoi in July 2001 formally adopted three papers on PD. Considering that the ARF had previously not been able to produce any notable progress on PD issues, the agreement gave the impression that the Forum had achieved a major breakthrough in moving itself toward the PD stage. However, whether the adoption of three PD papers was an indication of real progress was in question. In actuality, there still remained serious dissension among ARF countries over the definitions and measures of PD. This was expressed by the Eighth ARF Chairman's statement, which noted that 'the paper on the concept and principles of PD was adopted as a snapshot of the state of current discussion on PD in the ARF' and that 'the ISG on CBMs would continue discussing PD in the next intersessional year and focus on those issues where there remains divergence of views'.[60] Indeed, the concept and principles of PD adopted at the Eighth ARF remained only a working definition. It was reported that ARF countries were unable to reach an agreement on the paper on the concept and principles of PD without inserting the 'snap shot' clause in the Chairman's statement due to opposition from the US and Australia, which had insisted on the need to broaden the scope of PD to cover intra-state conflicts.[61]

Meanwhile, some ARF countries persisted in their reluctance to move the Forum fully toward the PD stage. Vietnamese Foreign Minister, Nguyen Dy Nien, the chair of the Eighth ARF, for instance, stated that 'the meeting agreed only on the concept of PD and the ARF still emphasised confidence building as the main thrust'.[62] This was also confirmed by the Chairman's statement, affirming that 'confidence building would remain the foundation and main thrust of the whole ARF process'.[63] In short, the adoption of the PD papers at the Eighth ARF was a result of neither the emergence of a common understanding of PD nor of a compromise between activist and reluctant countries. The ASEAN secretariat reportedly stated that the ARF needed to adopt the PD papers in order to deflect criticism of the Forum for not showing any concrete achievements on PD.[64]

Due in part to an overwhelming focus on the counter-terrorism issue after the September 11 terrorist attacks in the US, substantial discussion on PD has not taken place after the Eighth ARF. Activist countries have attempted to revitalise the momentum of the ARF's discussion on PD, but their initiatives have been so far not effective. At the Tenth ARF Ministerial Meeting held in Phnom Penh in June 2003, Japan called for other ARF countries to hold a more in-depth discussion on PD and proposed to organise an ad hoc workshop on PD.[65] It was convened in Tokyo in March 2004, but it yielded no impressive results. Activist countries also revived the earlier proposal for establishing an intersessional meeting on PD in the Ninth ARF meetings.[66] However, the proposal was still highly problematic because of a continued reluctance on the part of some ARF countries to move the Forum fully toward the PD stage. In the end, at the Twelfth ARF Ministerial Meeting in Vientiane in July 2005, ARF countries agreed to replace the 'ISG on CBMs' with the 'ISG on CBMs and PD' instead of forming the 'ISG on PD'.[67]

In addition, activist countries have continued to seek opportunities for the structural reform of the ARF, but opposition from both ASEAN and China has not been easily overcome. At the Eleventh ARF Ministerial Meeting in July 2004, for instance, Japan presented a proposal to set up a permanent secretariat in the ARF, consisting of staff from both ASEAN and non-ASEAN states.[68] However, the proposal again received cool responses from ASEAN states, which wished to maintain a position of diplomatic centrality within the ARF. In the end, it was agreed that an ARF unit comprising only ASEAN officials would be established within the ASEAN Secretariat.[69]

Conclusion

This chapter has examined Japan's experience in the ARF regarding the PD agenda. Like the CBM agenda, ARF countries were split roughly into two groups according to their views of PD with activist countries, most notably Japan, Australia, Canada, and the US, which sought to develop the ARF's potential in PD along the path developed by the Concept Paper on the one hand and reluctant countries, including China and most ASEAN countries, which wanted the ARF to focus on security dialogue on the other. Ostensibly, ARF countries reached an agreement on a working definition of the concept and principles of PD in 2001. However, due to oppositions from reluctant countries, the adopted paper excluded all intra-state disputes and even humanitarian contingencies from the scope of PD, thus eliminating the possibility of the ARF dealing with many potential regional conflicts. Just as disappointing, the enhanced role of the ARF chair, the key to the success of prompting practical PD measures, was limited to roles as discussion facilitator and liaison officer with external parties with little potential to actually play a good offices role in the events of regional crises. Indeed, the most important elements of the Japanese proposals for the enhanced role of the ARF chair were eliminated due to opposition from reluctant countries, which feared the possibility of interference in their domestic affairs. Finally, despite widespread recognition that the present institutional arrangements of the ARF were inadequate for the development of effective PD mechanisms, there have been no real prospects for the ARF seriously undertaking institutional reform due to stiff resistance from reluctant countries. Consequently, the ARF's potential to play an effective PD role has so far remained very limited.

The notable lack of progress on the PD in the ARF has stemmed not only from considerable misgivings about its active participation in conflict prevention on the part of reluctant countries but also ASEAN's principles of 'consensus decision-making' and maintaining 'the pace comfortable to all participants' both of which allow proposals to be easily vetoed. As we have seen, many PD proposals raised by activist countries were simply dropped or significantly watered down even though these proposals seemed to strike a fair middle point between the two parties. As a result, the consequence of negotiations has been, at best, the lowest common denominator, almost exclusively reflecting the preferences of reluctant countries. In other words, the accomplishments of the ARF have been a result of neither the emergence of a common understanding nor of a compromise between the two sides. Without any serious concessions from reluctant states, such results are almost inevitable in a forum that operates under the 'ASEAN Way'.

Overall, what Japanese officials have learnt through their experiences in the ARF is that promoting meaningful cooperative security measures, including military CBMs and PD measures, in a cooperative security forum, which operates on the principle of inclusive membership and under the

'ASEAN Way' of institution building, is extremely difficult. Inevitably, this realisation has served to dilute Japan's expectations for the ARF. Before entering into an investigation of the effects of this on Japan's conceptions of regional security multilateralism, the following two chapters of this study will look at another dimension of Japan's ARF policy, namely, diplomacy in the process of multilateral dialogues on regional security issues.

5 Japan and multilateral security dialogue in the ARF (1994–97)

Security dialogue as a means of reassuring, engaging or constraining China?

Introduction

As discussed in Chapters 1 and 2, Japan's growing enthusiasm for Asia-Pacific security multilateralism in the early 1990s was grounded not only in hopes for the promotion of cooperative security measures but also the expectation that multilateral security dialogue could be a means of addressing its wider security concerns. Firstly, Japanese policy makers saw multilateral security dialogue as an instrument for reassuring its Asian neighbours about the future direction of its security policy. Secondly, they also expected that it could be used as a vehicle for engaging or constraining non-like-minded countries, most notably China. And finally, Japan hoped that in the long-term, multilateral discussions on potentially destabilising issues, such as the South China Sea dispute, in the ARF would help facilitate policy coordination and cooperation among concerned countries on those issues.

This chapter is the first of two chapters that examine Japan's diplomacy in multilateral dialogues on regional security issues in the ARF. The focus of this chapter is Japan's diplomacy during the four years since its foundation (1994–97), with special reference to its security relations with China. This is because not only did China related security issues, such as its nuclear testing and the South China Sea disputes, become the main agenda of security dialogue process in the ARF during this period but also rising tensions in Sino-Japanese security relations, ignited by these issues, since the mid-1990s serve as a test of whether the ARF can actually meet Japan's expectations for multilateral security dialogue, specified in the above. While the focus is on Japan's diplomacy, this chapter also tries to examine China's conception of and policy toward the ARF and contrasts them with those of Japan. This undertaking will shed light on the difficulties and problems of reconciling Japan's multilateral security policy with the pursuit of the strengthening of the Japan-US Alliance.

This chapter argues that the ARF's security dialogue process contributed to Japan's policy of engagement with China to some extent, as exemplified by its rapprochement with China through the ARF meetings after bilateral collisions. However, Japanese policy makers also recognised the limitations of multilateral security dialogue as an instrument of addressing Japan's security interests, in particular regarding its attempts to constrain and reassure Beijing.

Resistance to multilateral security dialogues

The security dialogue process in the ARF got off to an extremely modest start. In the First ARF SOM, senior officials exchanged views on regional political and security issues. But they deliberately avoided discussing sensitive issues that might provoke certain participating countries on the grounds that the top priority for the First ARF was to get everybody around the table rather than to make concrete decisions regarding security issues. The ARF officials agreed to neither discuss sensitive issues nor set agenda in the First Ministerial Meeting in order to promote a frank discussion.[1] In actuality, however, this decision largely reflected China's opposition to placing any specific security issue, such as the South China Sea and the Korean Peninsula, on the ARF agenda. At the SOM, Chinese officials suggested that specific regional security issues be discussed on a bilateral basis and thus objected to the idea of using the ARF to address them.[2]

However, prior to the Ministerial Meeting, there was dispute between a number of ASEAN countries and China over the issue of whether the South China Sea should be discussed in the ARF. At the AMM held just before the ARF Ministerial Meeting, three ASEAN states: the Philippines, Malaysia and Brunei, called for discussion of the South China Sea issue in the Forum.[3] Chinese representatives rejected this insistence, stating at the press conference prior to the Ministerial Meeting that 'negotiation should be conducted bilaterally between China and the disputing parties, not during the ARF talks'.[4] Regardless of Beijing's objection, however, several countries touched on the South China Sea issue in the meeting, albeit very briefly. Japan and the US also raised the issue of North Korea's suspected nuclear weapons development in the absence of representatives from Pyongyang. By the summer of 1994, North Korea's nuclear problem turned to a crisis as Pyongyang rejected an important part of the inspection activities by the IAEA. In response to this the US proposed that the UN Security Council discuss the possibility of sanctions against North Korea. The Clinton administration was ready to impose new sanctions, including military blockade and even prepared for the possibility of hostilities with North Korea when Pyongyang signalled that any sanctions would be regarded as a declaration of war.[5] In this situation, US officials proposed to issue a critical statement against North Korea in order to press Pyongyang to settle the nuclear problem. However, though China tolerated brief discussion of the issues, it reacted negatively to the US proposal, reiterating that the ARF should not deal with specific regional security issues.[6] Nonetheless, due to the initiative of Thai Foreign Minister, Prasong Soonsiri, the chairman of the First ARF, the Chairman's statement successfully mentioned the issues of non-proliferation of nuclear weapons and the Korean Peninsula. However, the statement totally excluded other important security issues, such as the South China Sea dispute.[7]

China's nuclear testing and the South China Sea dispute

The second working session of the ARF was convened against growing tensions in relations between Japan, the US and China. A confrontation between the US and China was triggered by the US decision to grant a visa to Lee Teng-hui, the President of Taiwan, for a private visit to Cornell University. The Clinton administration had initially rejected Taiwan's request, but because of strong pressure from Congress, it reversed the decision. This provoked the Chinese government, which regarded the decision as not only interference in China's domestic matters but also a sign of its departure from the one-China principle. This led China to take retaliatory measures, such as the withdrawal of its ambassador to the US, the cancellation of high-level military visits to the US and the granting of business contracts to non-American firms.[8]

Meanwhile, Japan's diplomatic relations with China significantly worsened when Beijing conducted underground nuclear tests in May 1995. China's nuclear test outraged the Japanese government since it was conducted shortly after Prime Minister Murayama Tomiichi had asked Chinese Premier Li Peng for a moratorium on testing during a visit to Beijing. The nuclear test also took place against the backdrop of the UN decision, supported by more than 170 countries, to extend the NPT indefinitely.[9] This provoked an unprecedented strong reaction from Japan. The Japanese government called China's nuclear testing 'extremely regrettable' and in August decided for the first time to suspend ODA in protest.[10]

In parallel with this, Japan's perception of China was worsened by Beijing's increasing assertive behaviour in the South China Sea. In February 1995, Chinese forces entered the disputed waters and built military structures on Mischief Reef, an island also claimed by the Philippines. This was considered evidence of a marked shift in China's policy towards the South China Sea by Japan as well as other regional countries since it was the first time that China had taken action against an ASEAN country. Subsequently, in March 1995, the Malaysian Navy fired on a Chinese fishing boat in waters claimed by Malaysia.[11] The confrontation between China and ASEAN countries attracted a great deal of attention from Japan, which feared that the dispute would endanger the free passage of Japanese ships through one of the world's major shipping routes. Akiyama Masahiro, the then administrative vice minister of JDA, stated that 'Tokyo is closely watching the South China Sea disputes since the disputes will affect Japan's vital interests as most of the energy coming to Japan passes through sea lanes in the South China Sea'.[12]

It was inevitable that China's nuclear tests and its expansionist policy in the South China Sea would exacerbate Tokyo's unfavourable view of Beijing. In October 1995, Foreign Minister Kōno Yōhei stated in the National Diet that 'from the viewpoints of Japan's as well as regional security, Chinese military modernisation and its territorial policies could be a source of regional instability'.[13] The 1995 JDA's Defence White Paper, which had avoided mentioning China's threatening language, eventually expressed concerns over China's recent activities, including the modernisation of its naval, air and nuclear forces as well as its increasingly aggressive policy towards the South China Sea.[14] More importantly, earlier drafts of the 1995 NDPO indirectly mentioned the Chinese threat regarding its increasing military modernisation and highlighting its military activities.[15] In sum, China's assertive behaviour was enough to convince Japanese policy makers that China was a potential long-term threat, though not an immediate one, to Japan's security as well as that of the region.

Japan's increasing apprehension about China's aggressive security policy led MOFA to take decisive action in the ARF. While many countries were still hesitating to raise sensitive security issues in the ARF, Japan decided to utilise the meeting to apply collective criticism to China. Foreign Minister Kōno expressed the Japanese intention prior to the Second ARF Ministerial Meeting, saying that 'I must state that I am concerned about the issue of the nuclear testing by China and France and fear that this could easily have a very detrimental impact on the non-proliferation regime credibility. I intend to take the issue up vigorously at the ARF, the UN and other forums'. Kōno also argued that disputes over the South China Sea should be discussed in the ARF meetings, openly opposing China's stance.[16] For Japan, coaxing Beijing into multilateral discussion on these sensitive security issues was a test of whether the ARF was capable of discussing sensitive security issues with which Japan was seriously concerned and also of whether the Forum had the potential to be a useful diplomatic channel for gathering collective criticism against China.

At the Second ARF SOM in Brunei in May 1995, Japanese officials expressed explicitly their concerns about the situation in the South China Sea and joined the Philippines and the US in efforts to raise the issue on the agenda of the upcoming Ministerial Meeting.[17] Needless to say, their initiatives met strong objections from China. Chinese representatives reiterated that the South China Sea should be discussed exclusively in bilateral talks between claimants and China.[18] The ARF officials eventually refrained from pushing the South China Sea issue further, fearing that provoking China might lead its withdrawal from the Forum. Nevertheless, their collective pressures on China over the South China Sea issue at the SOM made Chinese representatives feel their diplomatic isolation, thus inducing China to soften its position on the issue. At the Second ARF Ministerial Meeting in Brunei in August 1995, while reiterating China's indisputable sovereignty over the Spratly Islands and their adjacent waters, China's

Foreign Minister, Qian Qichen, expressed willingness to discuss the South China Sea dispute with all ASEAN countries, reversing for the first time its long-standing opposition to multilateral discussion on the issue. Qian also publicly agreed to pursue a peaceful resolution on the disputes in accordance with international law, including the United Nations Convention on the Law of the Sea (UNCLOS).[19] The Chinese Foreign Minister also did not prevent the Chairman's statement from urging 'all claimants to reaffirm their commitment to the principles contained in relevant international laws and convention and the ASEAN's 1992 Declaration on the South China Sea.'[20] Considering that China had previously not even tolerated specific mention of the South China Sea dispute in the Chairman's statement, this was a significant concession on the part of Beijing.

Japan along with Australia also took the lead in the discussion of the nuclear tests conducted by China and France at the Ministerial Meeting in order to create collective pressure on China to halt the testing. Although Kōno did not refer to China by name at the meeting, he did criticise China indirectly, stating that 'the nuclear test undermines international efforts for nuclear proliferation and that nuclear powers should make efforts to win trust from non-nuclear countries'. Following Japan and Australia, several ARF countries explicitly aired concerns about the Chinese nuclear tests. Qian responded to the criticism by promising to sign the Comprehensive Nuclear Test-Ban Treaty (CTBT) in the near future.[21] Beijing also did not disrupt a consensus on the Chairman's statement, which indirectly condemned both China and France for their nuclear testing, stating that 'those countries that plan to conduct further nuclear tests were called upon by all other ARF member states to bring immediate end to such testing'.[22]

In addition, the Second ARF was also utilised by major powers to defuse tensions between Washington and Beijing stemming from the visit of Lee Teng-hui to Cornell University. On the sidelines of the Ministerial Meeting, US Secretary of State Warren Christopher had a one and half hour meeting with his Chinese counterpart, Qian Qichen, and the two sides agreed to initiate a senior official conference to repair the bilateral relationship. Christopher also proposed to hold a bilateral summit meeting in October of the same year.[23]

MOFA was of the opinion that the Second ARF had made notable progress on multilateral discussion on regional security. MOFA officials gave high marks to the fact that the ARF was actually capable of discussing specific security issues, including China's nuclear testing and the South China Sea issue, which were also addressed in the Chairman's statement.[24]

Collisions over the Taiwan crisis, the Senkaku Islands and the Japan-US Joint Security Declaration

Regardless of attempts by the US and China to restore their bilateral relationship, relations among the three major powers continued to deteriorate through to 1996. China-US ties had reached a low point when Beijing attempted to disrupt Taiwan's first presidential election by military coercion. Beijing conducted a series of missile tests and military exercises of their combined forces in and around the Taiwan Strait between July 1995 and March 1996 apparently in order to intimidate Taipei and to prevent it from moving toward independence. In response, the US dispatched two aircraft carrier groups to the coastal waters of Taiwan to express its strong resolve to protect Taiwan.[25] The Taiwan crisis featured prominently in Japan' security concerns over China. The crisis, which took place near to Japanese territory, impressed on Japan that any conflicts in the Taiwan Strait might influence the country's national security. In fact, one of the three missiles, which China fired in March 1996, landed in the sea off Taiwan, only 60 km from Japan's westernmost island.[26] The Chinese missile exercise also raised apprehensions about Beijing's willingness to use force to resolve issues involving its national sovereignty and security interest. Indeed, after China's missile diplomacy, many Japanese security analysts began to doubt the credibility of Beijing's non-first use policy.[27] Consequently, the Taiwan crisis further aggravated Japan's perception of China, which had already been damaged by its nuclear tests. LDP secretary general Katō Kōichi warned that 'China's missile testing in international waters in the Taiwan Strait was behaviour that cannot be tolerated'.[28]

In addition, Sino-Japanese tensions were heightened by territorial disputes over the Senkaku Islands (called the Diaoyu Islands in Chinese). Since 1995, Chinese oil exploration ships had regularly intruded and operated in Japan's claimed EEZ and territorial waters around the Senkaku Islands. In December 1995, Japanese Foreign Minister, Kōno Yōhei, formally protested against the intrusion of Chinese vessels into the Senkaku Islands.[29] Meanwhile, in July 1996, Japanese right wing groups constructed a lighthouse on one of the islands, provoking the Chinese government.[30] Beijing warned Tokyo that the construction of a lighthouse on the Senkaku Islands was a serious violation of Chinese sovereignty, but in response the Japanese government merely reiterated the country's sovereignty over the islands. Chief Cabinet Secretary, Kajiyama Seiroku, stated that 'anyone in Japan can build a lighthouse on the island as long as it is permitted by a landowner. Since Japan has made claims to ownership of the territories, it is not in a position to interfere in the matter'.[31]

Finally, strained relations between Japan and China were heightened by their collisions over the Japan-US Joint Declaration on Security, signed in April 1996 by President Bill Clinton and Prime Minister Hashimoto Ryūtarō. The declaration was issued as a result of attempts to reaffirm the bilateral security relationship in the context of the emerging new security environment of the post-Cold War era. It stated that 'the two countries reaffirmed that the Japan-US alliance continuously remains the cornerstone for achieving common security objectives and for maintaining a stable and prosperous security environment in the Asia-Pacific region in the twenty-first century'.

Among other things, the declaration stressed the need to enhance Japan-US military cooperation in dealing with 'situations that may emerge in the areas surrounding Japan, which will have an important effect on the peace and security of Japan'. In the declaration, the two countries thus agreed to review the 1978 Guidelines for Japan-US Defence Cooperation to clarify the role of US and Japan's forces on a concrete operational level in times of contingency that may emerge in the areas surrounding Japan.[32] The 1978 guidelines had actually promised to explore their military cooperation in contingencies in the Far East based on Article VI of the Japan-US Security Treaty. But the two countries had not conducted substantive research on joint operations beyond the narrow confines of the missions of Japan's national defence out of fear that the issue of joint operation outside Japanese territory would inevitably provoke a controversial debate over the right of collective self-defence.[33] In short, the joint declaration demonstrated Japan's new interest in expanding the bilateral defence cooperation in not only defending Japan's home islands but also dealing with a regional crisis not involving direct attacks on Japan. As for the first concrete step for enhancing the bilateral defence cooperation, just prior to the issue of the joint declaration, Japan and the US had signed an Acquisition and Cross-Servicing Agreement (ACSA). This agreement would allow the SDF and US forces to mutually supply goods and services, including fuel and military spare parts, in joint military training, UN peacekeeping operation, and other international humanitarian relief operations.[34]

Another important aspect of the declaration was its emphasis on the bolstering the Japan-US cooperation in other areas, including the development of multilateral regional security dialogues and cooperation mechanisms, such as the ARF and security dialogues in Northeast Asia, and of a close cooperation with China and Russia.[35] This expressed the Japanese and US intention to maintain their policy of simultaneously pursuing both bilateral and multilateral approaches to enhancing regional stability.

The primary motivation behind the reaffirmation of the Japan-US alliance was to prepare for contingencies on the Korean Peninsula. Japan's inability to provide clear commitments of logistical support for the US forces during the North Korea nuclear crisis in 1994 generated serious concerns among Japanese and US defence officials that the credibility of the alliance would be dangerously undermined if Japan's military roles were not specified. With the greatly heightened possibility of a new Korean conflict the two military forces required better integration in preparation for joint operations in the event of an emergency situation in East Asia.[36]

Beijing, however, reacted sharply to the joint security declaration, which was issued just one month after the Taiwan crisis, regarding it as a response to the crisis and a new tool for containing China.[37] China charged that the joint declaration expanded the scope of Japan-US security cooperation beyond that of the 1960 Japan-US security treaty because the 1960 security treaty only referred to 'Far East', not 'Asia-Pacific'. Moreover, a reference made to 'coping with situations in areas surrounding Japan' and the decision of the two countries to review the 1978 guidelines led China to suspect that the two countries might interfere in a crisis over the Taiwan Strait and even the South China Sea.[38] China's Foreign Minister, Qian Qichen, stated that 'the relevant discussions on the meaning of the (Japan-US security) treaty and the relevant joint statements that have been issued signify that the role of the treaty may be extended to cover the whole region. That is worrisome'.[39]

The Japanese-US decision to revise their defence guidelines also triggered concerns among other Asian countries, including South Korea and ASEAN countries, since it posed great uncertainty about what sort of role Japan's SDF would play in joint operations.[40] ASEAN states had mixed feelings about the new development regarding the Japan-US security relationship. While recognising the importance of the US military presence in the region, which they regarded as a stabilising factor for regional security, they did not want to see the expansion of Japan's military role in East Asia due to memories of the suffering caused by Japanese militarism during World War II.[41]

Though the joint declaration was not a direct response to the Taiwan crisis, China's missile diplomacy towards Taiwan inevitably generated further momentum for the review of the Japan-US defence guidelines as it convinced Japanese policy makers of the need to hedge against China's military power by reinforcing the nation's defence cooperation with the US.[42] In addition to stressing a military balancing approach, the Taiwan crisis also drove Tokyo to create strategic relationships with other Asian countries surrounding China. Indeed, Japanese policy makers began to undertake a policy of what Michael Green called 'soft containment'.[43] In January 1997, Prime Minister Hashimoto visited five ASEAN countries and proposed the establishment of an annual summit between Japanese and ASEAN leaders to promote multilateral cooperation on the preservation of the region's cultures and traditions and joint action to tackle transnational problems, such as terrorism and drugs. Hashimoto's proposal, dubbed 'the Hashimoto doctrine', envisaged a broader and more profound political and security relationship between Japan and ASEAN beyond mere economic cooperation. The main driving force behind the Hashimoto proposal was the desire to counterbalance growing Chinese power in East Asia with ASEAN support.[44] In sum, by bolstering the security dimension of its relationship with ASEAN, Japan intended to use ASEAN as a balancer to increasingly complex relations within the Japan-US-China triangle. However, ASEAN leaders paid little attention to the Hashimoto doctrine out of fear of involving themselves in the growing rivalry between Japan and China. Instead, ASEAN countries floated a counter-proposal to create a regional summit between ASEAN governments and their counterparts from Japan, South Korea and China.[45] This proposal came to fruition in December 1997, leading to the establishment of the 'ASEAN+3 summit'.

In addition, Japan also began to actively approach Russia in order to create a strategic balance against China. In 1996, the Japanese government announced a new policy toward Russia based on trust, mutual benefit and emphasis on the long-term perspective. In March 1996, Foreign Minister, Ikeda Yukihiko, visited Moscow and announced the initiation of regular Russo-Japanese meetings to discuss regional security issues. Moreover, at the Japan-Russia summit in 1997, the two countries agreed to promote high-level military exchanges and bilateral economic cooperation, including peaceful use of nuclear power.[46]

Ironically, while China's continuing assertiveness, illustrated by its nuclear testing and its coercive diplomacy towards Taiwan, further convinced Japanese officials of the significance of the alliance for Japan's national security, these incidents exposed the limitation of multilateral security diplomacy for constraining China. Tokyo's expectations that the ARF might serve to constrain China were dashed when Beijing conducted further nuclear tests in June 1996 despite collective criticism at the previous year's ARF meetings and Japan's decision to suspend its ODA. In addition, the ARF's failure to discuss the issue of the Taiwan Strait deepened Japan's disappointment. At the Third ARF SOM in Jakarta in May 1996, Japanese officials attempted to place the issue of the Taiwan Strait crisis on the SOM agenda by calling for China to use peaceful means to resolve the dispute. However, the Japanese initiative was discouraged by Beijing, which argued that the matter was exclusively within its domestic jurisdiction.[47] ASEAN countries were also reluctant to raise the Taiwan issue in the ARF although they were apprehensive about China's increasing assertiveness. With Beijing declaring the status of Taiwan to be a domestic issue, ASEAN, which traditionally abided by the principles of non-interference in the internal affairs of states, was hesitant about engaging discussion on the Taiwan issue in the ARF. In fact, among regional countries, only Japan and Australia criticised China's missile exercise.[48] Hence, it was revealed that the ARF had a very limited mandate to discuss one of Japan' major security concerns, namely the issue of Taiwan Strait.

Notwithstanding, while being conscious of the need to hedge against China's growing military power by strengthening its defence cooperation with the US, Japanese policy makers realised the need to continue its efforts to engage China politically and economically in order to alleviate increasing tensions between the two nations. Indeed, Japan began to pursue dual approaches, political and economic engagement and balancing, to manage the rise of China. In this sense, Japan's policy of engaging China on security issues through the ARF was still highly relevant to its overall China policy. Accordingly, MOFA officials saw the Third ARF as an opportunity to allay Chinese concerns about the reaffirmation of the Japan-US alliance. In the Ministerial Meeting in Jakarta in July 1996, Foreign Minister Ikeda attempted to reassure China by stating that 'the alliance is not directed against any other country and its reaffirmation does not entail any shift in

Japan's security policy'.[49] However, China did not seem convinced by this explanation.

In the meeting, Ikeda also proposed to establish a Track One forum for Northeast Asian Security dialogue based on the existing Track Two level security dialogue, namely the NEACD, which included Japan, the US, China and Russia and both North and South Korea. This proposal reflected Japan's growing willingness to incorporate China into multilateral security arrangements.[50] Tokyo expected that a sub-regional forum would create a more substantive security dialogue between the major powers than a region-wide security forum, thus helping to ameliorate their tensions.

The Japanese proposal for Northeast Asian security dialogue was also a sign of Tokyo's frustration with the lack of attention the ARF was giving to Northeast Asian security issues. As noted above, the past two ARF meetings revealed that the ARF agenda tended to be centred narrowly on Southeast Asian security issues whereas the great weight of the emergent regional security concerns came from Northeast Asia. Thus, it was expected that establishing a forum for Northeast Asian security dialogue would supplement the work of the ARF.[51] The Japanese proposal, however, received only scant attention from other participants, excepting South Korea which also floated a similar proposal. China rebuffed Japan's proposal by citing North Korea's reluctance to participate in such a forum as a major reason. Even the US showed little enthusiasm due partly to concerns that establishing such a sub-regional security forum might weaken the momentum for strengthening Japan-US defence cooperation, generated by the 1996 joint declaration.[52]

Japan also used the ARF to try to engage China in Japan's effort to address its other major security concern, North Korea's nuclear weapons development. The North Korean nuclear issue continued to remain one of the major security concerns for Japan in spite of the agreement on the establishment of the Korean Peninsula Energy Development Organization (KEDO), which was concluded by Japan, the US and South Korea in 1995 and under which the three countries promised to provide North Korea with two light water reactors as replacements for its existing nuclear reactors and nuclear weapon programme.[53] Japan intended to play an active role in addressing the North Korean nuclear and missile threats through KEDO, but despite its significance, KEDO faced a major shortfall in funding, which threatened the existence of the project. The tension in the Peninsula was further heightened by a series of North Korean provocations, including incursions into the buffer zone. In response to this, in April 1996, the US and South Korea proposed to establish four-party talks between the US, China and North and South Korea with the aim of creating a new system to guarantee permanent peace on the Korean Peninsula.[54] Reflecting this situation, in the bilateral meeting between Tokyo and Beijing held on the sidelines of the Ministerial Meeting, Ikeda asked Chinese counterpart Qian for China's support in the establishment of the four-party talks. This occasion was also utilised by Japan to attempt to allay Chinese concerns about the Japan-US alliance.[55]

The Third ARF also provided Japan, the US and South Korea with an opportunity to not only garner support from regional countries for their initiatives in the Korean Peninsula but also to coordinate their policies. The three countries held trilateral talks to orchestrate policy towards the KEDO as well as a joint US-South Korean proposal for the four-party talks.[56] At the Ministerial Meeting, Ikeda and Secretary of State, Warren Christopher, jointly appealed for more financial assistance from regional countries, which had not contributed to the KEDO. The two foreign ministers also called for political support for the four-party talks. Tokyo and Washington, in particular, targeted Beijing and Moscow in the hope that countries having special ties with Pyongyang could persuade it to join the four-party talks. Both countries reacted positively to their request. China pledged to play a constructive role in the Korean Peninsula although Beijing said that it would not force North Korea to take part.[57]

The issue of the Korean Peninsula also attracted significant attentions from ASEAN countries. Unlike previous ARF meetings, the Third ARF saw a vigorous exchange of views on the issue, which ASEAN countries had shown little willingness to discuss in the past.[58] Japan, the US and South Korea were also successful in leading the Chairman's statement to 'encourage ARF participants to consider giving further financial and political support to KEDO' and to stress 'the need to establish a peace mechanism in the Korean Peninsula (namely the four-party talks)'.[59]

In addition, the Third ARF witnessed some positive developments in terms of the South China Sea issue though it was continuously complicated by China's ambiguous intent. In May 1996, China ratified UNCLOS, but baselines for its territorial waters were extended to include the Paracel Islands in the South China Sea. China's definition of its maritime baselines posed serious concerns to a number of ASEAN countries, including the Philippines and Vietnam, since they saw China's ratification as potentially strengthening its territorial claim.[60] Nonetheless, Beijing took some efforts to defuse ASEAN concerns in the ARF, and this ameliorated the situation to some extent. In the Ministerial Meeting, Chinese Foreign Minister, Qian Qichen, agreed to discuss the details of a new Chinese territorial claim with ASEAN states and reiterated an earlier proposal for commencing joint development of resources while shelving the sovereignty question.[61] In addition, in the bilateral consultations between China and the Philippines, the two countries agreed to military exchanges, joint research on maritime science and cooperation on piracy control and to establishing a bilateral consultative mechanism to explore ways of cooperation in the South China Sea.[62] These encouraging changes in Chinese position on the South China Sea dispute were also reflected in the Chairman's statement, which recorded the Chinese acknowledgement of seeking solutions on the South China Sea by peaceful means in accordance with international law and UNCLOS.[63]

China's attack on the new defence guidelines and major powers collaboration on the Cambodia issue

Sino-Japanese collisions over the new developments in the Japan-US alliance were further exacerbated by China's criticism of the review of Defence Guidelines for Japan-US Defence Cooperation. The draft report of the defence guidelines, which was released in early June in 1997 by the Japan-US Security Consultative Committee, raised apprehensions about the possibility of Japan expanding its military role in the region since the draft report put a special emphasis on bilateral military cooperation in regional contingencies.[64] Under the new guidelines, Japan would not only provide rear-area logistical support for US forces engaged in regional crises but also play a greater role in intelligence gathering, minesweeping and surveillance.[65-] Moreover, the new defence guidelines further complicated the controversial concept of 'the areas surrounding Japan'. While the 1996 Joint Declaration sanctioned bilateral cooperation in dealing with 'situations in areas surrounding Japan that will have an important influence on Japan's peace and security', the new guidelines replaced this with the more general definition, 'cooperation in situations in the areas surrounding Japan' and specified no geographic boundaries.[66]

China saw this ambiguity as a deliberate ploy to allow Taiwan and the South China Sea to be included in the scope of the alliance, and consequently Beijing intensified its attacks on the Japan-US alliance.[67] The ISG on CBMs in Beijing in 1997 witnessed a serious clash between US, Japanese and Chinese officials over the role of bilateral alliances in regional security. Chinese officials strongly criticised the Japan-US alliance as destabilising and representative of a Cold War mentality.[68] Due to discord between Chinese, US and Japanese representatives over ASEAN's proposal to include language in the Chairman's statement stating that 'the US-Japan alliance plays a constructive role in maintaining regional peace and stability and is the foundation upon which regional multilateral mechanisms are established', the meeting was delayed for several hours.[69]

Needless to say, Tokyo and Washington recognised the need to allay apprehensions over the new defence guidelines and thus attempted to reassure Asian countries through both bilateral and multilateral channels. After the presentation of the interim report of the defence guidelines, the Japanese government dispatched MOFA and JDA officials to Beijing and ASEAN countries to brief them on its contents.[70] On the multilateral level, Tokyo attempted to reassure Asian neighbours about the review of the defence guidelines through the ARF. In the Forth ARF Ministerial Meeting in Malaysia in July 1997, Japan's Foreign Minister, Ikeda Yukihiko, stated that 'the defence guidelines will remain within the limitations set by the Constitution, and Japan intends to continue its efforts in enhancing the credibility of the Japan-US security arrangements'. Ikeda also contended that 'the Japan-US alliance constitutes an indispensable factor for regional security and stability since it has sustained the US military presence in the region'.[71] In short, Tokyo justified the Japan-US alliance by defining it as 'the common good' in the Asia-Pacific region, thus trying to convince Chinese leaders that it would ultimately serve China's interests in a more stable region.

Japan's explanation for the new defence guidelines was basically acceptable to ASEAN countries that supported the US military presence in the region, but not to China. Beijing continued to criticise the Japan-US alliance. In the Ministerial Meeting, China's Foreign Minister, Qian Qichen, indirectly denounced the alliance, stating that 'the new international situation has called for a new security concept. Security should depend neither on military build-up nor on military alliance, but rather it should be built on mutual trust and common interests'. Qian added that a traditional military alliance approach to security should be replaced with a new security approach, suggesting that regional countries increase security through the following ways: (1) respecting each other and treating each other as equals instead of pursuing power politics or imposing their wills on others, (2) expanding economic exchanges and cooperation among countries, (3) settling disputes through peaceful means, and (4) pursuing multilateral efforts to promote dialogue and cooperation.[72]

The emergence of this new way of thinking, dubbed the 'New Security Concept', was in part influenced by Beijing's experience in regional multilateral arrangements, including the ARF and APEC, and the ideas of security multilateralism, such as the concepts of cooperative or common security. However, more fundamentally, as Michael Yahuda has argued, it was designed to promote Chinese security interests rather than those of the region as a whole.[73] The new security concept, for instance, helped to fulfil China's need to allay the concerns of Asian neighbours about its growing military power and security policy, which would make them more inclined to align themselves with the US against China. By adopting the new security concept and projecting a better image of itself, China expected to reassure its Asian neighbours and thus discourage them from participating in a US-led containment policy.[74]

The new security concept also served to challenge the status of the US as the unipolar power in the post-Cold War world. On the cusp of the end of the Cold War, Chinese leaders envisaged that a multipolar regional order based on equality and partnership between regional major powers, including China, the US, Japan, India and Russia, would gradually emerge in the post-Cold War era. With the end of both rigid bipolarity and direct threat, China expected that they would be able to pursue a more independent foreign policy and focus on the task of economic development.[75] However, what the post-Cold War era witnessed was the emergence of American unipolarity, stemming from both US preponderant military power and the enviable performance of its economy. China became increasingly concerned about US primacy compromising China's strategic interests, as evinced by confrontations over the 1995–96 Taiwan crisis. The new security concept was therefore employed by China in an attempt to reduce the US military presence in the region and to weaken the ties between Asian countries and the US through lecturing them about the dangers of military alliances.[76]

China's views contrasted sharply with those of Japan and the US, which regarded America's alliance system as the cornerstone of regional security and stability. Hence, Chinese officials rebuffed Japan's attempts to justify the strengthening of the Japan-US alliance, stating that 'the reinforcement of military alliances should not be regarded a major factor for peace and stability in the region. We do not think that it is correct to see bilateral alliances as the foundation of regional security and the ARF as a supplement to them'.[77]

This fundamental difference of perspective on regional order between Japan, the US and China also highlighted their differing views of the ARF. Indeed, while China came to conceive the ARF as a vehicle to not only reduce regional suspicions about its rising power and promote multipolarity to counter US primacy in the region, Japan and the US primarily saw it as a tool for promoting CBMs and PD that would complement the existing bilateral alliances and of socialising China into international standards of behaviours. These differing views of the ARF were demonstrated by differing attitudes towards the issue of India's participation in the Forum. China supported the ASEAN decision to accept India as a new ARF member to dilute the influence of the US and promote a multipolar regional order; Tokyo and Washington opposed it. The allies were concerned that admitting India to the ARF would bring contentious South Asian security issues to the Forum and expand its membership, thus not only decreasing the weight of their own security agendas, such as the issue of the Korean Peninsula, but also making the task of promoting practical CBMs and PD measures more difficult.[78]

In addition, Japan's efforts to reassure China about the new defence guidelines were in part impeded by Japan's failure to clarify any specific scenario or geographic location around Japan, especially regarding Taiwan. In the Ministerial Meeting, Qian asked Japanese representatives whether the areas surrounding Japan included Taiwan, but they refrained from offering a satisfactory explanation.[79] China's concerns about the vagueness of the new guidelines were more or less shared by other ASEAN countries, which feared the possibility of Japan expanding its military role in the region. Citing Chinese antipathy towards the new guidelines, Indonesia and Thailand also asked Japan to clarify the meaning of the phrase, 'to defend the area surrounding Japan'.[80]

Overall, due to fundamentally different views of a desired regional security order between major powers and due in part to a lack of clarification on the scope of the Japan-US alliance, Japan's multilateral reassurance diplomacy ended with disappointing results. A Chinese Foreign Ministry spokesman expressed dissatisfaction after the Ministerial Meeting, stating that 'the explanation Japan and the US tried to give other countries is not clear, at least not yet'.[81] Yet China's new security concept also lacked credibility in the eyes of many Japanese officials. While acknowledging China's increasingly positive attitude towards the ARF, many Japanese officials regarded the Chinese discourse on regional security multilateralism as diplomatic rhetoric. China's opposition to greater military transparency in its security policy and the promotion of PD measures in the ARF, discussed in the previous chapters, reinforced these suspicions.[82]

Whereas the fourth working session of the ARF saw discord between the major powers over disagreements on the defence guidelines, the Forum again served as a useful vehicle through which major countries were able to defuse tension stemming from regional crises. Indeed, the Ministerial Meeting was utilised by Beijing and Washington to restore their strained relations in advance of the upcoming US-China summit between President Bill Clinton and Chinese President Jiang Zemin. On the sidelines of the Ministerial Meeting, US Secretary of State Madeleine Albright held a bilateral meeting with her counterpart, China's Foreign Minister Qian Qichen, in which they expressed their willingness to develop 'strategic partnership' between the two countries.[83] Qian also pledged Chinese support for the four-party talks on the Korean Peninsula.

In the Ministerial Meeting, the US and China also collaborated on the issue of the Cambodian crisis, a product of their attempts to rebuild the bilateral relation.[84] In July 1997, Second Prime Minister Hun Sen seized control of the Phnom Penh government by launching a violent military coup to depose First Prime Minister, Prince Nordom Ranariddh. Washington took a tough stance towards Hun Sen. Soon after the coup the US government announced its decision to suspend aid for 30 days, a total of around US$35 million, to Cambodia for the purpose of pressing it to respect the Paris accord.[85] Meanwhile, the US expressed full support for ASEAN's decision to send the Indonesian Foreign Minister to Cambodia and itself dispatched a special envoy, Stephen Solarz, to explore the possible resolution of the crisis. Beijing had been highly critical of US policies towards Cambodia on the grounds that they would amount to interference in Cambodia's domestic affairs. However, China appeared to coordinate its position on the Cambodian issue with the US by the time of the ARF Ministerial Meeting. Qian expressed for the first time 'deep concern' about the political turmoil in Cambodia. Moreover, the Chinese Foreign Minister publicly endorsed ASEAN's initiative to promote political stability in Cambodia, which came as a surprise to other participants, though he still stressed the importance of the non-interference principle.[86]

The ARF also provided an opportunity for the US and Japan to coordinate their differing policies towards Cambodia. In contrast to the US position, Tokyo showed a relatively benign posture towards the Hun Sen government. Although Japan, Cambodia's biggest aid donor accounting for about half of all aid to Phnom Penh, promptly suspended its aid after the coup, Tokyo soon showed signs of resuming aid in the face of US requests for international support for economic sanctions. The Japanese government announced that Japan would restart aid if the Hun Sen regime would comply with certain conditions, such as the maintenance of the constitutional government and holding general elections. Japan even avoided calling the event a coup and acknowledged the legitimacy of the Hun Sen's government.[87] Upset by this, Washington sent Stephen Solarz to Tokyo to persuade Japanese leaders not to resume aid, but Japan's Prime Minister Hashimoto Ryūtarō simply replied that 'though Japan and the US share the same goal of establishing peace in Cambodia, we may differ in our approaches. Japan and the US are entitled to hold different opinions'.[88] Japan's soft stance on the Hun Sen regime was mainly a reflection of its concerns about China's growing influence over Southeast Asia. Japan recognised that Hun Sen was the only power that would be able to restore political stability in Cambodia and was worried that Cambodia would move closer to the Chinese side if the Hun Sen government were overthrown.[89]

Despite discord over the resumption of aid to Cambodia, in the bilateral meeting held on the sidelines of the ARF, Japanese Foreign Minister Ikeda and US Secretary of State Albright reached a consensus on the view that the top priority for their Cambodia policy was to restore political stability in Cambodia rather than to impose economic sanctions against it. They thus agreed that the Hun Sen regime would remain as a caretaker government until the general election scheduled to be held in May 1998.[90] This agreement led the US to soften its hard line policy towards to the Hun Sen regime. In the bilateral meeting, Albright pledged to resume US humanitarian aid to Cambodia, while arguing that the suspension of economic aid should be continued. This clear shift in US policy towards Cambodia was due to Washington coming to share Tokyo's concern about the possible expansion of Chinese influence over Cambodia.

The collaboration of the major powers over the Cambodian issue had a positive impact on the mood of the meeting. The Fourth ARF successfully led to the issue of a Chairman's statement expressing concerns over the situation in Cambodia and support for ASEAN's role and initiative in helping restore political stability.[91] The emerging consensus in the ARF put sufficient pressure on Cambodia to accept ASEAN's ministerial delegations headed by Indonesian Foreign Minister Ali Alatas, which had initially been rejected.[92]

Confrontations among major powers over the new defence guidelines and their collaboration on the Cambodian issue in the Fourth ARF showed that their relationships had considerable influence over the success and progress of the ARF. The issue of the defence guidelines clearly demonstrated how deteriorating relations between the major powers negatively affected the mood of the ARF. In fact, 'the level of harshness between the US and China over the alliance issue at the ISG on CBMs in Beijing was so great as to lead many participants to worry that it had disrupted the ARF process'.[93] Such negative influence could also be found in the Fourth ARF Chairman's statement. Despite the heated debate on the proposed guidelines for enhanced US-Japan security cooperation, reference to the bilateral alliance was absent from the Chairman's statement, which included all other major regional agendas discussed at the meetings, such as Cambodia, Myanmar and the Korean Peninsula. The chairman conspicuously avoided including the most contentious issue in the statement since there was no way to find a wording that would satisfy both sides. Instead, the Chairman's statement signified regional concerns about growing tensions among the major powers, saying that 'the importance of the development of positive relations, particularly among the major countries in Asia Pacific, China, Japan, Russia and the US, for sustaining stability in the region'.[94]

Conclusion

The mid-1990s witnessed the deterioration of Sino-Japanese security relations, stemming from not only a series of assertive Chinese security policies, such as its nuclear tests, actions in the South China Sea and in the Taiwan Strait, but also new developments in Japan's security policy, marked by the redefinition of the Japan-US alliance. In this situation, the ARF, the only regional security institution including all the major powers, came to be regarded as a useful vehicle through which Japan actively tried to address its security concerns regarding China without provoking a direct confrontation. Japan played an active role in raising sensitive security issues in the ARF even in the face of strong Chinese opposition, in order not only to enhance the quality and efficacy of the security dialogue process in the ARF but also to use the Forum to put collective pressure on China to restrain its assertive security policy. Japan's diplomatic efforts gradually came to fruition as China increasingly became involved in multilateral security dialogues on those issues. Collective criticisms from Japan and other regional countries through multilateral security discussions in the ARF exerted sufficient pressures on Beijing to soften its posture towards the South China Sea disputes. Moreover, the ARF proved its usefulness to Japan's engagement policy towards China to some extent. Indeed, the ARF meetings were utilised by Japan and the US to encourage China to join in their collaborative diplomatic efforts to resolve the issue of the Korean Peninsula. And perhaps most importantly, the ARF provided the major powers with a precious opportunity for diplomatic contact at a time when their relations had reached a low point due to some crises.

However, Japan's ARF diplomacy also revealed the obvious limitations of multilateral security dialogue as an instrument for addressing Japan's security concerns. Collective diplomatic pressures formed through the ARF's dialogue process proved to be inadequate for fully constraining China. The ARF's total silence on the Taiwan Strait crisis further impressed upon Japanese policy makers the limited potential of multilateral security diplomacy in constraining China's behaviour. Moreover, Japan's attempt to use the ARF for reassuring China about the strengthening of the Japan-US alliance remained unsuccessful, in part because of entirely different views of what constituted their desired regional security order and a regional security institution. This shows the limitations of multilateral security dialogues as a tool for reassuring China about Japan's policy of strengthening the bilateral alliance since security dialogue alone is unlikely to alter China's underlying preference for a regional security order.

Overall, regardless of its shortcomings with reference to Japan's policy of reassurance and containment towards China, ARF developments for the first four years were satisfactory to Japanese policy makers. The achievements of the ARF during this period led Tokyo to hold the view that the Forum could contribute to Japan's policy of engagement with China and to the enhancement of the overall climate of the major powers' relationship to some extent.[95] These positive developments in the ARF for the first four years thus gave Japan hope that one of its major goals in multilateral security diplomacy, policy coordination on specific regional security issues, might be achievable. However, as we will see in the next chapter, in subsequent meetings, Japanese hopes finally began to fade away.

6 Japan and multilateral security dialogue in the ARF (1998–2005)

Eroding confidence in multilateral approaches to regional security issues

Introduction

This chapter deals with Japan's diplomacy in security dialogue process in the ARF from 1998 to 2005. The steady progress of its dialogue process during its first four years gave Japanese policy makers hope that the Forum might progress along the lines of their expectations and develop into an effective instrument for tackling Japan's security concerns in the future. Thus, Japan continued to press the ARF to discuss contentious security issues in order not only to address its security concerns but also to enhance the credibility of the ARF as a valid forum for security dialogue and cooperation. However, the Japan's experience of multilateral security diplomacy in the ARF from the late 1990s onwards was, overall, frustrating rather than satisfactory. Not only did Japan's initiatives in tackling regional security issues through the ARF prove to be abortive in most cases but also its momentum was weakened by a number of new developments occurring in and after the late 1990s.

Facing challenges of acute regional crises

India and Pakistan's nuclear tests

The fifth working session of the ARF was caught up with two regional crises, the nuclear tests conducted by India and Pakistan and the Asian financial crisis. The relationship between India and Pakistan was considerably aggravated in May 1998 when both countries conducted a series of nuclear tests. The heightened tension aroused regional fears of the likelihood of nuclear war between the two countries, which had fought three wars in previous fifty years. These nuclear tests also significantly undermined the credibility of the nuclear non-proliferation regime, which had been strengthened in prior years through international efforts to dissuade New Independent States, such as Ukraine and Kazakhstan, from maintaining nuclear weapons.[1]

The India and Pakistan nuclear tests provoked Japan, which being the only country to have suffered an atomic bomb attack and having committed itself to active diplomacy on non-proliferation and nuclear disarmament, to lunch a barrage of diplomatic offensives against the two countries. Immediately after their nuclear tests, Tokyo announced a freeze on new grant aid and yen loans to both New Delhi and Islamabad. This was a severe blow to both India and Pakistan since Japan was the largest provider of assistance to both countries. As a non-permanent member of the United Nation Security Council (UNSC), Japan also introduced with Sweden and Costa Rica a resolution in the UN, encouraging UN member states to refrain from providing India and Pakistan with technology for the development of nuclear weapons.[2]

While showing tough opposition to their nuclear tests, Japan also attempted to mediate in the disputes between the two countries, including the highly contentious issue of Kashmir. In June 1998, the Japanese government offered to host a meeting on India-Pakistan relations in Tokyo to help defuse tensions following their nuclear tests and encourage them to sign the NPT and the CTBT.[3] This proposal was in part motivated by Japan's diplomatic aspiration to raise its political profile in the international community. It was expected that showing leadership on nuclear non-proliferation issues would solidify Japan's long-standing claims for a permanent seat on the UNSC, which Japan wanted to match the country's international standing.[4]

Tokyo also tried to utilise the ARF to achieve its aspiration. In June 1998, Japanese Foreign Minister, Obuchi Keizō, formally asked Philippine Foreign Minister, Domingo Siazon, the chair of the fifth working session of the ARF, to invite Pakistan to the ARF Ministerial Meeting on an ad hoc basis so that the Forum could discuss the issues of nuclear crisis and Kashmir.[5] Parallel to these efforts, Japan also attempted to level strong criticism against New Delhi and Islamabad through the ARF. In the Fifth ARF SOM in Manila in May 1998, Japanese and Australian officials pushed the Philippines to issue a highly critical statement against India and Pakistan's nuclear tests. This initiative reflected Japan's intention to raise the reputation and effectiveness of the ARF rather than its diplomatic ambitions for a larger political role. Japanese officials worried that the ARF's failure to respond to India and Pakistan's nuclear tests would considerably undermine its credibility. MOFA's internal report for the Fifth ARF SOM, for instance, argued that 'whether the ARF will successfully insert a passage censuring the Indian nuclear testing in the Chairman's statement is critically important for assessing the future potential of the ARF to function as a venue for multilateral political and security dialogues'.[6]

ARF members, excepting India, were virtually unanimous in denouncing the two countries on the grounds that their nuclear tests were inconsistent with the ARF's principle of non-proliferation. However, despite this common recognition, there were deep divisions among ARF officials as to whether to actually include criticism of India and Pakistan in the Chairman's statement. India of course opposed any passage relating to nuclear testing even without being named in the statement, arguing that the ARF was not the proper forum to make such a statement. ASEAN was also split on this issue. While the Philippines supported Tokyo's strict posture towards India and Pakistan, Vietnam, Indonesia and Singapore pressed for a toned down statement, not mentioning the two countries by name. The reluctant countries were concerned that the harsh text of the statement would not only have adverse effect on the impartial and moderate role of the ARF in resolving sensitive security issues but also violate the ARF's principle of consensus decision-making.[7] The ARF SOM eventually failed to reach agreement on this issue, but Japanese officials continued to press ASEAN officials to issue a critical statement against India and Pakistan.[8]

Japan's ARF diplomacy regarding the South Asian nuclear tests ended with mixed results. The Chairman's statement expressed 'grave concern over and strongly deplored the nuclear tests in South Asia' and called for 'the total cessation of such testing and urged the concerned countries to sign the NPT and the CTBT'.[9] However, despite Japanese efforts, the statement failed to not only mention both India and Pakistan by name but also to make strong critical remarks against their nuclear tests, thus disappointing many Japanese observers.[10] Yet, Japanese officials were not totally disappointed with the result since the statement actually succeeded in referring to the nuclear tests in the face of opposition from India to the inclusion of any reference to them at all. This statement was a product of both the strong initiative taken by the Philippines, the chair of the Fifth ARF, and a compromise between activist countries, including Japan, Australia and the US, and reluctant countries, such as India and some ASEAN countries. The Philippines had made great efforts to issue a critical statement for the nuclear tests in South Asia by using the chair's discretion. Japan's *Diplomatic Bluebook* stated that 'at the chair's initiative, the Chairman's statement which expressed grave concern and strongly deplored the Indian and Pakistan's nuclear tests was a groundbreaking event given Indian participation in the ARF and the rule of consensus-decision-making'.[11] However, Japanese officials were discouraged by the fact that their initiative to promote the resolution of India-Pakistan disputes through the ARF was rejected by other ARF countries. The Philippine Foreign Secretary dismissed the Japanese proposal for inviting Pakistan to the Ministerial Meeting, stating that 'we do not wish to involve ourselves in Kashmir, it is outside our footprint'.[12] Consequently, the lack of enthusiastic support from other ARF countries for its initiative further eroded Japan's confidence in the efficacy of multilateral security diplomacy for addressing major security issues in the region.

The detrimental effect of the Asia Financial crisis

Another major topic of discussion at the Fifth ARF meetings was the Asian financial crisis. The crisis began with the floating of Thailand's currency in mid-1997, which brought about currency clashes with Indonesia, Malaysia and finally South Korea. As a result of this, many ASEAN countries, in particular Indonesia, Malaysia and Thailand, underwent severe economic downturns and suffered from social and political unrest. Indonesia's economy, for example, shrank by 20 percent in 1998 and Thailand's by 8. Moreover, the rate of regional unemployment increased by nearly 20 million in 1998, and 15 million in Indonesia alone. The political turmoil in Indonesia even forced President Suharto to step down from power after thirty-two years.[13]

The Asian economic crisis had profound implications for the ARF, undermining ASEAN's solidarity and capacity to commit to the ARF process. The crisis considerably decreased the level of ASEAN commitment to the ARF since domestic turbulence led to a redirection of attention from external to domestic environments. For them, the first priority was to deal with their domestic problems, not to invest their limited energies in the ARF. Moreover, financial problems contributed to a reduction in ASEAN's participation in the ARF's activities, including defence exchanges, thus damaging its efforts to promote CBMs and PD measures.[14]

More worrying, however, was the significant damage to political cohesion brought about by the rekindling of tensions between ASEAN countries due to the economic crisis. Long-standing rivalries within ASEAN resurfaced after the economic crisis as demonstrated by the deterioration of relations between Singapore, Indonesia and Malaysia. Singapore was criticised by its neighbours over a perceived shortfall in its financial assistance and was accused of being unwilling to help them while Singapore simply dismissed the charge. The bilateral strife between Malaysia and Singapore even spilled over to their defence relationship. Malaysia not only announced its withdrawal from the joint exercises in the Five Power Defence Agreement but also rescinded long-standing agreements that allowed Singapore's military and rescue planes to fly over Malaysian territory without prior authorisation.[15] The collapse of the Suharto regime also damaged ASEAN's cohesiveness, undermining Indonesia's capacity to sustain its former leadership role in ASEAN.

In addition, ASEAN's political cohesion was also jeopardised by intra-mural disputes over ASEAN's norms, most notably the principle of non-interference in the internal affairs of states. The principle came to be seen as the primary cause of ASEAN's failure to promote cooperation in addressing the economic crisis and the Indonesian haze. This led two ASEAN countries, Thailand and the Philippines, to challenge the non-interference principle. At the ASEAN Ministerial Meeting (AMM) in Manila in July 1998, Thailand's Foreign Minister, Surin Pitsuwan, proposed 'the flexible engagement approach', intending to allow ASEAN to openly discuss and deal with the internal matters of member countries which could have negative effects on neighbours or ASEAN as a whole, such as the issues of human rights, environmental degradation and refugees. Pitsuwan argued that these problems required an approach that would go beyond ASEAN's traditional policy of non-intervention. However, other ASEAN members, excepting the

Philippines, rebuffed the proposal because of their concerns that a flexible engagement would not only subvert ASEAN's long-standing principles of non-interference but also reawaken tensions among ASEAN countries with intra-mural problems.[16] In the end, ASEAN foreign ministers reaffirmed the sanctity of the principle of non-interference and adopted 'enhanced inter-action' instead of flexible engagement as a policy framework to cope with transnational issues. The notion of enhanced interaction was to stick to the principle of non-interference, but the debate on flexible engagement pointed out that consensus about this old principle within ASEAN had begun to weaken.

The Asian financial crisis, undermined ASEAN's capacity to play a central role in the ARF. Japan's expectations of the Forum were lowered as a result. One Japanese diplomat in charge of ARF policy wrote in 1999 that 'the Asian economic crisis has weakened ASEAN's commitment to the ARF in both financial and psychological terms ... this has been one of the major causes of its stagnation'.[17]

Disputes over ASEAN's constructive engagement with Myanmar

Finally, the Fifth ARF meeting witnessed tension between ASEAN and Western countries over how to deal with the human rights issue in Myanmar. The confrontation was first provoked by ASEAN's decision to award Myanmar observer status in ASEAN in 1996, which put it one step away from full membership and, by implication, membership of the ARF. ASEAN's decision angered the US and the EU, which had tried to isolate the country for Myanmar's dismal human rights record, such as the oppression of pro-democracy activists led by Aung San Suu Kyi's National League for Democracy (NLD) by the State Law and Order Restoration Council (SLORC). Western countries were deeply frustrated with ASEAN's policy of 'constructive engagement' towards Myanmar, which sought to bring about internal change through dialogue and persuasion without any threat of sanction or coercion. In their view, such soft measures were not likely to produce any concrete results. They, thereby, called for more forceful actions, including economic sanctions.[18] Western criticism, however, served only to irritate ASEAN countries. The Western approach to Myanmar was not palatable to many ASEAN countries since such an approach would contravene its traditional way of coping with security, which maintained intra-political cohesion by avoiding interference in the internal affairs of member states and intervention in bilateral tensions between members. Indonesian Foreign Minister, Ali Alatas, represented this view when he stated that 'ASEAN prefers quiet diplomacy, the Southeast Asian Way never tries to interfere in their internal affairs, never makes them feel cornered publicly'.[19]

In the Fourth ARF SOM in Kuala Lumpur in May 1997, Western countries led by the US put pressure on ASEAN not to admit Myanmar as a formal member, but ASEAN was unmoved. Myanmar eventually became a new member of ASEAN and the ARF in July 1997 along with Laos. Western countries conceded to ASEAN's decision to admit Myanmar, but they continued to criticise its approaches to Myanmar's junta, which failed to make progress with the country's problems. As Myanmar's entry to ASEAN and the ARF failed to produce any visible changes in its policy, in the Fifth ARF Ministerial Meeting, US Secretary of State, Madeleine Albright along with the foreign ministers of other Western members again criticised Myanmar's policies and urged ASEAN to press for political reform.[20] However, most ASEAN countries apparently did not wish to get involved in the domestic situation of one of its member states. Ali Alatas reiterated that 'ASEAN's current policy towards Myanmar was working and ASEAN must be careful not to intervene in domestic affairs'.[21] Despite the heated debate on Myanmar issues in the Ministerial Meeting, any reference to Myanmar was conspicuously absent from the Chairman's statement.

Tokyo took a different approach to the Myanmar issue, supporting ASEAN's constructive engagement policy. While Tokyo and Washington coordinated their different positions on the Cambodia issue as discussed in Chapter 5, Japanese officials recognised that it would harder to reconcile their differences regarding Myanmar. Japan supported Myanmar's entry into ASEAN while the US strongly opposed it. Although expressing deep concerns about human right violations in Myanmar, Tokyo rejected the US request to impose economic sanctions. Japanese support for the ASEAN approach to Myanmar, again, reflected Japan's considerations regarding balance of power with China. Tokyo shared ASEAN concerns that political isolation would make Myanmar drift into the Chinese orbit. Beijing's attempt to deepen its economic and military relations with Rangoon provided Japan with the justification to back up ASEAN's engagement policy towards Myanmar.[22]

Yet, this did not mean that Japan was satisfied with ASEAN's extremely soft approach to Myanmar. There was growing frustration among Japanese political leaders about ASEAN's muted response and the unchanging situation in Myanmar. In August 1998, Japan's Foreign Minister requested his counterpart in Thailand, perhaps the only ASEAN member being willing to resolve the political turmoil in Myanmar, to play a more active role in persuading Myanmar's military junta to hold talks with Aung San Suu Kyi.[23]

Corrosion of the ARF's credibility

North Korea's missile launch

Japan's diplomacy in the Sixth ARF meetings was almost exclusively devoted to the task of building international criticism of North Korea's missile launch. In August 1998, North Korea launched a medium range 'Taepodong' ballistic missile over Japan into the Pacific Ocean. Pyongyang claimed that it was a test for placing a satellite into orbit, but Tokyo rejected the claim, arguing that it was a ballistic missile test and was thus a significant threat to Japanese security. With a sense of great outrage, Japan took a tough line towards North Korea. The Japanese government not only suspended normalisation talks with Pyongyang and Japan's financial support for a KEDO project to build a light water nuclear reactor but also rejected the North's request for food aid. Moreover, the Japanese government began seriously to seek the possibility of a more robust economic sanction, namely the suspension of financial remittances from the North Korean community in Japan. However, heavy pressure from the US and South Korea forced Japan to soften its stance. In November 1998, the Japanese government signed the KEDO cost sharing agreement, indicating Tokyo's intention to restart financial contributions to the project. Japan also determined to restart normalisation talks with Pyongyang in January 1999.[24]

However, by the summer of 1999 tensions between the two countries were heightened again due to further provocative actions on the part of North Korea. In March 1999, North Korean spy ships entered Japanese waters. The Japanese government dispatched SDF vessels to capture the ships, but they escaped after the Japanese vessels fired warning shots. The situation was further aggravated in August 1999 when it was reported that North Korea was preparing to launch a new ballistic missile, which was capable of reaching Alaska.[25]

Despite this, Japan's options for responding to North Korea's missile threat were highly limited. Talks held in the second half of 1998 between the US and North Korea aimed at eliminating suspicions regarding North Korean nuclear weapon and missile development had been unsuccessful. Moreover, it was not expected that the four-party talks on the Korean Peninsula would address Japanese security concerns at all. Prime Minister Obuchi Keizō expressed these frustrations, saying that 'dialogue between North and South Korea alone will not ensure the security of Northeast Asia. It is good to hold the US-DPRK talks and the four-party talks but we cannot carry out our responsibilities if we are not allowed to participate in them even when a missile is launched into the sea near Japan'.[26] In order to play a more direct role, Tokyo proposed to establish six-party talks, involving South and North Korea, the US, China, Russia and Japan. However, neither Washington nor Beijing was enthusiastic about the proposal, citing North Korea's reluctance to participate in multilateral dialogues.[27]

In this situation, diplomatic campaigning through existing multilateral forums became one of a limited number of options open to Japan for dissuading North Korea from conducting a new missile launch. While strengthening diplomatic coordination with Seoul and Washington, Tokyo attempted to gather international criticism against the North through the ARF. Japanese officials expected that the issue of a strong statement criticising Pyongyang, instead of a very general statement on the Korean Peninsula that had been the norm in past chairman statements, would help to discourage North Korea from further aggressive behaviour since the ARF included several countries having special relationships with the North, namely China, Russia and Cambodia.[28]

Tokyo's diplomatic efforts in the ARF began with bilateral talks with China on the sidelines of the Ministerial Meeting in Singapore in July 1999. Japanese Foreign Minister, Kōmura Masahiko, met with his Chinese counterpart, Tang Jiaxuan, and asked for Chinese support for the issue of a critical statement directed at North Korea's missile threat. Tang did not oppose Japan's proposal to include concerns over the North in the Chairman's statement, but showed reservations about the inclusion of overly strong criticisms that could provoke Pyongyang.[29] In the Ministerial Meeting, Kōmura stressed the implications of North Korea's missile threat for regional stability in order to gain regional attention and cultivate widespread support for the Japanese initiative, stating that 'the North Korean missile programme poses a significant security threat to the Asia-Pacific region as the whole since not only is its ballistic missile actually capable of reaching most of the countries of the region but also its missile programme encourages a proliferation of missile technology and weapons of mass destruction in the region'. Kōmura also delivered a warning against North Korea that 'any missile launch by North Korea will not only damage its diplomatic relations with its neighbouring countries but also lead to a suspension of Japanese contributions to the KEDO, amounting to around US$1 billion'.[30]

In addition, Tokyo launched trilateral talks with Washington and Seoul on the sidelines of the meeting in order to coordinate their policies towards North Korea's missile threat. This resulted in the issue of a joint statement, warning that 'any missile test will have very serious consequences for North Korea … Japan, the US and South Korea will take decisive action should North Korea carry out a test'.[31] Japan's diplomatic campaign was successful to the extent that ARF countries came to agree that North Korea's missile launch was a threat to regional stability. However, this did not mean that Japanese concerns about North Korea were shared to the same degree amongst them. Indeed, Japan's efforts to incorporate strong criticism of North Korea in the Chairman's statement were impeded by China. The Chairman's statement consequently failed directly to refer to North Korea by name. Instead, it stated that 'the minister expressed concern over the August 1998 payload launch and other missile-related activities which could heighten tensions and have serious consequences for stability in the Korean Peninsula and the region'.[32]

Nonetheless, Japan considered the statement an important achievement since the ARF was actually able to send a clear message of warning to Pyongyang.[33] At the same time, however, Japan's ARF diplomacy on the issue of North Korea's missile launch as well as India and Pakistan's nuclear tests led Japan to recognise the difficulties of attaining a common stand on specific regional security issues in a cooperative security forum like the ARF, within which regional countries having different threat perceptions sit together.[34]

Tension over the North Korea's missile programme was eventually relieved when Washington and Pyongyang reached an agreement in Berlin in September 1999, under which North Korea promised to freeze its missile tests in return for a partial lifting of sanctions.[35]

ASEAN's lack of cohesion over the South China Sea territorial dispute

Another important issue discussed at the Sixth ARF was the renewed tension in the South China Sea. The situation in the South China Sea deteriorated in November 1998 when the Philippines denounced Beijing for expanding its structures on Mischief Reef in the Philippines 200 mile EEZ and for increasing the number of Chinese vessels entering the area.[36] To ease the tension, the two countries organised an Experts Working Group on CBMs in March 1999. However, the dispute escalated further when the Philippine Navy sank two Chinese fishing boats operating in the waters close to a disputed shoal in May and again in July same year. Meanwhile, Malaysia also built structures on two shoals in the Spratly Islands, further complicating the situation. The heightened tensions in the South China Sea convinced a number of ASEAN countries of the need to set up guidelines to deal with this worsening territorial dispute. In the AMM SOM held in Singapore just before the ARF Ministerial Meeting, the Philippines presented the draft regional code of conduct in the South China Sea. The regional code of conduct, which was developed based on the code of conduct informally agreed in 1995 between China and the Philippines, prescribed that naval vessels and aircraft were not to navigate or fly close to those of the other countries in the area and called for no further occupations of these islands.[37]

The South China Sea disputes attracted much attention from Washington. In the past, although the US had consistently voiced its interest in maintaining freedom of navigation in the South China Sea, it had basically maintained neutrality. However, the escalation of the dispute led the US to adopt more active posture towards the South China Sea issue. In the Ministerial Meeting, US Secretary of State, Madeleine Albright, voiced strong concerns over rising tensions in the South China Sea, stating that 'the stakes are too high to allow a cycle to emerge in which each incident leads to another with potentially greater risks and graver consequences'. Albright also urged the claimant countries to discuss the South China Sea issue within the ARF, saying that 'we cannot simply sit on the sideline and watch. There is no doubt that the ARF is an appropriate forum for discussion of this issue. All members of the ARF have an interest in peace and stability in the South China Sea'.[38] Although Washington did not show any intention to intervene in the disputes, this statement signified US willingness to constrain Chinese activities in the South China Sea through a multilateral discussion. More specifically, US policy makers expected that initiating multilateral discussion on the South China Sea issue in the ARF would not only help induce ASEAN to act in concert against China but also allow Japan and the US to join ASEAN in pressing China to moderate its position on the dispute.[39]

However, despite clear US support for multilateral dialogue on the South China Sea issue, ASEAN itself failed to show solidarity. While the Philippines called for early adoption of the code of conduct, Malaysia expressed reservations. Malaysia even opposed multilateral discussion of the South China Sea disputes and appeared to move closer to the Chinese position, arguing that neither the ASEAN meetings nor the ARF were the proper forum to discuss the issue.[40] The lack of cohesion within ASEAN regarding the South China Sea disputes exposed its inability to create a common external security front even as China continued to upgrade its facilities in the South China Sea.

Japan's response to the South China Sea dispute was also passive in spite of the fact that its economic security depended on the political stability of the area. Being preoccupied with the task of forming collective criticism against North Korea, Tokyo did not display any enthusiasm for the South China Sea issue. Japan's statement regarding the issue did not go beyond a brief expression of concern about the situation. For instance, Japan's Foreign Minister Kōmura merely stated that 'Japan is supportive of a code of conduct so long as it facilitates a peaceful resolution of disputes and is based on maritime and other international laws'.[41]

Beijing, which had steadfastly refused to launch multilateral discussion on the South China Sea issue in the ARF, showed great irritation at the possibility of third party intervention in the dispute. China indirectly criticised the US, saying that 'conflicting claims to the Spratly Islands must be addressed through bilateral negotiation, and we are not in favour of the involvement of countries, which have nothing to do with the issue'.[42] China also responded coolly to the proposed code of conduct, saying that 'we have taken note of it, but we consider the 1997 China-ASEAN leaders' joint statement that touched on the South China Sea to be sufficient'.[43] At an ASEAN+1 Summit in Manila in November 1999, Beijing formally refused to accept the ASEAN proposed code of conduct, though agreeing to set up an ASEAN-China working group on a regional code of conduct.[44]

Total silence on renewed tensions in the Taiwan Strait

Meanwhile, the ARF failed to address two other regional trouble spots, the Taiwan Strait and East Timor. In July 1999, the relationship between China and Taiwan deteriorated after a provocative statement from Taiwanese President, Lee Teng-hui, that 'Taiwan's relationship with China is state-to-state relations or at least special state-to-state relations'.[45] Lee's remark antagonised Chinese leaders, who regarded it as a challenge to their country's one China principle. The following escalation of Chinese diplomatic offensives generated the worst tensions in the relationship between the two countries since 1996.

Although mounting tensions in the cross-strait relationship triggered fears of a military confrontation, the ARF was totally silent on the issue because of considerable diplomatic pressure from China. Beijing exerted strong pressure on ASEAN countries, having the prerogative to set agenda for the ARF, not to raise the Taiwan issue in advance of the ARF Ministerial Meeting. There was, seemingly, a tacit agreement between China and ASEAN countries not to bring the Taiwan issue to the ARF as no ASEAN countries were willing to raise the issue in the Ministerial Meeting. Beijing also successfully prevented other ARF participants from internationalising the Taiwan issue by showing an overtly aggressive posture. In the Ministerial Meeting, Chinese Foreign Minister, Tang Jiaxuan, warned that 'the Taiwan problem is an internal matter of China. China will not sit back and do nothing if there are any attempts by foreign forces to separate Taiwan from the motherland'.[46] Japan also hesitated to bring the Taiwan issue to the ARF, which was in stark contrast with the robust stance taken towards Chinese coercion in the 1996 Taiwan Strait crisis. Even in the bilateral meeting with China held on the sidelines of the Ministerial Meeting, Foreign Minister Kōmura merely emphasised Japan's policy of maintaining the 1972 Japan-China joint statement declaring that Taiwan was a part of China. Japan's weak posture in part reflected its concern that taking up the Taiwan issue in the ARF would reignite Chinese denunciations of the Japan-US alliance.[47] Even the US, which expressed strong concerns about the South China Sea dispute, hesitated to raise the Taiwan issue in the ARF. Washington seemed to be worried that touching on the Taiwan problem, which was a far more sensitive matter than the South China Sea issue, would only exacerbate its diplomatic relations with Beijing. In fact, one of the main US policy objectives in the Sixth ARF was to repair its bilateral relationship with China, which was in the danger of breaking down due to the accidental bombing of China's embassy in Belgrade by the US in May 1999. Hence, in the bilateral meeting between Washington and Beijing held on the sidelines of the ARF, Albright reassured Tang by reaffirming the US commitment to its one-China policy.[48]

The ARF and ASEAN's lukewarm response to the East Timor crisis

The East Timor crisis gave ASEAN and the ARF a great opportunity to restore the credibility that had been damaged by a series of failures to address major regional problems. The violence in East Timor had been escalating since January 1999 when Indonesia's President Jusuf Habibie unexpectedly decided to hold a referendum on its autonomy and independence from Indonesia. Habibie's decision, which was made without consulting the military, upset pro-integrationist groups in Indonesia which had consistently refused to compromise on the issue of Indonesian sovereignty. The UN established its mission in East Timor to supervise the referendum. However, despite this, the months leading up to the referendum witnessed acts of violence committed by pro-Indonesia militia groups, alongside the police and army. After the pro-independence group won the referendum in September 1999, pro-integrationist militias and the Indonesian military unleashed a campaign of violence at a much more destructive level throughout East Timor.[49]

ASEAN's initial response to the bloodshed in East Timor was muted. Most ASEAN countries held the position that the crisis was a problem internal to Indonesia. Even after Jakarta's surprise announcement of a referendum, ASEAN remained silent on the issue, arguing that it should be left to the disputing parties. Jakarta was also loath to accept ASEAN's interventions in the East Timor issue. Ironically, it was not ASEAN member states but Australia that offered to deploy a large contingent of troops to East Timor as a peacekeeping force to prevent violence. The International Force for East Timor (INTERFET), which was mainly comprised of Australian forces, was eventually deployed in September 1999 under the auspices of the UN. Thailand, the Philippines, Singapore and Malaysia all participated in the INTERFET, but ASEAN did not act as a cooperative entity.[50]

The ARF also failed to assume any constructive role in helping the concerned parties to resolve the East Timor crisis. Most ARF countries showed no interest in the issue until crisis point had been reached. The meetings of the Sixth ARF discussed the East Timor problem only briefly and the Chairman's statement did not even touch on it. Ironically, extensive discussions on the East Timor crisis took place in APEC, not the ARF. APEC held a special ministerial meeting on East Timor in early September 1999 at which a consensus was reached among ministers that the international community should intervene in the crisis.[51] The inability of the ARF to respond to the East Timor issue further damaged its credibility. As G. V. C. Naidu put it, 'if the ARF had been able to take constructive initiatives, at a minimum through convening informal meetings to facilitate dialogue between Indonesia and the ARF members supporting the UN intervention, or to play some role regarding the peacekeeping operations in East Timor, this could have established a foundation for such activities in the future. However, the Forum missed the opportunity and thus disappointed many of its supporters'.[52]

An arena for power politics

North Korea joins the ARF: An impetus or an obstruction to the ARF's progress?

The most notable event of the seventh working session of the ARF for Japan was North Korea's entry to the ARF. The groundwork for North Korea's ARF admission was laid by Thailand, the chair of the Seventh ARF meetings. In March 2000, Thailand's Foreign Minister, Surin Pitsuwan, visited Cambodia, a nation with strong links to Pyongyang, and asked

Prime Minister Hun Sen to persuade North Korean leaders to join in the ARF. Thailand's initiative was also backed by the Philippines, which pledged to establish diplomatic ties with North Korea. This was followed by their collaborative efforts to bring North Korea into the ARF. Cambodia, Thailand and the Philippines each initiated bilateral meetings with North Korea during the Non-Aligned Movement (NAM) summit in Havana in early April 2000. These efforts paid off that same month when North Korea formally applied for membership of the ARF. Thailand then circulated the letter to all ARF participants to obtain formal admission from them.[53] North Korea's application was not, however, accepted without reservations from some ARF countries, particularly Japan. Though Japan had urged North Korea to join the ARF in the years of its inception, relations between the two nations had deteriorated considerably since that time due to the issues of the North Korea's missile launch over Japanese territorial waters and its abduction of Japanese nationals. Japan's cautious stance was also due in part to its suspicion that North Korea might not fully recognise the ARF's objectives and respect ARF's principles.[54] Yet, Japan later softened its opposition to North Korea's participation on the grounds that in the long-term, incorporating North Korea into a multilateral security setting was much better for Japan's national security than isolating it.[55]

Thailand and the Philippines' collaborative initiative for the admission of North Korea into the ARF was motivated primarily by their aspirations for restoring the credibility of ASEAN's leadership role within the Forum which had been considerably undermined since the Asian economic crisis. It was also due in part to their expectations that the North's participation in the ARF would enhance the quality of the ARF's discussion on regional security issues. Philippine Foreign Secretary, Domingo Siazon, stated that 'Pyongyang's entry to the ARF enables the Forum to have more serious dialogue on regional security issues since we will deal with real issues'.[56] The admission of North Korea did in actual fact have a positive effect on the ARF process. Most importantly, it provided ARF member countries with a precious opportunity for diplomatic contact with North Korea. Indeed, on the sidelines of the Seventh ARF Ministerial Meeting in Bangkok in July 2000, Japan's Foreign Minister Kōno Yōhei and his North Korea's counterpart Paek Nam Sun held the first ever foreign ministerial meeting between the two countries and agreed during the meeting to resume normalisation talks which had been suspended due to the missile launch issue.[57] The US also held its first ever foreign ministerial meeting with North Korea on the sidelines of the Ministerial Meeting. In their bilateral meeting, Albright and Paek agreed to launch normalisation talks.[58] This led to more in-depth diplomatic exchanges between the two countries, including the visit of a North Korean envoy to Washington and Albright's trip to Pyongyang in October that year.

Yet Pyongyang's participation in the ARF made no tangible contribution to the enhancement of the efficacy of its multilateral security dialogues.

Ironically, while ASEAN's principles of non-interference and consensus decision-making served as a crucial factor in North Korea's decision to enter the ARF, those principles also prevented the Forum from seriously addressing contentious issues involving Pyongyang. In the Ministerial Meeting, for instance, Tokyo raised the unresolved issue of North Korea's missile and nuclear programmes but extensive discussion of the issue was not pursued due to ASEAN's reluctance to provoke Pyongyang. Consequently, the tone of the Chairman's statement regarding the North Korean issue was considerably watered down compared to that of the previous year. Instead of touching on the missile issue, the statement simply mentioned the historic summit meeting between South and North Korea in Pyongyang in June 2000.[59] It can be said that North Korea gained full benefits from incorporating itself into the ARF, which operated under the ASEAN's rules of consensus decision-making.

Major powers' collisions over Theatre Missile Defence

Ironically, North Korea's participation in the ARF resulted in more confrontation than collaboration among the major powers. Beijing used the presence of North Korea to build an ad hoc coalition with Moscow and Pyongyang against US plans to develop a Theatre Missile Defence (TMD) or a Ballistic Missile Defence (BMD) system, which was designed to protect the US and its allies from incoming ballistic missiles by intercepting and destroying them with missiles or other means. China's criticism of TMD began in the mid-1990s around the time that Japan and the US had begun to cooperate in the study of ballistic missile defence. However, the tone of its criticism became far more severe from December 1998 when the Japanese government decided to fund joint technical research on TMD with the US. This was followed by their agreement in August 1999 to launch a five-year research and development program, focusing on a Navy Theatre-Wide Defence (NTWD) system, which would be deployed on Aegis ships.[60]

The Japanese government had initially been reluctant to participate in the US TMD project. There were several reasons for this. First, Japanese officials doubted the technical feasibility and effectiveness of TMD. A series of unsuccessful missile tests led them to hold the view that the TMD system would be easily overcome if adversaries launched a large number of missiles or deployed Multiple Independently targetable Re-entry Vehicles (MIRVs). Secondly, the huge cost of deploying the TMD system, estimated at over US$15 billion, was not acceptable to the Japanese government especially as the country was undergoing a severe economic recession. Thirdly, Japanese policy makers were concerned that the co-development and implementation of TMD would involve legal and constitutional issues, such as the ban on arms exports, the 1969 Diet resolution limiting the use of outer space to peaceful purposes, and perhaps most importantly the prohibition on the exercise of the right of collective self-defence. For instance, the operation of the TMD system, which would require greater integration of command and control functions and military connectivity between SDF and US forces, might not be feasible without lifting the prohibition on collective self-defence. Finally, there were serious concerns among Japanese officials that Japan would inevitably be embroiled in a US-China conflict if TMD were extended to Taiwan.[61] However, North Korea's missile launch over Japan's main islands in August 1998 convinced Japanese policy makers of the potential danger of ballistic missile attack and changed their views of the utility of TMD. This thus provided a major catalyst for Japanese participation in the research project.[62]

China's opposition to the US TMD project basically stemmed from its concerns that the TMD system would undermine China's nuclear deterrence by neutralising its ballistic missile forces. However, Japan's involvement in TMD further reinforced Chinese apprehensions mainly for the following reasons. First and foremost, Beijing was anxious that US-Japan co-development of an Aegis ship based NTWD system might be used for defending Taiwan from Chinese ballistic missiles in a crisis situation since such a ship based system could be moved easily to the Taiwan Strait. If that were the case, TMD would eliminate China's military means of dissuading Taiwan from pursuing its independence. Secondly, there were serious concerns on the part of China that Japanese participation in TMD would lead Tokyo to develop a more independent military capability, including offensive weapons, on the grounds that the TMD project would improve its military industry and technology. It was China's opinion that TMD would enable Japan to develop both a 'shield' and a 'sword'. Japan's decision to develop an independent reconnaissance satellite capability in 1998, which was in part influenced by North Korea's 1998 missile launch, amplified these apprehensions. Finally, China voiced concerns that TMD would be a new tool in the US-Japan containment strategy towards Beijing. It was feared that the co-development and implementation of TMD, which required greater military connectivity between their military forces than ever before, would more fully integrate Japan into the US military strategy in East Asia, thus further strengthening the bilateral alliance against Beijing.[63]

The Seventh ARF meeting presented a golden opportunity for China to unite with Russia and North Korea in opposition to the TMD campaign. In the Ministerial Meeting, Chinese Foreign Minister, Tang Jiaxuan, indirectly criticised both the US and Japan, stating that 'some countries are hawking the TMD program against the tide of our times, and such developments are compromising regional confidence building efforts and aggravating the instability of the region'.[64]Beijing also held bilateral meetings individually with both Russia and North Korea and showed their solidarity against TMD.[65] Russia supported Chinese opposition to TMD since it was perceived by Moscow as not only a violation of the 1972 Anti Ballistic Missile (ABM) treaty, which prohibited the development of anti-ballistic missile systems, but also a significant challenge to Russia's nuclear deterrence capability.[66] At the Ministerial Meeting, Russian Foreign Minister, Igor Ivanov, contended that 'the US plan to develop TMD will spark a new arms race and thus make strategic offensive arms reduction impossible and undermine the entire system of arms reduction'.[67]

China and Russia's denunciations of TMD were, however, not acceptable to Washington and Tokyo which considered TMD to be a potentially effective measure for stabilising the status quo in the face of new threats. In response to these criticisms, US Deputy Secretary of State, Strobe Talbot, defended TMD by stating that 'the TMD was not designed as a measure for containing a certain country but rather was deployed as a counter-measure against new threats of weapons of mass destruction'. Meanwhile, Japan's Foreign Minister Kōno backed up the US position, stating that 'the real problem was the development and proliferation of ballistic missiles, not TMD'.[68] The US and Japan's justification of TMD, however, did nothing to halt the wave of criticism. Neither was TMD welcomed by other regional countries, including ASEAN members. ASEAN countries offered no official pronouncement on the TMD issue in the ARF meetings, fearing that this might involve them in a confrontation with major powers. None-theless, ASEAN signalled its concern in the AMM in July 2000. Thai Foreign Minister, Surin Pitsuwan, stated that 'ASEAN is concerned about TMD because it will affect mutual confidence and might have negative effects on the ARF's achievements'.[69] In short, ASEAN believed that TMD had a high potential to damage relationships between the major powers, which in turn would have profound implications for the progress of the ARF.

Unfortunately rows among the major powers over TMD further solidified the image of the ARF as a 'talking shop' since it was a sign that the Forum was being dominated by rising tensions between the major powers. As a Japanese newspaper lamented, 'as Russia and China's stern criticism of TMD suggests, the ARF has increasingly become a venue for major powers' self assertion with little prospect of it developing into a practical security institution which could play effective preventive diplomacy roles'.[70]

Waning interest in multilateral security diplomacy?

The meetings of the Eighth ARF were dominated by renewed tension between the US and China. Sino-US relations were once again put under great strain by the collision of a US EP-3E surveillance plane and a Chinese jet fighter in April 2001 near the coast of Hainan Island. The incident threw their relations into crisis as China detained the US plane and aircrews, which landed at a Chinese military base on the island. The crews were eventually released after negotiations between the two governments had been concluded, but the plane was detained until July in the same year. This incident led to a flaring up of tensions between the two countries in part because of the change in US policy towards China with the advent of the

Bush administration in January 2001. The new Bush administration labelled China as a 'strategic competitor' rather than a 'strategic partner' and thus shifted its China policy from the Clinton administration's combination of engagement and containment to greater containment with a special emphasis on the Japan-US alliance as the core of its military strategy in East Asia. The Bush administration also strengthened American support for Taiwan through the approval of a robust arms sales package, provoking much anger among Chinese leaders. Thus, the EP-3E incident was seen by Washington as a challenge to the US presence in the South China Sea while Beijing regarded it as a manifestation of US containment policy.[71]

The ARF was once again utilised by the US and China to ease political tensions among them and to reassure other regional countries. On the sidelines of the Ministerial Meeting in Hanoi in July 2001, US Secretary of State, Collin Powell, and China's Foreign Minister, Tang Jiaxen, held the first foreign ministerial meeting between the two countries since the advent of the Bush administration. In the meeting, the two foreign ministers acknowledged improvement in bilateral relations and pledged to make joint efforts for further amelioration at a summit to be held during the forthcoming APEC meeting scheduled for Shanghai in October of the same year.[72] Significantly, Tang stated in the Ministerial Meeting that 'China welcomes US positive and constructive roles in the Asia-Pacific region', making a break from its past policy, which had sought to diminish American presence in the region.[73] However, this does not mean that China came to see the US military presence as a stabilising factor for regional security and to accept pervasive American primacy. For instance, in a statement after the conclusion of 'the Good Neighbourly Treaty of Friendship and Cooperation' between China and Russia in July 2001, Chinese President Jiang Zemin called for the building of 'a multipolar world' and 'a rational international order', implicitly expressing China's concerns about US unipolar status in the world.[74] In addition, China and Russia again used the Ministerial Meeting to express their opposition to the US TMD project though the tone of their criticisms had softened compared with the previous year.[75]

Though again giving Washington and Beijing a chance to defuse their tensions, the ARF failed to facilitate the addressing of specific regional security issues in meaningful ways. There were high expectations among regional countries that the Eighth ARF Ministerial Meeting would make a tangible positive contribution to the volatile situation in the Korean Peninsula by giving impetus for the resumption of high-level talks between North Korea and the US and its allies. Talks between the two camps had stalled in early 2001 due in part to Pyongyang's hostility towards the new Bush administration which had openly expressed its distrust of Kim Jong Il.[76] However, these hopes were dashed by the absence at the meeting of North Korean Foreign Minister Paek Nam Sun. Pyongyang instead sent Ambassador Ho Jong who was placed much lower in North Korea's hierarchy than Paek.

The Ambassador used the meeting to criticise US policy without actively seeking the possibility of reopening the talks.[77] In the end, the Chairman's statement called for the early commencement of the second Korean summit and went as far as to state that 'the Ministers noted with satisfaction the recent positive developments in the situation on the Korean Peninsula, including increased dialogue and cooperation between Seoul and Pyongyang following the Korean summit in June 2000',[78] regardless of the fact that reunification talks between the two Koreas were stalling.

Moreover, whereas tensions in the South China Sea still persisted, there was no intense discussion of the issue at the ARF meetings. This was due in part to a lack of interest from non-concerned countries, including Japan. By the time of the Eighth ARF, discussions between China and ASEAN on framing a regional code of conduct had not progressed significantly because of dissensions among concerned countries over its geographical scope. Vietnam's proposal for the application of the code of conduct to the Paracel Islands for instance was rejected by China, which occupied those islands and thus wished to limit its scope to the Spratly Islands.[79] There were also disagreements between the Philippines and Malaysia over the issue of whether the code of conduct should be binding or not. In the ASEAN summit in Phnom Penh in November 2002, China and ASEAN eventually signed a 'Declaration on the Conduct of Parties in the South China Sea', developed based on Malaysia's non-binding draft code of conduct. However, not only did it not make any reference to its geographic scope, even failing to specify the Spratly Islands by name, but also it failed to ensure countries' commitments not to construct new structures on the islands.[80]

Japan's ARF diplomacy in this year was neither active nor energetic, showing no particular interest in pressing for specific regional security issues. Foreign Minister Tanaka Makiko did mention the issue of North Korea's alleged abduction of Japanese nationals, which was a first for Japan in a multilateral venue involving Pyongyang.[81] However, Tanaka's remark was a personal statement and did not represent the intentions of MOFA, which wished to avoid to bringing this extremely contentious issue to the ARF on the grounds that this would merely provoke Pyongyang.[82]

Japan's ARF diplomacy after September 11

The growing threat of international terrorism

After the Eighth ARF meetings, the ARF's dialogue process has largely been dominated by two issues, namely counter-terrorism and the North Korean nuclear crisis. The momentum of its security dialogue process was somewhat invigorated after the terrorist attacks on the US on September 11 2001 since not only provided the threat of international terrorism for the first time regional countries with a common interest in promoting regional cooperation against common threats but also many regional countries came to see the ARF, the only security institution in the Asia-Pacific region, as an ideal venue for promoting such regional cooperation, as mentioned in Chapter 3. In particular, the US, which regarded Southeast Asia as 'the second front' of its war on terror, strongly pushed the ARF to promote multilateral counter-terrorism measures. For instance, in March 2002, the US hosted the workshop on 'Financial Measures Against Terrorism' with Malaysia, examining the financial systems of terrorist organisations. Then, US Secretary of State, Colin Powell, used the Ninth ARF Ministerial Meeting in Brunei in July 2002 as an opportunity to create a common threat perception of international terrorism among regional countries and to urge them to give full support to the US counter-terrorism initiatives. Consequently, the Ninth ARF Chairman statement acknowledged that 'the terrorist acts of September 11 2001 in the US had a tremendous impact on the overall security environment' and stressed 'the need for the ARF to find ways and means to cooperate further in the fight against terrorism'.[83] The Ninth ARF also adopted a statement on 'Measures against Terrorist Financing', which committed ARF countries to promote regional cooperation on blocking the financing of terrorism, and endorsed a US proposal for the formation of ISM on Counter-Terrorism and Transnational Crime (CTTC), thus significantly increase the ARF's capacity to develop greater counter-terrorism measures.[84] In addition, parallel with these initiatives, the US also boosted its efforts to promote bilateral and multilateral counter-terrorism cooperation with ASEAN states. In August 2002, for instance, the US and ASEAN issued 'the United States-ASEAN Joint Declaration for Cooperation to Combat International Terrorism', which specified six areas of multilateral cooperation, such as intelligence sharing, capacity-building, and border and immigration controls.[85]

As discussed in Chapter 3, Japan was previously reluctant to bring non-traditional security issues to the ARF, believing that expanding the scope of the ARF's activities would undermine its efforts to tackle many traditional security issues existing in the region. However, the September 11 attacks and the immediate need for promoting practical cooperation for fighting terrorism have led Tokyo to change its position. Since then, Japan has embarked on active efforts to promote counter-terrorism cooperation in the ARF while recognising the importance of advancing other important agenda, including CBMs and PD. For instance, in the Ninth ARF, Japan presented the idea of producing the ARF dossier on counter-terrorism measures, aiming to facilitate the exchange of information on terrorists among the participating countries. Japan also organised a Second ARF Workshop on Counter-Terrorism in Tokyo in October 2002, which drew on experiences gained from anti-terrorism efforts during the Japan-South Korea World Cup soccer tournament.[86]

The bombing in Bali in October 2002 by Jemaah Islamiyah (JI) that killed over 200 people further intensified the ARF's discussion on counter-terrorism as these incidents not only proved the real threat of terrorist networks existing in the region but also exposed the inadequacies of regional counter-terrorism efforts. Indeed, at the Tenth ARF Ministerial Meeting in Jakarta in June 2003, foreign ministers reaffirmed 'their resolve to strengthen further regional cooperation in the fight against international terrorism',[87] and issued a statement on 'Cooperative Counter-Terrorist Action on Border Security', in which they agreed to cooperate on information sharing and capacity-building regarding border controls against the cross-border movement of terrorists.[88] Moreover, reflecting the increasing perceived threat of terrorist attacks on transport networks in the region, the Eleventh ARF Ministerial Meeting in July 2004 adopted a statement on 'Strengthening Transport Security against International Terrorism', which specified a number of regional cooperation in this field, such as conducting simulation and joint exercise for enhancing institutional capacity-building of coastal states against piracy, maritime and aerial terrorism.[89] At the Twelfth Ministerial Meetings held in Vientiane in July 2005, ARF countries also put out a statement on 'Information Sharing and Intelligence Exchange and Document Integrity and Security in Enhancing Cooperation to Combat Terrorism and Other Transnational Crimes' in order to enhance the effectiveness of information and intelligence exchange among them.[90]

The issue of these statements inspired hope in some observers that the ARF has finally taken steps in progressing beyond a mere forum for multilateral security dialogue to that for security cooperation. Singapore's Foreign Minister, Shanmugam Jayakumar, for example, argued that 'in my view, at least on non-traditional security issues, we have moved from CBM to preventive diplomacy'.[91] Yet, the achievements of the ARF's discussion on counter-terrorism cannot be assessed only by looking at statements since many agreements in these statements remain dependent on the voluntary compliance of participating nations. Thus, there is still the serious question as to whether positive-sounding statements can actually be translated into concrete actions. Indeed, many ASEAN countries, in particular Indonesia and Malaysia, have encountered enormous difficulties in fully implementing agreed counter-terrorism measures due mainly to the existence of large Islamic population in these countries, which has been hostile to the US military operations against the Taliban and al-Qaeda in Afghanistan. These countries have thus worried that closer security collaboration with the US and its allies on counter-terrorism would severely endanger their domestic political environment.[92] In addition, the effectiveness of the ARF's cooperation on counter-terrorism would also be inhibited by ASEAN's adherence to the principle of non-interference in the internal affairs of states and sovereign equality. Some of ASEAN states do not entirely welcome direct involvement of outside powers, especially the US, in the war against terrorism in Southeast Asia, being worried that it would allow foreign intervention in their domestic affairs and thus undermine the legitimacy of their governments.[93] Their deep sensitivity to state sovereignty surfaced when the US proposed to carry out counter-terrorism patrols in the Malacca Strait with

Singapore. The proposal drew strong opposition from Indonesia and Malaysia, worrying that the US patrol activity in the strait would violate their national sovereignty.[94]

Hence, real progress of the ARF's discussion on counter-terrorism rests on whether the agreements concluded in the statements are successfully implemented by the participating countries, in particular ASEAN countries, or remain on paper only. Some ARF countries, including Japan, already expressed concerns regarding the issue of implementation. For instance, at the Twelfth ARF Ministerial Meeting, Japan's Vice Foreign Minister, Aizawa Ichirō, stated that 'in order to move the ARF beyond the stage of CBMs to that of PD, the ARF has to do more than simply having discussions on various non-traditional security issues. The ARF must function as a venue for concrete cooperative actions, such as joint exercises and capacity-building'.[95]

The North Korea's nuclear crisis

Another major topic for the ARF's dialogue process since 2001 has been the North Korea's nuclear crisis. Notwithstanding the first ever inter-Korean summit meeting in June 2000, the beginning of the twenty-first century witnessed no major progress in the rapprochement process in the peninsula. This was due mainly to growing confrontations between the US and North Korea over Pyongyang's nuclear weapons programme. The tension between the two countries rose dramatically in January 2002 when President George W. Bush, in the State of the Union Address, labelled North Korea as part of an 'axis of evil' along with Iran and Iraq. With the success of the US military campaign in Afghanistan, the Bush's speech raised serious anxieties on the part of North Korea as well as many regional countries that the US might extend its 'global war on terrorism' to the Korean Peninsula. In June 2002, Washington decided to send a special envoy to Pyongyang for new bilateral talks, but the US plan stalled because of a naval clash between North and South Korea in the Yellow Sea in the same month.[96] The US, however, still did not completely lose its interest in engaging the North and thus used the ARF to renew contact with Pyongyang. Indeed, the Ninth ARF Ministerial Meeting provided US Secretary of State, Colin Powell, with a chance to hold an informal meeting with North Korea's Foreign Minister, Paek Nam Sun, the highest-level diplomatic contact between the two countries since the inauguration of the Bush administration. It was reported that they agreed to resume their bilateral dialogues as a result of this meeting.[97]

There were also some positive developments in Japan-North Korea relations in 2002. Their normalisation talks had been suspended since their meeting in Beijing in October 2000 due mainly to the burning issues of the alleged abduction of Japanese citizens by North Korea. Japan had requested the North Korean Red Cross Society to launch an investigation of situations regarding Japanese 'missing people', but it conducted no serious investigations.

However, from early 2002, signs of change appeared in the North's policy towards Japan. In March 2002, Pyongyang announced the resumption of the investigation and proposed holding the Japan-North Korea Red Cross talks. Reflecting this positive move, Japan revived its active engagement policy toward Pyongyang. In April 2002, Japan's Prime Minister, Koizumi Junichirō, expressed a strong interest to resume the normalisation talks with North Korea, and over the summer Japanese officials hold a series of informal and formal negotiations with their North Koran counterparts.[98] Tokyo then utilised the ARF to initiate high-level talks with Pyongyang. On the sidelines of the Ninth ARF Ministerial Meeting, Japan's Foreign Minister, Kawaguchi Yoriko, had a bilateral meeting with Paek, and the two foreign ministers agreed to make serious efforts to resume bilateral normalisation negotiations.[99] These efforts finally came to fruition when in September 2002, Koizumi visited to Pyongyang for the first summit meeting with Kim Jong Il. In the meeting, Kim admitted that North Korea abducted thirteen Japanese nationals and offered his apologies for the incidents. The historical summit also resulted in the issue of Japan-North Korea Pyongyang Declaration, which confirmed the resumption of normalisation talks, the extension of the North's moratorium on missile testing and a resolution of the nuclear issues in the Korean Peninsula.[100]

However, the North's relations with the two major powers were soon deteriorated in October 2002 when North Korea proclaimed that it had secretly pursued its nuclear weapons programme, in violation of the Agreed Framework accords of 1994. The tension was further escalated by a series of provocative actions taken by the North during the following two months, including its withdrawal from the NPT and its missile tests in the Sea of Japan. Moreover, in the three-party talks, involving the US, China and North Korea in Beijing in April 2003, North Korean officials informed American counterparts that Pyongyang had already developed nuclear weapons.[101]

With the escalation of the crisis, the focus of Japan's and US ARF diplomacy was shifted from engaging to containing Pyongyang. Japan and the US employed the Tenth ARF Ministerial Meeting to gather support from other participating countries for issuing a critical statement against North Korea with the aim of putting collective pressure on Pyongyang to abandon its nuclear weapons programme. They mainly targeted ASEAN participants, expecting that criticisms from ASEAN states, most of which had normal diplomatic relations with the North, would bring undue pressure to bear on Pyongyang. Their initiatives succeeded, as the chairman statement explicitly called for Pyongyang to reverse its decision to withdraw from the NPT and resume its cooperation with the IAEA.[102] Meanwhile, the US and Japan were not enthusiastic about ASEAN's proposal to mediate the North Korean nuclear issue at an ad hoc meeting involving North Korea, China, Russia, Thailand and Malaysia within the framework of the ARF.[103] Instead, Washington and Tokyo pushed for six-party talks between

Japan, the US, South Korea, China, Russia and North Korea outside the ARF while using the Tenth ARF meeting as an occasion for their policy coordination. The first six-party talks on North Korea's nuclear development were held in Beijing in August 2003.

In addition, Tokyo also raised the abduction issue in the Tenth Ministerial Meeting. Despite North's apology for its abduction of Japanese nationals, the issue still remained controversial because not only was the Japanese public outraged by the North's statement that only five abductees survived but also Pyongyang refused Japan's request for the release of the family members of the five survivors who had returned to Japan in 2002. In the meeting, Kawaguchi called for regional support for the resolution of the issue and was successful in securing the first ever mention, albeit indirect, of the abduction issue in the ARF Chairman's statement.[104]

The crisis over the North Korea's nuclear development persisted during 2004. In this year, the six-party talks were held in Beijing in February and June, but these meetings produced no significant results because of sharp disagreements between the US and North Korea over the way of ending Pyongyang's nuclear programme. North Korea demanded that the US government remove the North from the list of states sponsoring terrorism and resume energy assistance in return for the 'freeze' of its nuclear program while the US officials demanded for 'the complete, verifiable, and irreversible dismantlement' (CVID) of the program. At the June meeting, in order to break its standoff with Pyongyang, Washington made some concessions, suggesting that North Korea take necessary steps towards dismantling its nuclear programmes in the three-month preparatory period in exchange for energy assistance from South Korea, China, Russia, and Japan, and provisional multinational security guarantees. However, the US proposal was simply rejected by North Korea.[105]

Reflecting this situation, Washington and Tokyo again employed the ARF to exert international pressures on Pyongyang. At the Eleventh ARF SOM in Jakarta in May 2004, the US officials took the initiative for issuing 'the ARF Statement on Non-proliferation', for the purpose of not only strengthening regional cooperation on the prevention of terrorists' access to WMD but also expressing regional solidarity against its nuclear weapon programme. During the drafting exercise, officials from some ARF countries attempted to include a phrase 'CVID of North Korea's nuclear programme' in the statement, but it was eventually removed from the final draft because of strong resistance from North Korean officials.[106] In addition, on the sideline of the Eleventh ARF Ministerial Meeting, US Secretary of State, Colin Powell, and North Korea's Foreign Minister, Paek Nam Sum, had a bilateral meeting, the first minister level contact between the two countries since the Ninth ARF meeting. The meeting, however, simply ended with the reiteration of their different positions on the nuclear issue.[107]

In the meantime, the normalisation talks between Japan and North Korean continued to stall because of the contentious abduction issues.

Japan's Prime Minister Koizumi made a second visit to Pyongyang in May 2004 in order to move the normalisation talks forwards and to settle the abduction issue.[108] The summit meeting generated an agreement that North Korea would return the family members of the five abductees and conduct a new investigation regarding the fate of other Japanese 'missing people' in exchange for humanitarian aid from Japan.

The year of 2005 saw continuing tension over the North Korea's nuclear problem. In January, North Korea officially claimed that it possessed a nuclear weapon and declared in February that it would indefinitely suspend its participation in the six-party talks. Moreover, in May, North Korea asserted that it had removed 8000 spent fuel rods from its Yongbyon nuclear plant in order to increase its nuclear weapons. In response, the US began to seriously explore the possibility of referring the nuclear issue to the UN Security Council. The six-party talks eventually restarted in July, but the talks broke off again as Washington and Pyongyang were unable to reach an agreement on the scope and pace of denuclearisation. North Korea began to assert the right to promote nuclear development for peaceful purposes and even insisted on a light-water reactor. The US and Japan rebuffed the North's demands and called for the abandonment of all nuclear programmes, including peaceful nuclear activities.

The six nations entered into negotiations again in September. The fourth round of the six-party talks made some achievements, issuing a joint statement agreed by all participating countries for the first time since its foundation. The joint statement stipulated that Pyongyang would abandon all nuclear weapons and existing nuclear programs and return to the NPA and IAEA safeguards. It also committed other participating countries to respect North Korea's right to develop civilian nuclear power and to discuss providing the North with a light-water reactor at an appropriate time. There was also agreement that the other five countries would provide energy assistance to Pyongyang. The issue of the joint statement impressed some observers that the talks finally made a major breakthrough after the two years negotiations. However, such optimism evaporated on the night after the issue of the statement when North Korea announced that it would not abandon its nuclear programs before the US provided North Korea with a light-water reactor that would take years to build. By the end of the year, the six-party talks seemed to lose its momentum as Pyongyang again declared its boycott of the talks in retaliation for the US sanctions against the North Korea's alleged money laundering.[109]

Like previous meetings, North Korea's nuclear issues featured high on the agenda of the Twelfth ARF Ministerial Meeting. The discussion was, however, not intensified because of the absence of foreign ministers from the three major powers, namely the US, Japan and China. Japan's Foreign Minister, Machimura Nobutaka, skipped the ARF meeting due to his attendance at a meeting on a Group of Four (G 4) resolution in the UN headquarter while US Secretary of State, Condolezza Rice, gave it a miss owing to her visit to

Africa and Middle East. Whether or not their absence indicated their diminished interest in the ARF, it actually raised regional concerns about their future commitments to the Forum. Indonesian Foreign Minister, Hasan Wirayudha, stated just before the Ministerial Meeting that 'we regret the two important ASEAN partners do not attend this meeting. I hope their absence from the ARF does not indicate their less heed to ASEAN countries'.[110]

Conclusion

Japan's diplomacy in the process of multilateral security dialogues in the ARF from the late 1990s onwards was a largely disappointing rather than satisfactory experience. Japan's initiatives proved to be abortive in most cases, as represented by its fruitless efforts to promote a discussion of the disputes between India and Pakistan. At the same time, the momentum of multilateral security dialogues in the ARF was considerably weakened by the Asian financial crisis, which undermined ASEAN's intra-mural solidarity and its capacity to play a leading role in the ARF. The legitimacy of ASEAN's leading position was also challenged by growing frustrations among activist countries, including Japan, with the ASEAN Way of coping with regional security issues which they blamed for the failure to solve even intra-mural problems, namely Myanmar and Cambodia. After the financial crisis, the credibility of the ARF was further damaged by its incapacity to respond effectively to major regional crises, including the bloodshed in East Timor and the renewed tensions in the South China Sea and the Taiwan Strait. The momentum of discussions on the South China Sea territorial dispute was weakened in the late 1990s not only by the erosion of ASEAN's solidarity but also the absence of keen interests on the side of non-concerned countries, including Japan. Moreover, the clash between major powers over TMD and defence guidelines suggested, multilateral security dialogues were sometimes employed by China to attack the Japan-US alliance, indicating that the Forum had become an arena for major powers' self assertion rather than policy coordination on regional security issues. The momentum of the dialogue process has partially regained since the September 11 as counter-terrorism has provided the ARF with a new focal point for cooperation. Although the ARF's discussions on counter-terrorism have produced numerous statements on regional cooperation in this field, however, whether the statements can actually translate into concrete actions has still remained in question since the issue of implementation has not been addressed. The ARF's security dialogue process has still served Japanese diplomacy by providing precious opportunities for Japan to engage in diplomatic contact with non-like-minded countries, most notably North Korea, and to apply collective pressure on them. However, such limited utility after the twelve years suggests that its security dialogue process had matured little since its foundation.

How have Japan's experiences in the ARF influenced or altered their conceptions of and policy towards regional security multilateralism? What have been the implications of this for the course and direction of Japan's overall security policy, if any? These questions will be answered in the next chapter.

7 Japan's changing conception of the ARF

From an optimistic liberal to a pessimistic realist perspective on security multilateralism

Introduction

In the previous four chapters, this book has examined Japan's actual diplomacy in the ARF over twelve years. We now turn to examine the question of how have Japan's experiences in the ARF influenced its initial conception of and policy towards regional security multilateralism. In order to answer this question, this chapter first evaluates in more detail the ARF's achievements and limitations with respect to Japan's expectations, objectives and goals for ARF policy, as discussed in Chapter 2. This chapter argues that though the ARF has served a number of Japan's policy objectives, in general terms, it remains no more than a venue for multilateral security dialogues or, to put it more cynically, 'a talking shop' for Japanese policy makers because of its highly limited capacities for promoting meaningful cooperative security measures and for addressing Japan's major security concerns. As a result of certain disappointing experiences, Japanese conceptions of the ARF have shifted from an optimistic 'liberal' to a more pessimistic 'realist' perspective, which has in turn resulted in Japan's ARF policy becoming considerably more tentative and less energetic. This chapter also considers other factors accounting for Japan's waning enthusiasm for regional security multi-lateralism. It examines the internal and external constraints that have been placed on Japan's ARF policy, including US misgivings about Japan's tilt toward security multilateralism, Japan's domestic organisational limitations, growing dissensions within MOFA over the value of the ARF, the lack of political support for bureaucratic initiatives for regional security multi-lateralism, and the unexpected frictions between bilateral and multilateral security approaches in Japan's overall security policy.

The effectiveness and limitations of the ARF from the Japanese perspective

Generally speaking, from a Japanese perspective, the ARF can serve security interests in the following ways. Firstly, the ARF is for Japan an important tool for reassuring its neighbouring countries. As discussed in Chapter 1, Japan's initial motivation to establish a region-wide security forum was to reassure its Asian neighbours about the future direction of its security policy. It was expected that multilateral security dialogue would give regional countries a useful opportunity to express their concerns about Japan's security policy as well as for Japan to convey its intentions and explain its policy. As seen in Chapter 5, in order to deal with its Asian neighbours' concerns about the revised guidelines of the Japan-US alliance, Japan utilised ARF meetings to reassure them. The ARF, which included all major countries in the region, proved to be a convenient tool for this purpose. It also became clear, however, that multilateral security dialogue had obvious limitations as a means of reassurance, especially when there were fundamental differences between concerned parties over security interests. For instance, Japan's reassurance diplomacy regarding the redefinition of the Japan-US alliance was more or less successful for ASEAN countries, which agreed with Japan in considering the alliance as the cornerstone of regional security, but not for China, which envisaged a multipolar regional order. It is hardly to be expected that Japan could persuade China to accept the supremacy of the Japan-US alliance and alter the Chinese underlying preference for regional order through multilateral dialogue. Nonetheless, generally speaking, from the perspective of Japanese officials, the exchange of views and concerns about each country's intentions and threat perceptions through multilateral dialogue has served the cause of confidence building among regional countries to some degree.[1]

Secondly, the ARF has provided Japan with an important opportunity to form collective criticism against the policies of certain countries, in particular China. As discussed in Chapter 2, Japanese policy makers had expected to use a regional security institution as a diplomatic means to constrain target countries by exerting collective pressure on them through the formation of international criticisms. As seen in Chapter 5, in the Second ARF meeting, Japan built an ad hoc coalition with Australia and a number of ASEAN countries to press the issues of the South China Sea and of China's nuclear testing in order to indirectly apply collective pressure on and criticisms against China. Moreover, as discussed in Chapter 6, Tokyo repeatedly used the ARF to garner support from other regional countries to bring international criticism to bear on North Korea's missile and nuclear developments.

Collective criticism and pressure formed through multilateral security dialogues were, on occasion, effective in encouraging regional countries to exercise more restraint in their behaviour. At the Second ARF, China publicly admitted that there were overlapping claims over islands in the South China Sea and agreed to pursue a peaceful resolution to the dispute in accordance with UNCLOS. Beijing has also been compelled to discuss the South China Sea issue in the ARF since that time. Considering that Beijing had once been adamantly opposed to even touching on the issue in the ARF, this was a notable change in China's position. As Rosemary Foot put it, 'China's public endorsement that there are overlapping claims over islands in the South China Sea would have been unlikely in the absence of the ARF'.[2]

However, Japan's experiences in the ARF also exposed the shortcomings of multilateral security dialogue as an instrument for constraining state policy. Collective criticisms against China's 1995 nuclear test, for example, were not effective in dissuading Beijing from conducting the second nuclear test in 1996. Moreover, despite some changes in its policy toward the South China Sea, China has maintained its opposition to multilateral negotiations on the issue and has further expanded its structure on Mischief Reef, thus reinforcing its claims in the sea while ASEAN has failed to act as a collective entity. As noted in Chapter 6, China and ASEAN signed a Declaration on the Conduct of Parties in the South China Sea, but due to Chinese opposition, the declaration failed not only to make any reference to its geographic scope but also to ensure their commitment not to erect new structures on the islands. In this regard, multilateral security dialogue has so far failed to provide adequate pressure on or incentive for China to fully restrain its behaviour. Despite these shortcomings, Japanese officials have still seen the Forum as a potential instrument of constraining the policies of target countries, namely China and North Korea. This is because multilateral security dialogues have permitted Japan to press sensitive security issues and level strong criticism at their policies in a way that may not have been feasible in bilateral talks, given its weak diplomatic position due to the historical legacy of its aggression.

Last, but not least, the ARF has helped Japan to improve the climate of its diplomatic relations with other regional countries to some extent by providing opportunities for bilateral meetings at foreign-minister level, which might otherwise have been politically difficult to set up. As seen in Chapter 6, the Seventh ARF Ministerial Meeting offered a venue for a bilateral meeting between Japan's Foreign Minister, Kōno Yōhei, and his North Korean counterpart Paek Nam Sum, which was the first ever foreign ministerial meeting between the two countries. This paved the way for the resumption of their normalisation talks, which had been suspended due to North Korea's suspected plan to launch a new missile. One Japanese official later stated that 'it would be unlikely that Japan and North Korea could have held a foreign ministerial meeting if the ARF did not exist since it was hardly expected that Japan's Foreign Minister would visit Pyongyang at that time'.[3] The ARF has also been consistently utilised by the US to repair its diplomatic relations with China after certain crises, including the visit of Lee Teng-hui to the US in 1995, the 1996 Taiwan crisis, the accidental bombing of the Chinese embassy in Belgrade in 1999 and the EP3 incident in 2001, and to renew its contact with North Korea. Overall, these achievements have led Japanese officials to hold the view that the ARF has contributed to the expansion of Japan's foreign policy options and the enhancement of minimal confidence building among member countries by facilitating the exchange of security perceptions and increasing opportunities for interaction among them.[4]

However, Japanese officials certainly do not overstate the ARF's accomplishments, suggesting that the Forum has actually not made substantive progress on its agendas outlined in the Concept Paper. It is fair to say that the quality of the dialogue process in the ARF has steadily improved as participating countries have become accustomed to discussing sensitive security issues. The dialogue process, however, has made almost no tangible contribution to the addressing of specific regional security issues in meaningful ways since it has never resulted in policy coordination or concerted action. For instance, proponents of the 'ASEAN Way' stress the importance of dialogues and consultation as an instrument of regional security and thus suggest its application to the ARF. Through ARF meetings, Japan also supported ASEAN's initiative to promote peace and stability in Cambodia and Myanmar. However, ASEAN's constructive engagement through dialogue proved to be ineffective in the case of Myanmar and Cambodia. The idea of extending the ASEAN Way to the ARF further lost its credibility due to the ARF's failure to respond effectively to major regional crises, including the East Timor crisis and the renewed tensions in the South China Sea. Furthermore, Japan's major security concerns have not fully reached the ARF agenda. Although the issues of the Korean Peninsula, including North Korea's nuclear developments, became one of its major agendas, the potential of the ARF to address the Taiwan Strait issue was nullified by China's opposition to Taiwanese participation in the Forum. As seen in Chapter 5, Japan once attempted to raise the Taiwan issue in the ARF immediately after the 1996 Taiwan crisis, but both China and even ASEAN countries, which regarded the issue as a matter of Chinese domestic jurisdiction, opposed its initiative. Since then, no ARF countries, including Japan, have ever attempted to raise the Taiwan issue.

In addition, the recurrent skirmishes between major powers over TMD and the defence guidelines have impressed upon Japanese officials the fact that the ARF has increasingly become an arena for major powers' self-assertion and confrontation rather than for policy coordination. In order to overcome these limitations, Japan has repeatedly proposed to establish a Northeast Asian forum for multilateral security dialogue, but proposals have thus far not come to fruition. In 1998, after a period of continued opposition to the Japanese proposal, Beijing finally agreed to set up a Track Two trilateral meeting with Japan and the US. However, prospects for the establishment of a Northeast Asian security forum at the Track One level are still poor. In addition, contrary to the expectations of many observers, Track Two forums, such as CSCAP, have also failed to discuss sensitive issues, such as Taiwan and the South China Sea, because of Chinese opposition. Japanese representatives are increasingly frustrated with the tactics of Chinese participants, who 'are in general reluctant to take part in discussions except to block them whenever they veer towards sensitive security issues'.[5]

Japanese officials have also doubted the utility of the ARF in terms of increasing military transparency among participating countries, which was the primary goal of Japan's ARF's policy. As we have seen in Chapter 3, it is clear that the ARF has not functioned as a facilitator for the flow of reliable information about each country's military capabilities, such as defence strategies and arms purchases. Agreed CBMs in the ARF are modest and largely irrelevant to the transparency of each country's defence policy, and some measures cannot even be regarded as CBMs. Japan and many Western countries have been ready to adopt more meaningful CBMs, such as a regional arms register, and notification of and observer exchanges in military exercises, which are explicitly listed in the Concept Paper, but there have been no real prospects for the development of these measures in the ARF owing to strong opposition from reluctant countries, including China and many ASEAN countries. Moreover, contrary to the wishes of Japanese policy makers, the focus of the CBM process has increasingly moved to non-military areas, such as environmental and economic security issues, further limiting the ARF's ability to promote military CBMs. Of greater concern is the fact that many countries have not regularly implemented important agreed CBMs, including the publication of defence white papers. Though China and ASEAN countries have occasionally published defence white papers, information provided by them has been highly unrevealing. Japanese Foreign Ministers have repeatedly urged other member countries to properly implement agreed CBMs, but the situation has not improved. Consequently, CBMs that have so far been agreed to and implemented have been severely limited in scope. A modest set of CBMs may help exchange views and increase the frequency of interaction between member countries, but it is obviously far short of reducing the mutual suspicion among them stemming from uncertainties about each country's military capabilities.[6]

The ARF's failure to build substantial confidence and trust among member countries has made the task of moving itself toward the next stage of security cooperation, namely the promotion of PD measures, considerably more difficult. The Eighth ARF reached agreement on a working definition of the concept and principles of PD, but all intra-state disputes and humanitarian contingencies were excluded from the scope of PD due to strong opposition from reluctant countries which feared the possibility of interference in their domestic affairs. Just as discouraging were the unsatisfactory results of Tokyo's initiatives towards an enhanced role for the ARF, which ended with the most important elements of its proposals being shot down by reluctant countries. The chair's enhanced roles approved at the Eighth ARF were mostly confined to that of a discussion facilitator and a liaison officer with external organisations. The only role on which agreement was reached that would be potentially useful in the event of a crisis was the power to 'convene an emergency meeting on prior consent of directly involved states and the consensus of all the ARF members'. However, it is highly implausible that China would allow the ARF chair to convene an emergency meeting in the case of a regional crisis, which closely involved issues of sovereignty, such as the territorial disputes in the South China Sea. Consequently, in the views of Japanese officials, the ARF's capacity to address potential regional conflicts has been so far extremely limited.

As we have seen in previous chapters, the focus of the ARF agenda has shifted from traditional to non-traditional security issues, most notably counter-terrorism, in particular since the terrorist attack of September 11. By the Twelfth ARF Ministerial Meeting, the ARF had achieved some positive results, adopting a number of statements that committed member countries to take concrete cooperative actions in this area. However, although the ARF has made some progress in multilateral cooperation on non-traditional security issues, this does not mean that the prospect for the ARF has suddenly improved in the eyes of Japanese officials. This is because, as discussed in Chapter 6, real progress in the ARF depends on whether agreements concluded in those statements are successfully implemented by the participating countries, and more importantly, whether or not this kind of cooperation can be extended to the enduring traditional security problems of the region. Because most agreements remain dependent on the voluntary compliance of participating nations, there is question as to whether these agreements can be fully implemented by them. Moreover, some ARF countries are reluctant to support agreements that may undermine the principle of national sovereignty and constitute interference in their internal affairs. In short, the problems that the ARF may encounter in promoting practical cooperation on non-traditional security issues are the same as those that have obstructed the ARF's work for developing cooperative security measures in traditional security areas, including military CBMs and PD measures.

Using the ARF as a means of socialising China into international norms of behaviour has been one of Japan's as well as other countries' long-term aims. As discussed in the introduction to this book, by referring to China's increasingly positive attitude towards the ARF, some scholars have contended that China's involvement in the Forum has brought about partial changes in its preferences and interests regarding its commitment to security multilateralism. As seen in Chapter 3, China did begin to actively involve itself in the CBM process from the late 1990s, co-sponsoring the 1997 ISG on CBMs and proposing various non-military CBMs. Beijing also began to play active roles in the PD agenda. It would be, however, a mistake to simply assume that China's growing activism in the ARF does indicate that Beijing has been increasingly socialised to norms of cooperation. The careful analysis of the evolution of the ARF has revealed that

China's changing approach towards the Forum has still largely been reflection of its desire to control the pace and the direction of the ARF according to its own preferences. As we have seen, while actively proposing various modest CBMs and pushing the focus of the CBM process towards non-military security issues, China has quashed many important proposals for military CBMs and successfully avoided serious commitment to military transparency. By 2002, Beijing published three defence white papers, but the level of transparency in the Chinese papers was still low even compared with those submitted by ASEAN countries such as Singapore and Thailand. China also began to actively participate in the discussion on PD, but again Chinese diplomacy was largely self-serving, pressing its own preferences without making any significant concessions. By taking full advantage of the rule of consensus decision-making, China has successfully emasculated the ARF's concept and principles of PD, thus eliminating any possibility that the Forum might play a mediating role in regional disputes and conflicts. In sum, China's ARF policy has mainly mirrored its self-interests and preferences rather than the interests of the region as a whole. In fact, Japanese officials as well as those in other activist countries have seen China as the main impediment to the development of PD in the ARF.[7] Hence, there has been no convincing evidence of changes in China's fundamental preferences and interests. This very fact not only casts doubt on the credibility of the constructivist argument but also confounds Japan's long-term expectations for the socialisation of China.

Finally, there has also been growing discontent among Japanese officials about ASEAN's diplomatic centrality in the ARF, which has not only constrained the role of non-ASEAN members but also prevented a higher degree of institutionalisation. In the inception years of the ARF, Japan had basically supported ASEAN's managerial role since it was the only way of ensuring China's regular participation in the Forum. ASEAN's leading role also contributed to North Korea's entry to the ARF in 2000, which made the Forum a truly region-wide venue for security dialogue. Nonetheless, as discussed in Chapter 4, Japanese officials became increasingly frustrated with the 'ASEAN Way' of institution building. This is because not only the fact that the principles of 'consensus decision-making' and 'pace comfortable to all participants' allowed reluctant states to easily veto many important proposals for cooperation but also their realisation that the successful development and implementation of cooperative security measures might not be achieved without certain degree of institutionalisation of the ARF, in particular the establishment of a permanent secretariat. In order to overcome these structural limitations, activist countries have called for a sharing of the leadership role of the ARF and the creation of a secretariat. However, ASEAN's leading position has been strongly supported by China and, so far, no significant changes have been brought about.

Japan's changing conception of the ARF: The rise of pessimistic realism

It is inevitable that such a low opinion of the utility of the ARF among Japanese policy makers would affect their perspectives on Asia-Pacific security multilateralism. Morimoto Satoshi, a leading Japanese participant in Track Two regional security forums and a consultant to MOFA regarding Japan's ARF policy, wrote in 2000 that:

> a multilateral security arrangement centred on ASEAN, which had been developing since the end of the Cold War, has increasingly stalled in recent years with the weakening of ASEAN's leadership role caused by Indonesia's domestic instability and weakness. Moreover, the momentum of regional cooperation for addressing sources of regional instability has also lowered ... Over five years, regional countries have undertaken efforts to promote CBMs centred on the ARF. However, the possibility of concrete cooperation on CBMs has been improbable ... and consequently a sense of suspicion and unease has increasingly prevailed in the relationships between regional countries. Meanwhile, some argue that regional hopes for multilateral cooperation have risen under such security conditions.[8]

Morimoto's pessimistic view of the future prospect of regional security multilateralism is widely shared by many Japanese policy makers. Many Japanese officials no longer expect the ARF to move beyond the stage of CBMs, at least in the foreseeable future. One Japanese official, for instance, stated that 'it is unlikely that ARF countries will ever become willing to establish preventive diplomacy and conflict resolution mechanisms unless a major event shaking regional security environment occurs'.[9] Japan's willingness to develop meaningful PD mechanisms through the ARF was also questioned by its formal accession to the TAC, which stressed the principle of non-interference in the internal affairs of states, in July 2004. Although the acceptance of the TAC contributed to the strengthening of Japan-ASEAN relations, it would constrain Japan's initiatives for not only advancing the PD agenda in the ARF but also promoting regional cooperation on counter-terrorism issues. In fact, there were serious disagreements between MOFA's bureaus as to whether Japan should join the treaty.[10] Moreover, Japan's interest in promoting multilateral military CBMs through the ARF has also been significantly lowered. Realising the limitations of promoting multilateral military CBMs, Japanese officials have become more willing to advance CBMs on a bilateral basis, such as Japan-Russia and Japan-China relations, rather than a multilateral basis while leaving the ARF as a forum for security dialogue.[11] In addition, the ARF's inability to address Japanese security concerns has reinforced previously held beliefs that specific regional security issues should be better addressed by meetings of the concerned parties rather than a region-wide security institution.

Some Japanese officials even describe the ARF as something similar to the G8 summit, in which the primary objectives of member countries are to participate in a diplomatic salon and to exert their influences over a joint statement.[12] Accordingly, Japan's recent ARF diplomacy suggests that Japanese officials have been more concerned with the language of the chairman's statement than with addressing common security concerns in the region. For instance, as seen in Chapter 6, Japan gave only scant attention to recent developments regarding the South China Sea issue while they were preoccupied with the task of building regional support for the issue of critical statements against North Korea's missile launch. The interest that Japan had in addressing the South China Sea issue through the ARF in the mid-1990s seemed to have evaporated by the beginning of the twenty-first century. Meanwhile, Tokyo has continued to utilise the ARF mainly as an instrument for engaging non-like-minded countries, in particular North Korea.

Overall, in the views of Japanese policy makers, the ARF remains a mere venue for multilateral security dialogues or, to put it more cynically, 'a talking shop'. It can, at best, contribute to a minimal level of confidence building among participating countries by providing them with an opportunity to exchange their security perceptions and establishing additional diplomatic channels to hold bilateral talks. Japan's view of the ARF after twelve years since its formation tends to confirm what realists, who are pessimistic about the future prospect of Asia-Pacific security multilateralism, have assumed to be the maximum value of the Forum. This suggests that over the period, Japan's originally optimistic 'liberal' conception of the ARF has given way to a more pessimistic 'realist' perspective from which it could only make a modest contribution to the regional balance of power by performing certain limited functions.

Other factors behind dwindling enthusiasm for regional security multilateralism

This section examines other factors accounting for Japan's waning enthusiasm for regional security multilateralism, which can be found in both domestic and international environments of its security policy making.

US misgivings about Japan's tilt toward regional security multilateralism

Japan's diminished enthusiasm for regional security multilateralism has also been influenced by US suspicions regarding Japan's long-term commitment to the Japan-US alliance. As seen in Chapter 2, the US view of Japan's initiative for regional security multilateralism had gradually become positive during the early 1990s, due mainly to Japanese work in persuading US policy makers that it was not intended to undermine the bilateral alliance. However, the US government, in particular the Pentagon, still remained sensitive to bold multilateral security initiatives from Japan especially when the two countries' security relations were under strain. These continuing misgivings surfaced in Washington's harsh reaction to the Higuchi report, which was drafted by Prime Minister Hosokawa's advisory group in 1994. As mentioned in Chapter 2, the Higuchi report placed a special emphasis on the promotion of multilateral security cooperation at both international (UN) and regional (ARF) levels and on the enhancement of autonomous defence capabilities while it stressed that the Japan-US alliance remained a major pillar of Japan's security policy. However, the first draft of the Higuchi report actually mentioned the possibility of a US withdrawal from East Asia and questioned its ability to lead in multilateral security cooperation.[13] Thus, the report gave the misleading impression that Japan was beginning to give precedence to multilateralism over the bilateral alliance and to drift away from the US, thereby arousing strong suspicion on the part of US defence officials even though the members of the advisory group had no such intention.[14] The American reaction to the report was strident in its opposition to the upsurge in security multilateralism coming out of Japan's policy making community, and the content of the draft was revised, albeit not drastically, due to pressures from MOFA and JDA which worried about US criticism.[15]

The Higuchi report alerted both Japanese and US officials to a potential endangering of bilateral security relations, which had already been harmed by the serious trade frictions during the first years of the Clinton administration. The administration, which intended to promote the liberalisation and deregulation of the Japanese economy, set numerical targets in each key sector of the economy for fixing the trade deficit, but the Japanese government resisted and even criticised the proposal. The tension between the two countries reached its peak in 1994 when bilateral trade negotiations at the Hosokawa-Clinton Summit broke down. Though the Clinton administration officially denied its intention to connect economic issues with military security issues, serious concerns emerged among both US and Japanese defence officials that the continuation of economic and trade disputes might corrode bilateral relations in political and security spheres.[16]

The Higuchi report was drafted at the height of the trade friction between Tokyo and Washington, thus amplifying US concerns about Japan's tilt toward multilateralism. These misgivings eventually acted as a catalyst for the two countries' collaborative initiatives for revitalising the bilateral alliance. In February 1995, the Pentagon released the East Asian Strategic Review (EASR), which confirmed the US commitment to the Japan-US Security Treaty as well as its intention to maintain 100,000 troops in East Asia, thus reassuring Japan about the US commitment to East Asian security. In response to this, in November 1995, the Japanese government delivered the new NDPO, which emphasised the importance of the Japan-US alliance much more clearly than ever before, mentioning the alliance thirteen times while the 1976 NDPO did so only twice.[17] At the same time, a reference to multilateral security, explicitly made by the Higuchi report, was significantly diluted in the NDPO.[18] This bilateral collaboration resulted eventually in the 1996 Japan-US Joint Declaration and the 1997 revised guidelines. In addition, in late 1995, the two countries also established the Special Action Committee on Okinawa (SACO) to reduce the US bases in order to rescue the alliance from widespread public protests against its military presence in Japan, provoked by the rape of a school girl in Okinawa committed by three US servicemen in September 1995.[19]

Japan's unpleasant experiences regarding the US criticism of the Higuchi report and the drift of bilateral security relations during this period had a profound impact on the thinking of Japanese policy makers, making them consider more carefully the maintenance of the bilateral alliance. This, in turn, made Japanese officials cautious about their approach to the development of the ARF for fear of rekindling Washington's suspicions of their intentions.[20] One Japanese official in charge of ARF policy, for instance, wrote in 1999 that

> 'there is a need to carefully examine how the development of the ARF process will influence Japan's national security as well as the US military presence in the region. This is related to a question of how Japan should commit to the ARF for the sake of its national security. ... To develop the ARF into a more robust security institution or organisation might impose certain kinds of limitation on US military activities. Hence, it should be carefully considered whether such development is acceptable to the US and is more desirable for Japan's national security than the status quo. At present, developing countries put the brakes on the progress of the ARF. However, if they change their ARF strategies and start to call for substantial progress in its processes, this will raise a question as to whether Japan as well as the US should unconditionally welcome it'.[21]

This is not to say that Japanese officials were glad to see the ARF remain a mere venue for multilateral security dialogues. As discussed in Chapters 3 and 4, both Japanese and US officials strongly pushed the ARF to develop military CBMs and move itself towards the stage of PD. However, after the revitalisation of the bilateral alliance, whether Japanese officials still support the ARF in achieving the third stage of its security cooperation, namely 'the development of conflict resolution mechanisms' has become open to question. This is because any initiative from Japan for establishing such robust institutional mechanisms, which might constrain US military activities, would undermine the credibility of its commitment to the bilateral alliance.

The limitations to the organisational capabilities available to Japan's ARF policy

Japan's domestic organisational limitations have diluted bureaucratic motivation to boost its ARF policy. As discussed in the Introduction, MOFA not only plays a dominant role in devising Japan's ARF policy but also assumes overall responsibility for the formulation of the nation's security policy. Despite its huge responsibilities for foreign and security policy, MOFA's policy making capabilities are severely limited due in part to a shortage of organisational resources and manpower. The scarcity of manpower is obvious, compared to that of other developed countries. For instance, in 1989, MOFA had about 4,500 personnel while there were 16,000 employees in the US, 7,200 in France about 6,200 in Germany.[22] Regardless of the expansion of Japan's international role over the past decade, the number has expanded only to 5,300 by 2003.[23]

As discussed in Chapter 2, in 1993, MOFA created the National Security Policy Division in the Foreign Policy Bureau in order to boost its organisational capability to handle multilateral security activities in the Asia-Pacific. However, despite this, the problem of insufficient manpower has prevented MOFA from channelling sufficient organisational resources to the ARF. The National Security Policy Division usually has about eight overworked officials with only two of them working exclusively on preparing for the ARF.[24] Compared to the Japan-US Security Treaty Division in the North American Affairs Bureau, consisting of more than fifteen personnel, its organisational weakness is evident. The differences between the two divisions over manpower clearly reflect the order of priority in Japan's security policy.[25] As we have seen, it is fair to say that MOFA officials have made vigorous efforts to maintain the momentum of the ARF since its initiation. However, with the sheer scarcity of manpower, those officials have tended to be bound by day-to-day administration and thus have not been able to afford to invest much energy in undertaking a daunting task of revitalising the momentum of the ARF.[26]

The growing dissent within MOFA over the value of Asia-Pacific security multilateralism

Japan's waning enthusiasm for Asia-Pacific security multilateralism has also stemmed from an eroding consensus on its value within MOFA. As seen in Chapter 2, in the early 1990s, the idea of promoting regional security multilateralism enjoyed strong backing from Japan's policy making community, in particular MOFA. However, in the late 1990s, with the deep stagnation of the ARF process, consensus among MOFA officials on the potential effectiveness of a cooperative security approach began to fade away.

Generally speaking, the level of enthusiasm for and interest in the ARF differs between MOFA's bureaus. MOFA's decision-making system is operated under the rule of non-interference between its internal bureaus. For instance, geographic bureaus, such as the North American and Asian Oceanian Affairs, are given their own responsibility to maintain and promote good relations with the countries that they deal with.[27] In this condition, their views of the ARF are primarily influenced by their own policy priorities and preferences. For instance, while officials in the Asia-Pacific Affairs Bureau, which seeks to create special ties with Asian countries, (and of course those in the National Security Policy Division) tend to support Japan's more active role in the ARF, those in the North American Affairs Bureau, which is devoted to the work for the maintenance of stable bilateral relations with the US, are disposed to show little interest in or are simply indifferent to the ARF. For officials who support regional security multilateralism, Japan's greater activism in the ARF is worthwhile in its long-term promotion of a more benign security environment and its enhancement of Japan's political profile in the region, regardless of persistent criticisms of its ineffectiveness. However, for those who are highly sceptical about the value of the ARF and thus wish to see greater emphasis on Japan-US defence cooperation, expending energy on such a stagnant process is a misplacement of limited resources and manpower.[28] The Foreign Policy Bureau,[29] established in 1993 with the aim of articulating more independent diplomacy and of consolidating the functions regarding the planning and coordination of medium- and long-term policy, is supposed to coordinate these different stances on regional security multilateralism within the Ministry to ensure the effective implementation of the 'multifaceted approach'. However, considering a recent overwhelming emphasis on the bilateral alliance in Japan's overall security policy, its capacity or willingness for policy coordination has remained in question. This has probably mirrored the fact that an increasing number of officials have lost interest in the ARF, even in the Asian-Pacific Affairs and Foreign Policy Bureaus.

The lack of political support

A lack of political support has also served to reduce Japan's interest in regional security multilateralism. It is generally argued that Japanese politicians, including the prime minister, have little power over the process of security policy making. This is primarily because of the bureaucrats' control of information indispensable for policy making and a shortage of staff.[30] Moreover, many politicians have little interest in security policy making since security policy issues, which seldom lead to votes, are usually a second or third order priority. National security issues are placed high on the political agenda only when acute external security crises involving Japan arise and attract voters' attention.[31] Due to the absence of widespread interest in security issues at the political level and of a solid basis of political leadership in either government or in a political party, prime ministers often set up advisory commissions on security policy, generally consisting of retired bureaucrats, academics and prominent businessmen, in order to coordinate differing interests between ministries and exercise greater influences on policy making.[32] This was particularly true in the Cold War era when Japan could concentrate on the task of economic development under the Pax Americana and thus security issues were not very attractive for politicians.[33]

Since the end of the Cold War, however, national security issues have increasingly been moved to the centre stage of the political debate as a growing number of politicians have begun to aspire to take the lead in security policy making. As discussed in previous chapters, the collapse of the bipolar structure induced Japanese political leaders to seek more active roles in Asia-Pacific political and security affairs. The 1991 Gulf War activated the political discussion on Japan's security policy, bringing the divisive issue of the SDF's overseas missions to the Diet as well as to public debate. The situation has changed further since the end of the LDP one party rule in 1993 or so called 'the 1995 system', which weakened parties' factions and hierarchy, thus allowing younger politicians in and outside the LDP, who develop greater expertise in security issues, to exert more influence over the policy making process.[34] In addition, because of a number of regional crises since the mid-1990s, such as North Korea's nuclear and missile developments and the Taiwan Crisis, the general public have become more sensitive to external security threats, thus turning the attentions of politicians to security policy issues.

During the early 1990s, MOFA's initiatives for regional security multi-lateralism enjoyed generous support from some influential politicians, seeking a new role for Japan in Asia-Pacific political and security affairs. As seen in Chapter 2, Prime Minister Miyazawa Kiichi, and Foreign Minister Kōno Yōhei, among others, showed strong interest in regional security multilateralism. Moreover, the ruling political parties' policy commissions as well as the Prime Minister's advisory groups presented numerous papers, calling for Japan to take an active role in establishing a regional security institution. These political voices helped invigorate MOFA's new initiatives for regional security multilateralism from the early to mid-1990s.

However, political backing weakened considerably as their political influence diminished in the late 1990s. Due to growing perceived threats from North Korea and China, which once again convinced Japanese policy makers of the significance of the Japan-US alliance, and the rise of a new generation of politicians, who called for the nation to take greater military responsibility through the enlargement of the bilateral security cooperation, the focus of the political debate on Japan's security policy was shifted significantly to the Japan-US alliance, whereas it had been more balanced in the early 1990s. This was evident in a number of LDP policy papers on Japan's national security issued in the late 1990s. Among others, in March 1996, the LDP's Security Research Council released a policy paper, enti-tled 'the current importance of the Japan-US security arrangement'.[35] The paper urged both the Japanese and US governments to reconfirm the importance of bilateral security arrangements not only for the security of Japan but also for that of the Asia-Pacific region and to reinforce bilateral defence cooperation. In particular, it stressed the need to revise the 1978 Guidelines for the Japan-US Defence Cooperation in order to cope with the uncertainty of the region surrounding Japan. The paper, which manifested the ruling party's official view of national security policy, gave strong political support to MOFA and JDA officials, who had hesitated to seek a review of the defence guidelines under the premiership of the dovish Social Democratic Party's (SDP) leader Murayama Tomiichi (1994–96), and it helped lead the government to put 'joint cooperation between Japan and the US in the situation in the area surrounding Japan' into the 1996 Japan-US Joint Declaration on Security. With this, MOFA and JDA successfully put their initiatives for the review of the guidelines on track.[36]

This kind of political backing has not been supplied to Japan's regional multilateral security policy since the late 1990s. This does not mean, however, that Japanese interest in regional security multilateralism at the political level suddenly evaporated. For instance, a LDP foreign policy strategy paper, released by the LDP Commission on Foreign Affairs in April 1997, placed 'the promotion of multilateral security frameworks in the region', most notably the ARF, as the second highest priority for the nation's Asia-Pacific policy under 'the maintenance and strengthening of the Japan-US alliance'.[37] However, by the beginning of the twenty-first century, the diminution of political attention to Japan's role in regional multilateral security became more obvious. In March 2001, the LDP's Policy Research Council proposed a set of specific measures regarding Japan's security policy towards the Asia-Pacific region. While the report devoted large sections to the importance of the enhancement of the Japan-US defence cooperation, it touched on multilateral security cooperation in only a few sentences.[38] In short, regional security multilateralism is no longer fashionable in Japanese security debate, and without powerful domestic political constituencies, initiative for the ARF has been difficult to sustain.

The friction between the bilateral and multilateral security approaches in Japan's overall security policy

Finally, Japan's efforts to develop the ARF have been discouraged by unexpected frictions between the bilateral and multilateral approaches in its overall security policy. As discussed in Chapter 2, the architects of Japan's multifaceted approach to regional security expected that enhancing the Japan-US defence cooperation and developing cooperative security frameworks, most notably the ARF, would work in complement and the combination of the two approaches would effectively ensure Japan's national as well as regional security. However, unfortunately, although it is theoretically possible to boost two approaches at the same time, in practice the greater emphasis on a bilateral security approach was not reconciled easily with Japan's efforts to promote regional security cooperation in the ARF.

As discussed in Chapter 5, since the 1996 Japan-US Joint Declaration on Security, the bilateral alliance has come to be seen by China as the one of the greatest threats to its national security. Beijing has regarded the new developments in the bilateral alliance, including the 1997 revised defence guidelines and Japan's participation in the US TMD project, as new instruments in the US-Japan containment strategy towards China, thus generating acute tensions in their relations. Considering the fact that stable relations among the major powers are critical to the success of regional security cooperation, strained relations between them have the inevitable consequence of undermining Japan's efforts to move the ARF process forward. Indeed, disagreements between Japan, the US and China (and sometimes Russia) had already hindered the progress of the ARF. For instance, as seen in Chapter 3, the diplomatic strife among major powers often hampered the development of meaningful military CBMs in the ARF, evinced by serious disagreements between China and the US and its allies over proposals for notification of and observer exchanges in military exercises. Moreover, Japan's proposal for a Northeast Asian forum for security dialogue was rejected by China due to mistrust between the two countries stemming from their tensions over the bilateral alliance. Chinese security analysts, for example, argued that 'the time was not yet ripe for formal trilateral security dialogue between China, the US and Japan, given the collision between them over the issues of the revised defence guidelines, TMD and the lack of basic trust between China and Japan, and China's concern that it would be isolated in a two against one situation'.[39] In addition, as seen in Chapters 5 and 6, the ARF often became merely a venue for major powers' self-assertions and confrontations, caused mainly by Chinese offensives against the defence guidelines and TMD, rather than for their collaborations on certain security issues. These diplomatic skirmishes with China discouraged Japanese officials who had expected to be able to promote more constructive discussions on regional security issues and cooperative security measures in the ARF. These disappointments disposed them to see the Forum as 'a talking shop'. In short, Japan's policy of strengthening the bilateral alliance has indirectly undermined its efforts to promote regional security cooperation through the ARF.

This unexpected friction between the two approaches clearly highlights problems and difficulties inherent in the actual implementation of Japan's policy of the multifaceted approach. Contrary to the wishes of the proponents of the multifaceted approach to Asia-Pacific security, in practice, bilateral and multilateral security approaches have worked 'competitively' rather than 'complementarily'. As discussed above, given that there is no real prospect for the ARF moving beyond a mere venue for security dialogue and the Japan-US alliance have actually been recognised by most regional countries as the principal factor for preserving peace and stability in the region, Japan's policy of enhancing the bilateral defence cooperation would be the only available and reliable policy for ensuring its national and regional security. However, considering China's fundamentally different view of what constitutes a desired regional order and its basic lack of trust in Japan due primarily to the historical issue, Japan's growing focus on its hedging strategy against China through the strengthening of the bilateral alliance inevitably arouses tension and suspicion and has thus created considerable difficulties for the pursuit of the twin aspirations of Japan's overall security policy. It would seem that Japan's multifaceted approach cannot work successfully unless Japan persuades Beijing to accept the Japan-US alliance as the main component of regional order.

Conclusion

It is fair to say that the ARF, so far the only region-wide security institution to include all of the major regional powers, has served a number of Japanese policy objectives. However, the limited achievements of the ARF over twelve years since its formation suggest that that the Forum has not actually made substantial progress in the agendas outlined in the Concept Paper. Indeed, despite Japan's efforts, the ARF has failed to promote any meaningful CBMs or PD measures. Moreover, its dialogue process has made almost no actual contribution to the addressing of Japan's major security concerns in meaningful ways. As a result of disappointing experiences in the ARF, Japan's enthusiasm for regional security multilateralism, though intense in the early 1990s, began to fade from the late 1990s onwards, and Japan's optimistic 'liberal' conceptions of the ARF have shifted to a more pessimistic 'realist' perspective, from which it can at best contribute to make a minimal level of confidence building among the participating countries.

Conclusion

The main objective of this book is to explore the changes in Japan's conceptions of and policy towards Asia-Pacific security multilateralism since the end of the Cold War with special reference to the ARF. To understand the complex processes behind the changes in and formation of these perceptions, this study has adopted an eclectic theoretical approach and worked on multiple levels of analysis rather than focusing solely on either ideational or material, domestic or international level factors. By conducting an empirical analysis of Japan's diplomacy in security institution building over twelve years, the aim of this study can be extended not only to illuminate the direction of Japan's security policy in the post-Cold War era, but also to provide an empirical basis for examining the validity of three theoretical perspectives on the role and efficacies of security institutions, namely realism, neoliberal institutionalism and constructivism. This concluding chapter returns to and addresses these three main issues of the book raised in the Introduction.

Understanding Japan's changing conceptions and policy towards Asia-Pacific security multilateralism in the post-Cold War era

The dramatic shift in Japan's conceptions of and policy towards regional security multilateralism at the beginning of the 1990s, displayed by the Nakayama proposal, can be understood only by looking at the interaction between international level and individual level factors. As discussed in Chapter 1, the end of the Cold War not only aroused Japan's latent ambition to play a larger political role in the region but also provided regional countries with better conditions for expanding their political and security cooperation in the view of Japanese policy makers. At the same time, however, Japanese policy makers realised that such an aspiration would not easily be achieved as it would be likely to be faced with deep-rooted scepticism and concern amongst Asian neighbours, who had suffered as a result of past Japanese aggression. While the external factors are crucial in accounting for Japan's motivation to search for a new policy instrument for overcoming these challenges, its move toward regional security multilateralism as a response

cannot be fully understood without reference to the ideational force generated at the individual level, namely the concept of the 'multifaceted
approach' to regional security articulated by one senior MOFA official.

Japan's enthusiasm for regional security multilateralism grew considerably
during the early 1990s. Indeed, many in Japan's policy making community,
including politicians, bureaucrats, academics and journalists, began to call for
Japan's more active role in establishing a region-wide security framework.
MOFA continued to pursue this aim by not only convincing the US of the
importance of promoting multilateral security dialogue in the region but
also shoring up Singapore's initiative to expand the ASEAN PMC structure
to the wider Asia-Pacific, thus making a significant contribution to the
establishment of the ARF in 1994. By the mid-1990s, MOFA even established a new division in order to give impetus to its regional multilateral
security policy. As discussed in Chapter 2, Japan's increased interest in
regional security multilateralism was shaped by various factors at both the
international and domestic levels, but during this period it was motivated
primarily by security rather than political reasons. New security challenges,
such as the rise of China's military power, further underlined the need to
promote a multilateral security framework in the region. Moreover, the rapid
progress on regional cooperation in both political and economic fields and
the dissemination of the concept of 'cooperative security' amongst Japan's
policy making community naturally encouraged Japanese officials to be more
willing to incorporate multilateralism into their Asia-Pacific policy making.
The new security challenges also brought about a change in Japan's initial conceptions of regional security multilateralism, generating new policy needs for
more meaningful functions beyond mere security dialogue. In fact, Japanese
policy makers began to conceive the ARF as a potential instrument for
promoting multilateral CBMs, policy coordination and cooperation among
regional countries on certain security issues rather than as a mere vehicle
for reassuring Asian countries about Japan's intention and policies.

Rising expectations for regional security multilateralism among Japanese
policy makers also had profound implications for the course of Japan's
overall security policy in this period. Japanese officials began to incorporate
regional security multilateralism more explicitly into the nation's security
policy by carefully considering how it would operate alongside the Japan-
US alliance. Indeed, Japan formally embarked on the multifaceted approach
to regional security, with the aim of simultaneously strengthening both
Japan-US defence cooperation and multilateral security arrangements,
working on the assumption that the combination of two distinct approaches
was critical to the enhancement of Japan's national and regional security in
the post-Cold War period. This also indicated Japan's long-term expectations of erecting a new regional security order in which the two separate
security arrangements would mutually reinforce each other by providing
complementary functions. Japanese officials did not consider the ARF to be
a mere adjunct to the existing bilateral alliances as realists assume – at least

not at this time. It was considered to have the potential to evolve into a cooperative security institution playing a significant role in the promotion of post-Cold War regional stability.

However, notwithstanding strong multilateral impulses arising in Japanese policy thinking in the early 1990s, Japan's enthusiasm for regional security multilateralism faded in the late 1990s as quickly as it had grown. In order to understand this rapid change, a detailed examination of Japan's actual experiences in the ARF has been conducted in Chapters 3 to 6. The positive developments in the ARF during the first three years gave Japan the impression that progress towards security cooperation along the lines of the Concept Paper was possible, but Japan's experiences in the Forum from the late 1990s onwards were, overall, deeply frustrating. Indeed, what Japanese policy makers learnt through their search for Asia-Pacific security multilateralism over the twelve years since the formation of the ARF was that multilateral security diplomacy had only limited value in addressing Japan's regional security concerns and that the promotion of meaningful cooperative security measures such as military CBMs and PD in the ARF, which operated not only upon the principle of inclusive membership but also under the 'ASEAN Way', was a highly problematic undertaking. As seen in Chapter 7, a number of internal and external factors also played a part in dampening Japan's enthusiasm for regional security multilateralism, including US suspicion of Japan's tilt toward security multilateralism, its domestic organisational limitations, growing dissent within MOFA over the value of the ARF, the lack of political support, and the unexpected frictions between bilateral and multilateral security approaches in Japan's overall security policy.

In the end, Japan's optimistic 'liberal' conception of the ARF gave way to a more pessimistic 'realist' perspective from which the ARF could, at best, be seen to contribute only to a minimum level of confidence building among participating countries by providing them with an opportunity to exchange their views of regional security issues and establishing additional diplomatic channels to hold bilateral talks.

Of course, this is not to suggest that Japan's enthusiasm for Asia-Pacific security multilateralism has entirely disappeared. The Japanese government continues to express firm support for the ARF in spite of widespread criticisms of its ineffectiveness. Japan's Prime Minister, Koizumi Junichirō, for instance, stated in Singapore in January 2002 that 'the ARF has made steady progress in building confidence on security matters. Now is the time to aim for a higher degree of cooperation. Japan is eager to consider how together we can develop this forum for the future'.[1] Japan's continuous support for the ARF reflects its long-standing thinking that strengthening Japan-US security cooperation alone is inadequate for enhancing Japan's as well as regional security in the post-Cold War era. To put it another way, the multifaceted approach to regional security remains a basic imperative in Japan's Asia-Pacific security policy making, at least in principle, as the recent Japan's *Diplomatic Bluebook* indicates.[2]

However, despite continuing rhetorical support for Asia-Pacific security multilateralism, whether Japanese policy makers will or can really take greater efforts to strengthen multilateral security arrangements, most notably the ARF, for the success of the multifaceted approach is in question. As the findings of this book have revealed, Japanese policy makers face enormous difficulties in seriously undertaking such efforts, demonstrated by unexpected frictions between the bilateral and multilateral approaches in Japan's overall security policy and Washington's misgivings about its multilateral security initiatives. More serious questions about Japan's commitment stem from internal rather than external barriers placed on ARF policy, namely its domestic organisational limitations and the marked decline of interest in it at the bureaucratic and political levels.

There is no doubt that MOFA and JDA will continue to keep assigning resources to the task of moving the ARF process forward and that the Japanese government will continue to float proposals for regional security multilateralism inside and outside the ARF, given in particular that the rise of non-traditional security threats, most notably terrorism, has created an immediate need to promote practical security cooperation among regional countries through the ARF. However, as we have seen, the sections in charge of multilateral security initiatives are relatively small and weak in terms of bureaucratic resources and manpower, and this limits their actual capabilities mainly to day-to-day administration, preventing them from pursuing intensive follow-up measures to materialise their proposals, as they did in the case of the Nakayama proposal. A greater effort towards regional security multilateralism would certainly require more extensive bureaucratic resources and solid political backing.

However, given widespread disillusionment with regional security multilateralism among Japanese policy makers, it is unlikely that Japan will allocate greater resources to its initiatives for strengthening the ARF. In short, regional security multilateralism no longer receives strong backing from the Japanese government or even from MOFA as a whole, in the way that it did in the early 1990s. It has been left to a relatively small division within Japan's security policy making agents and not been placed high on the list of their policy priorities. Asia-Pacific security multilateralism is likely to remain low in Japan's security policy priorities as long as the ARF and other regional multilateral arrangements fail to make the kind of tangible progress on security cooperation that could alter the pessimistic realist conceptions of them that have increasingly prevailed in Japan's policy thinking.

The future direction of Japan's security policy

What have been the implications of Japan's dwindling expectations for regional security multilateralism for recent trends in its overall security policy? What have been their effects on the direction of Japan's security policy? This is one of the major issues that this book has intended to address. As discussed in Chapters 1 and 2, with the end of the Cold War, Japanese policy makers articulated the multifaceted approach to regional security, which intended to simultaneously strengthen Japan-US defence cooperation and promote multilateral security frameworks, most notably the ARF. However, although in the early 1990s they had vigorously supported regional security multilateralism and even made great efforts to convince the US to support it, the focus of their attentions was massively shifted to the bilateral security approach after the mid-1990s. The beginning of this shift was evident in the 1995 NDPO and the 1996 Japan-US Joint Declaration on Security, recognising that the alliance was not only the lynchpin of Japan's security strategy but also vital for peace and stability in the Asia-Pacific region. As seen in Chapters 5 and 6, since then, Japanese policy makers have devoted great energy to the enhancement of Japan-US defence cooperation. The two governments adopted the final report of the revised defence guidelines in September 1997 and in April 1998 signed a revised ACSA, which expanded Japan's logistical support to include contingencies in areas surrounding Japan.[3] In April 1998, the Japanese government submitted the bill for the new defence guidelines, which was composed of three elements: the Law on Emergencies in Surrounding Areas, the revision of the Self-Defence Law, and the ratification of the revised ACSA. Although the implementation of the revised guidelines proved to be controversial, in April 1999, the Diet eventually passed the bill. This was followed by the agreement between Tokyo and Washington in August 1999 to initiate a joint research programme on TMD.

The bilateral security cooperation has been further bolstered since the terrorist attacks of September 11 2001. Just two months after September 11, the Japanese government enacted the Anti-Terrorism Special Measures Law, which enabled it to dispatch SDF vessels to the Indian Ocean to provide rear-area logistical support to the US led war in Afghanistan. This deployment broke new ground in both the role of the SDF and the Japan-US security relationship since it was the SDF's first overseas mission in support of a US military operation. The US invasion of Iraq also provided an occasion to cement bilateral security relations. Immediately after the eruption of the war, the Koizumi administration announced clear support of the US War against Iraq and thus drafted the Iraq Reconstruction Assistance Special Measure bill in order to send the SDF in Iraq to assist in reconstruction efforts. The bill was made law in July 2003, and Japan sent its ground troops to Iraq in January 2004. Again, this move marked a significant development in Japan's security policy because, unlike the overseas dispatch of the SDF in Cambodia and elsewhere under the 1992 PKO law that allows Japanese participation in PKO activities if all parties involved in the conflicts have agreed to a ceasefire and to the deployment of SDF, Japan, for the first time since the end of World War II, sent its ground troops to a country in which fighting was still going on. The deployment of the SDF to Iraq as well as to the Indian Ocean can also be seen as a turning point in Japan-US security ties since these two policies have worked to broaden the scope of Japan-US security cooperation from the Asia-Pacific region to global areas. Indeed, at the meeting of the Security Consultative Committee (SCC) in May 2006, Japan and the US issued a joint statement that proclaimed their intent to strengthen the bilateral security cooperation to ensure that the Japan-US alliance plays 'a vital role in enhancing regional and global peace and security'.[4]

Equally significant has been Japan's decision to deploy a TMD system, consisting of the Standard Missile-3 (SM-3) launched from Aegis-equipped destroyers to intercept ballistic missiles in outer space and the ground-based Patriot Advanced Capability-3 (PAC-3) missile, by 2007.[5] The decision to employ TMD not only highlighted Japan's willingness to further boost the Japan-US alliance but also demonstrated the erosion of Japanese adherence to the basic principles of the nation's security policy. The Japanese government announced the revision of the ban on exports of weapons in order to expedite the movement of components to the US that Japan would be tasked with developing under the joint TMD program. Moreover, the introduction of the TMD system prompted the government to review the NDPO. The new NDPO, which was released in December 2004, presented the government plan to build a new defence capability based on the concept of 'multi-functional, flexible and effective defence forces' in order to deal with new security threats, such as ballistic missiles, international terrorism and the proliferation of WMD. The new NDPO represented a significant departure from Japan's traditional policy of building up a minimum defence capability against limited scale foreign attacks.[6]

In addition, Japan's decision to deploy TMD posed a fundamental question as to Japan's adherence to the prohibition on the exercise of the right to collective self-defence. This is because the actual operation of the TMD system, which would require greater integration of command and control functions and military connectivity between SDF and US forces, would certainly blur the distinction between individual self-defence and collective self-defence.[7] It seems to be a matter of time before the government will lift the ban on the right of collective self-defence given that political debate on the issue is no longer taboo[8] and that public support for the revision of the Constitution, including Article 9, has grown dramatically in recent years.[9]

Furthermore, Japan has taken major steps in enhancing its own military capabilities. In March 2003, Japan launched its first ever spy satellites to monitor North Korea's missile activities, and it has continued to pursue the possibility of acquiring refuelling tanker aircraft that would allow its fighters to operate over the Korean Peninsula.[10] In addition, the Japanese government set out the legal framework for the national defence. In June 2003, the Diet passed the war contingency bills, which clarified government measures and the SDF's roles in response to armed attacks on the country. The passage of the bills can be said to mark a new era in Japanese defence policy since the establishment of a military contingency legal framework had long been regarded as a sign of a return to militarism by many in the Japanese public and had been considered a taboo subject.

Japan's greater focus on the military dimension of its security policy, most notably the strengthening of the Japan-US alliance, has in part reflected the emergence of perceived security threats and the disillusionment of a multilateral security approach to the addressing of its security concerns. As discussed in Chapters 5 and 6, the North Korean nuclear crisis and missile launches not only posed a serious threat to Japan's national security but also exposed Japan's inability to respond to any contingencies involving the Korean Peninsula. China's missile diplomacy in the Taiwan Strait crisis and its assertiveness over the territorial disputes in the South China Sea demonstrated, in the eyes of Japanese policy makers, China's willingness to utilise military power as a primary instrument of pursuing its security interests. While these events convinced Japanese policy makers of the need to prepare for security contingencies involving Japan and to balance China's growing military power through the expansion of Japan-US defence cooperation, they exposed the shortcomings and deficiencies of the ARF as a means of addressing its security concerns. Moreover, though these events heightened Japan's perception of the need to promote meaningful military CBMs and PD measures, the prospects for such developments in the ARF actually diminished year by year. Needless to say, a growing disillusionment with Asia-Pacific security multilateralism among Japanese policy makers is not the sole factor accounting for recent trends in Japan's security policy. They have reflected various factors, among others, the inauguration of the Bush administration in 2001, which has called on Japan to make a robust military contribution to its military operations, the rise of the new generation of politicians in Japan who call for a more reciprocal military role in the Japan-US alliance and a review of the county's defence capabilities, and the decline of its economic resources as an instrument of security policy.[11] However, Japan's lowering expectations for regional security multilateralism has certainly been an important cause for them, making Japanese policy makers more inclined to devote their attentions to the enhancement of the Japan-US defence cooperation. This was expressed in a LDP security policy paper:

> China continues to modernize and strengthen its military capability. It has conducted nuclear tests despite the international trend to conclude the Comprehensive Nuclear Test Ban Treaty and has conducted missile launch exercises near Taiwan. Such military activities may affect the security of Japan. Moreover, China has stepped up its operational stations on the Spratly Islands over which territorial disputes exist among neighbouring nations. ... ASEAN members have been increasing their defence expenditure and modernizing their military capabilities through

the introduction of new equipment backed by economic development. Disputes still exist among related nations on the territorial rights of the Spratly Islands. ... Under such circumstances, it is necessary to promote mutual confidence building, but it is hardly feasible that an Asia-Pacific multi-national security framework will be formulated soon. In such uncertain global times, the United States, as sole superpower, contributes to the world's peace and stability. The cooperative relationship between Japan and the United States, based on the Japan-U.S. Security Arrangements, continues to play a key role for all in the international community, by securing and ensuring the engagement of the United States and its military deployment in the Asia Pacific region.[12]

This is not to say that Japan's policy thinking has been narrowly focused on the military aspect. As mentioned above, the concept of the multifaceted approach to regional security has still remained a basic imperative in Japan's policy making. More importantly, anti-militarist sentiment has still endured in broad segments of the Japanese public though it has been weakened. These factors will force Japanese policy makers to continue to see non-military instruments, in particular economic tools, as primary instruments for contributing to the enhancement of regional and international security.[13] Nonetheless, given growing disillusionment with the effectiveness of non-military security approaches – including regional security multilateralism, it is likely that Japanese policy makers will invest greater energies in the expansion of the military dimension of security policy, in particular its defence cooperation with the US, in order not only to counter China's growing military power and North Korea's missile and nuclear threats but also to cope with new security threats, including international terrorism and the proliferation of WMD. In short, Japan's pursuit of a 'normal' security policy is mostly likely to be accelerated.

The ARF and three major theoretical perspectives

Finally, using Japan's experiences in the ARF as a case study, this book has aimed to assess the validity of three major theoretical approaches to measuring the utilities of the ARF and the nature of state approach to the ARF, namely realism, neoliberal institutionalism and constructivism. The findings of this study, in particular, highlight the weaknesses of both constructivist and neoliberal institutionalist approaches. Japan's experiences in the process of security dialogues and of CBMs clearly show the limitations of the neoliberal institutionalist perspective on the ARF, holding that the Forum can contribute to regional stability by facilitating the flow of information about states' defence policy and diffusing norms that define acceptable state behaviours. As we have seen, the ARF is obviously incapable of performing such a task, and there has been no convincing evidence that the very limited information provided by the ARF has actually helped to reduce the level of mutual suspicion or altered the policies of member countries. The institutionalists' expectations that the Forum may contribute to ameliorate the security dilemma and increase the chances of security cooperation among regional countries are far from being met. The widespread aversion to greater military transparency for fear of the weakening of deterrent capabilities shows how balance of power thinking has prevailed in the policy thinking of many ARF countries.

Japan's experiences in these areas also pose serious questions to the validity of the constructivist position, which assumes that social interaction within the ARF will redefine interests of participating countries and thus help to develop common identities that may enable them to overcome balance of power politics and the security dilemma. Given that the redefinition of identities is a process measured in decades, it might be too early to judge the accomplishments of the ARF in this area.[14] Nonetheless, findings based on Japan's experiences suggest that the ARF's potential for socialisation is limited. John Garofano argues that focusing on the extent and quality of interactions within the ARF is critically important to assessing its utility from a constructivist approach.[15] The extent of interaction that the ARF provides is limited. For instance, senior officials get together only twice a year at a Ministerial Meeting and SOM. The mid-level officials who actually handle the ARF policy have more chances for interactions, getting involved in intersessionl activities, such as the ISG on CBMs and ISM on CTTC. Regardless of this, however, the extent of interactions is still restricted since these officials do not hold the same positions for more than a few years. In the case of Japan, officials in charge of ARF policy are usually replaced every two years and often moved to entirely different positions.[16]

Without greater continuity of interactions among officials, the redefinition or formation of collective identities is unlikely to take place. The poor quality of interactions has also posed problems for the constructivist perspective. Although the ARF has set up various intersessional working groups, there has been far more speech making in these meetings than concrete actions.[17] It is highly improbable that regional countries can develop common identity without engaging in much deeper interactions, including collective experiences in actual security cooperation. The low density and poor quality of interactions within the ARF may account for why many ARF countries have not yet begun to share feelings of growing trust and community even though they have sat together for more than twelve years.

This is not to say that the constructivist argument that ideational factors, such as the norms of multilateralism and cooperative security, are crucial in understanding the evolution of regional institutions[18] is not cogent. As seen in Chapter 1 and 2, the idea of 'the multifaceted approach to regional security' and of 'cooperative security' actually played a critical role in leading Japan as well as the US to give full support to regional initiatives in establishing the ARF. However, despite its significance, the constructivist argument overlooks the fact that the norm of multilateralism has not embedded or has even become less important in their regional security policy thinking, due in part to disappointing experiences in the ARF.

As this study has uncovered, Japanese policy makers have become more willing to put emphasis on a power balancing approach while their expectations for regional security multilateralism have been lowered. The same can be applied to the case of China. As discussed in Chapter 7, although Chinese officials have increasingly adopted positive attitudes toward the ARF, China's ARF policy, in particular regarding the PD agenda, has still been largely self-serving. Furthermore, whilst China's Foreign Ministry has begun to play active roles in the ARF, the PLA has vigorously pursued the build-up and the modernisation of the nation's military capabilities. These tendencies among major powers have increased mutual concerns and suspicion, but such concerns have not been alleviated either by security dialogue processes or by modest CBMs existing in the ARF. In short, there have been no real signs that regional institutions have actually led them to begin to seriously reduce their dependence on a traditional power balancing approach. In addition, it is also important to note that the continuity of major powers' engagement with regional institutions is not an appropriate yardstick for the success of institutions, though some constructivist scholars have referred to it as evidence for the significance of regional institutions. This is because participation is not a demanding enough task for true commitment to be judged by. For Japan and the US, for instance, it is worthwhile to keep commitment to the ARF even though they cannot gain more than additional points of diplomatic contact since the political and financial cost of participation is reasonably low.[19]

For China too, participation in the ARF, which operates under ASEAN's rule of 'consensus decision-making' and maintaining 'the pace comfortable to all participants' is relatively a risk free as these rules allow Beijing to veto any proposals that it dislikes. Beijing has thus begun to see the Forum as a useful venue, in which it can pursue its own national interests without making substantial concessions. These factors indicate that the effects of the ARF on policies of major powers as well as on regional security order have been so far only marginal. These findings would indicate that it is still premature to fully assess the utilities of the ARF from constructivist perspectives.

Ironically, constructivism may be much more useful when it is used as an analytical framework for explaining how Japan's fundamental beliefs about the ARF have changed from a liberal to a more realist perspective than when it is employed as that for explicating the utilities of the ARF. It is argued by constructivists that actors may adopt new norms and beliefs through the processes of social interactions (e.g. persuasion and learning) inside international institutions.[20]This constructivist argument can be applied to the case of Japan. Indeed, as we have seen, changes in Japanese beliefs about the ARF have occurred as a result of their social interactions with other states (repeated unsuccessful negotiations and failures to promote efficient cooperative outcomes) inside the ARF through which they have *learnt* that promoting practical cooperation in a security institution that operates not only on the principle of inclusive membership but also the 'ASEAN Way' of institution building is a highly problematic undertaking. Japan's case, which runs counter to standard constructivist interpretation that usually argue for the diffusion of cooperative norms inside international institutions, may open up new avenues for constructive research on their role regarding the question of when and under what conditions social interaction inside international institutions are likely to change actors' behaviour in more cooperative or non-cooperative directions. On the basis of findings from this case study, it may be said that an inclusive, informal and consensus based institution like the ARF is sometimes counter-productive in promoting significant cooperation, weakening the political commitments of actors who enter the institution in the expectation of achieving such cooperation. This is because such an institution tends to repeatedly produce outcomes that are overwhelmingly favourable to reluctant cooperators and thus create social environments where the preferences of reluctant actors rather than those of cooperative actors prevail.

Social interaction (learning processes) under such unfavourable conditions may change cooperative actors' fundamental beliefs about the utilities of the institution or multilateralism in a negative way and thereby discourage their motivation for cooperation. Constructivist scholarship may need more empirical studies of how continuous unsuccessful negotiations and repeated failures to promote cooperative outcomes inside international institutions affect cooperative actors' fundamental beliefs about their choices and strategies. While constructivist scholarship tends to present a one-sided analysis, focusing on how social interaction in international institutions diffuse 'cooperative' norms and belief, it seldom pays attention to an adverse case that actors come to adopt more 'realpolitik' beliefs as a consequence of social interaction. If identities and interests of potential defectors can change through social interactions, so too can those of genuine cooperative actors.

Finally, a realist perspective is also not free from problems. For Japan as well as other regional countries, the ARF is not merely an instrument for constraining China. Despite a marked lowering of expectations for the ARF, Japanese policy makers still see the Forum as a useful vehicle for enhancing the overall diplomatic climate between regional countries and as an important element of its policy of engagement with China and North Korea, as noted in Chapter 7. In addition, realism cannot fully explain why a major power like Japan had endeavoured to establish a multilateral security institution and to promote security cooperation in the ARF without fully being caught in the dilemma of relative gains.

As discussed above, Japan's conceptions of and policy towards regional security multilateralism in its inception years are better construed through the lens of neoliberal institutionalism and constructivism. However, with respect to the theoretical question about the role of ARF, its highly limited utility for Japan's national as well as regional security from the viewpoint of Japanese policy makers after twelve years since its formation tend to confirm what realists have assumed regarding the maximum value of Asia-Pacific security institutions. To make a decisive judgement regarding the explanatory power of these three IR theories is not the task of this study. On the basis of the empirical findings of this book, however, it may be said that realism has, at least so far, offered more persuasive assumptions about the nature and prospects of the ARF than neoliberal institutionalism and constructivism although the continuity of its superiority vis-à-vis other two perspectives depends on the future condition of the ARF as well as Asia Pacific security affairs.

Overall, though there is certainly a need to look beyond material factors in understanding the roles of security institutions as well as state approach towards them, it is important not to overemphasise the significance of one particular force since placing special focus on a single factor neglects important aspects of the evidence. Whereas engaging in a controversial debate on the epistemological issue is beyond the scope of this book, the fact that any specific theoretical perspective cannot fully explicate the connection between Japanese security and the ARF highlights the disadvantages of the American social science positivist approach to IR, which is represented by the privileging of parsimony and the paradigmatic battle, in terms of dealing with the very complicated international phenomenon.

These findings indicate that sufficient understanding requires an eclectic theoretical approach to IR rather than a single analytical perspective. It has been proved that such an approach, which places a premium on understanding the interplay of powers, interests, and norms in international politics and thus takes a cross-paradigmatic approach, has met the objectives of this study.

Notes

Introduction

1 Paul Midford, 'Japan's Leadership Role in East Asian Security Multilateralism: The Nakayama Proposal and the Logic of Reassurance', *The Pacific Review*, vol. 13, no. 3, 2000, p. 368.

2 The First meeting of the ARF was held in Bangkok Thailand in July 1994. It brought together foreign ministers from Japan, the United States, China, Australia, Brunei, Canada, the European Union, Indonesia, Laos, Malaysia, New Zealand, Papua New Guinea, the Philippines, South Korea, Russia, Singapore, Thailand, and Vietnam. Cambodia joined in the Forum in 1995, India and Burma in 1996, Mongolia in 1999, North Korea in 2000, and Pakistan in 2004.

3 According to John Ruggie, 'multilateralism' is defined as 'an institutional form that coordinates relations among three or more states in accordance with generalised principles of conduct: that is, principles that specify appropriate conduct for class actions'. Such principles include non-discrimination, an indivisibility among the members of an institution in terms of appropriate behaviour, and diffuse reciprocity indicating the arrangement where members can yield roughly equal benefits over time. This definition corresponds with Robert Keohane's interpretation of an 'institution' that has a 'persistent and connected sets of rules (formal or informal) that prescribe behavioural roles, constrain activity, and shape expectations'. Using these definitions, this book defines promoting 'security multilateralism' as an undertaking to establish a multilateral security institution that coordinates the policies of states belonging to it, based on generalised principles of conduct or rules. These definitions also allow us to see the ARF as a multilateral *institution* despite its highly imperfect institutionalised form since, at least in principle, it is premised on non-discrimination, diffuse reciprocity, and indivisibility. See, John Gerard Ruggie, 'Multilateralism: The Anatomy of an Institution', in John Gerard Ruggie (ed.) *Multilateralism Matters: The Theory and Praxis of an Institutional Form*, New York, N.Y.: Columbia University Press, 1993, p. 11–12. Robert O. Keohane, *International Institutions and State Power: Essays in International Relations Theory*, Boulder, Co.: Westview, 1989, p. 163.

4 See, *inter alia*, Yoichi Funabashi, *Domei Hyouryu*. Tokyo: Iwanami Shoten, 1997. Mike Mochizuki, *Toward a True Alliance: Restructuring U.S.-Japan Security Relations*, Washington DC: Brookings Institution Press, 1997. Michael J. Green and Patrick M. Cronin, *The U.S.-Japan Alliance: Past, Present, and Future*, New York: Council on Foreign Relations Press, 1999. Masashi Nishihara (ed.) *The Japan-U.S. Alliance: New Challenges for the 21st Century*, Tokyo and New York: Japan Center for International Exchange, 2000. Anthony DiFilippo, *The Challenges of the U.S.-Japan Military Arrangement: Competing Security*

Transitions in a Changing International Environment, Armonk, NY: M. E.Sharpe, 2002. Ted Osius, *The U.S.-Japan Security Alliance: Why It Matters and How to Strengthen It*, The Washington Papers, no. 181, Westport, Conn.: Praeger, 2002.

5 For research on Japan's roles in the UN, see, *inter alia*, Akiko Fukushima, Japanese Foreign Policy: *The Emerging Logic of Multilateralism*, Basingstoke: Macmillan, 1999. Reinhard Drifte, *Japan's Quest for a Permanent Security Council Seat: A Matter of Pride or Justice?*, Basingstoke: Macmillan, 2000. Hugo Dobson, *Japan and United Nations Peacekeeping: New Pressures, New Responses*, London: Routledge, 2003. As for research on Japan's role in promoting regional multilateralism in the realm of political economic affairs, see Yoichi Funabashi, *Ajiataiheiyō Fyujon: APEC to Nihon*. Tokyo: Chuōkōronsha, 1995. Richard F. Donner, 'Japan in East Asia: Institutions and Regional Leadership', in Peter J. Katzenstein and Takashi Shirishi (eds) *Network Power: Japan and Asia*, Ithaca, NY: Cornell University Press, 1997, pp. 197–233. Takashi Terada, 'The Origins of Japan's APEC Policy: Foreign Minister Takeo Miki's Asia-Pacific Policy and Current Implications', *The Pacific Review*, vol. 11, no. 3, 1998, pp. 337–63. Ellis S. Krauss, 'Japan, the US, and the Emergence of Multilateralism in Asia', *The Pacific Review* 13, no. 3, 2000, pp. 473–94.

6 See, for instance, Masashi Nishihara, 'Ajiataiheiyō Chiiki to Takokukan Anzenhoshō Kyōryoku no Wakugumi: ASEAN Chiiki Forum wo Chyūshin ni', *Kokusai Mondai*, no. 415, October 1994, pp. 60–68. Yoshide Soeya, 'The Evolution of Japanese Thinking and Politics on Cooperative Security in the 1980s and 1990s', *Australian Journal of International Affairs*, vol. 48, no. 1, May 1994, pp. 87–95. Ken Jinbo, 'Nichibeichu no Ajiataiheiyō Takokukan Anzenhoshō Kyōryoku: Kyōchō to Tairitsu Soui no Kouzu', *Shin-Bōeironshū*, vol. 25, no. 3, December 1997, pp. 48–66. Sheldon W. Simon, 'Multilateralism and Japan's Security Policy', *Korean Journal of Defense Analysis*, vol. 11, no. 2, 1999, pp. 79–96. Akiko Fukushima, 'Japan's Emerging View of Security Multilateralism in Asia', in Rulph Cossa, Akiko Fukushima, Stephan Haggard and Daniel J. Pinkston (eds) *Security Multilateralism in Asia: Views from the United States and Japan*, Institute of Global Conflict and Cooperation, University of California, Multi-Campus Research Unit, 1999, pp. 1–44. Midford, 'Japan's Leadership Role'. Kuniko Ashizawa, 'Japan's Approach toward Asian Regional Security: From "Hub-and-Spoke" Bilateralism to "Multi-Tiered"', *The Pacific Review*, vol. 16, no. 3, 2003, pp. 361–82.

7 Kawasaki argued that there existed three major perspectives on the ARF in Japan in its inception years (1991–95). For instance, idealists saw the ARF as a first step for achieving the long-term objective of replacing the traditional bilateral alliance system in the region with a new regional security system that might grow to become a security community. On the contrary, Realists regarded the ARF as a policy instrument for practicing balance-of-power politics with China. Finally, Liberals in the Ministry of Foreign Affairs (MOFA) saw the ARF as a vehicle to decrease the level of distrust and suspicion among regional countries and thus as a complement to the existing balance of power in the region. He concluded that this liberal conception of the ARF constituted the ideational backbone of Japan's ARF policy. Tsuyoshi Kawasaki, 'Between Realism and Idealism in Japanese Security Policy: The Case of the ASEAN Regional Forum', *The Pacific Review*, vol. 10, no. 4, 1997, pp. 367–97.

8 Christopher Hill, *The Changing Politics of Foreign Policy*, New York: Palgrave MacMillan, 2002, pp. 127–29.

9 The term 'normal' with regards to the debate on Japanese security policy refers to the widely held position that Japan should assume a more active or normal role in international security by weakening or lifting the legal constraints on its

military capabilities. The concept of a 'normal country' was originally articulated by Ichiro Ozawa, formerly of the LDP and now one of the leaders of the Democratic Party of Japan (DPJ). Immediately after Japan's failure to respond to the 1990 Gulf War, Ozawa organised an LDP study group on Japan's Role in International Society. Its controversial report argued that Japan has the right to fully participate in UN PKO and even in its collective security activities including military operations for contributing to the maintenance of international peace and security since the Japanese Constitution is itself based on the UN Charter. For details of Ozawa's vision of a normal country, see Ichiro Ozawa, *Blueprint for a New Japan*, Tokyo and New York: Kodansha International, 1994.

10 For a review of recent research on Japan's security policy, see Michael J. Green, 'State of the Field Report: Research on Japanese Security Policy', *Access Asia Review*, vol. 2, no. 1, September 1998, pp. 1–39.

11 Kenneth N. Waltz, 'The Emerging Structure of International Politics', *International Security*, vol. 18, no. 2, Autumn 1993, pp. 55–70. See also Christopher Layne, 'The Unipolar Illusion: Why New Great Powers Will Rise', *International Security*, vol. 17, no. 4, Spring 1993, pp. 5–51.

12 Peter J. Katzenstein, *Cultural Norms & National Security: Police and Military in Postwar Japan*, Ithaca, NY: Cornell University Press, 1996. Thomas U. Berger, *Cultures of Antimilitarism: National Security in Germany and Japan*, Baltimore, Md: The Johns Hopkins University Press, 1998. For another excellent study focusing on the role of the norm of antimilitarism in Japan's security policy, see Glenn D. Hook, *Militarization and Demilitarization in Contemporary Japan*, New York: Routledge, 1995.

13 Berger, *Cultures of Antimilitarism*, p. 209. Katzenstein, *Cultural Norms & National Security*, p. 208.

14 Katzenstein, *Cultural Norms & National Security*, pp. 204–8. This view is shared by some British based scholars, such as Glenn D. Hook, Julie Gilson, Christopher W. Hughes and Hugo Dobson. While acknowledging that changes in the regional structural environment and US pressure have compelled Japanese policy makers to seek greater military responsibilities in the Asia-Pacific region mainly through the strengthening of its defence cooperation with the US, they argue that the norm of anti-militarism embedded in domestic society has continued to constrain Japanese policy makers from fully committing to the use of military forces in line with a US war fighting strategy despite its pressure. Hence, they conclude that Japanese policy makers will continue to assume a direct security role in international affairs based on economic rather than military power. See Glenn D. Hook, Julie Gilson, Christopher W. Hughes and Hugo Dobson, *Japan's International Relations: Politics, Economics and Security*, London: Routledge, 2001, p. 149 and 224.

15 For the concept of strategic culture, see Alastair I. Johnston, *Cultural Realism: Strategic Culture and Grand Strategy in Chinese History, Princeton Studies in International History and Politics*, Princeton, NJ: Princeton University Press, 1998.

16 Michael J. Green, *Japan's Reluctant Realism: Foreign Policy Challenges in an Era of Uncertain Power*, New York and Basingstoke: Palgrave, 2001, pp. 271–74. This view is echoed by Reinhard Drifte and Christopher W. Hughes. Drifte argues that Japan's China policy has increasingly been motivated by balance of power considerations and it is likely that Japan will further integrate itself into the Japan-US alliance and strengthen political and military power against China. Reinhard Drifte, *Japan's Security Relations with China since 1989: From Balancing to Bandwagoning?*, London: RoutledgeCurzon, 2003. Hughes also contends that Japan has moved towards a more assertive or 'normal' military

power mainly through the strengthening of the Japan-US alliance. This trend
has been, according to him, mainly developed by Japan's concerns about
North Korea's nuclear programme and China's military intentions, the September 11 terrorist attacks, the US led global war on terror, and the emergence
of a newly proactive policy making system in Japan. See, Christopher W.
Hughes, *Japan's Re-emergence as a 'Normal' Military Power*, Oxford and New
York: Oxford University Press for the International Institute of Strategic Studies, 2004.

17 Green, 'State of the Filed Report', pp. 8–9.
18 Celeste A. Wallander and Robert O. Keohane, 'Introduction', in Helga Haf-
tendorn, Robert O. Keohane and Celeste A. Wallander (eds) *Imperfect Unions:
Security Institutions over Time and Space*, Oxford and New York: Oxford
University Press, 1999, pp. 3–4. Robert O. Keohane and Lisa L. Martin, 'The
Promise of Institutionalist Theory', *International Security*, vol. 20, no. 1,
Summer 1995, pp. 43–44. For further discussions of Institutionalist theory, see
Robert O. Keohane, *After Hegemony: Cooperation and Discord in the World
Political Economy*, Princeton, NJ: Princeton University Press, 1984. Lisa L.
Martin and Beth A. Simmons, *International Institutions: An International
Organization Reader*, Cambridge, Mass.: MIT Press, 2001.
19 See, for instance, Sheldon W. Simon, 'Security Prospects in Southeast Asia:
Collaborative Efforts and the ASEAN Regional Forum', *The Pacific Review*, vol.
11, no. 2, 1998, pp. 195–212. Yuen Foong Khong, 'Making Bricks without Straw
in the Asia-Pacific?', *The Pacific Review*, vol. 10, no. 2, 1997, pp. 289–300.
20 Realists argue that relative gain is much more important than absolute gain
especially in the realm of security, since one state may use its disproportionate
gain to implement a policy intended to damage others, and this makes states
prone to adopting more narrow self interested behaviour and intolerant and
wary of imbalances in benefit. Keneth N. Waltz, *Theory of International Politics*, Reading, Mass.: Addison-Wesley, 1979, pp. 105–6. Joseph M.Grieco,
'Anarchy and the Limits of Cooperation: A Realist Critique of the Newest Liberal
Institutionalism', in David A. Baldwin (ed.) *Neorealism and Neoliberalism: The
Contemporary Debate*, New York: Columbia University Press, 1993, pp. 124–30.
21 For example, See, John J. Mearsheimer, 'The False Promise of International
Institutions', *International Security*, vol. 19, no. 3, Winter 1994/1995, pp. 13–14.
22 Mearsheimer, 'The False Promise of International Institutions', p. 13.
23 See, *inter alia*, Barry Buzan and Gerald Segal, 'Rethinking East Asian Security',
Survival, vol. 36, no. 2, 1994, pp. 3–21. Paul Dibb, *Towards a New Balance of
Power in Asia*, Adelphi Papers, no. 295, London: International Institute for
Strategic Studies, 1995, pp. 66–67. Michael Leifer, *The ASEAN Regional
Forum: Extending ASEAN's Model of Regional Security*, Adelphi Papers, no.
302. London: Oxford University Press, 1996. Gerald Segal, 'How insecure is
Pacific Asia?', *International Affairs*, vol. 73, no. 2, 1997, pp. 235–50. Robyn R.
Lim, 'The ASEAN Regional Forum: Building on Sand', *Contemporary Southeast
Asia*, vol. 20, no. 2, 1998, pp. 115–36. For a discussion on the role of balance of
power factor in the evolution of the ARF, see Ralf Emmers, *Cooperative
Security and the Balance of Power in ASEAN and the ARF*, New York: Routledge
Curzon, 2003.
24 Leifer, *The ASEAN Regional Forum*, pp. 57–58.
25 Ibid, p. 59.
26 Alexander Wendt, 'Anarchy Is What States Make of It: The Social Construction
of Power Politics', *International Organization*, vol. 46, no. 2, Spring 1992, pp.
414–18. Alexander Wendt, 'Collective Identity Formation and the International
State', *The American Political Science Review*, vol. 88, no. 2, June 1994, pp.
388–90. Andreas Hasenclever, Peter Mayer, and Volker Rittberger, *Theories of*

International Regimes, Cambridge: Cambridge University Press, 1997, pp. 186–92.

27 For further discussions regarding security community, see Emanuel Adler and Michael N. Barnett. *Security Communities*, New York: Cambridge University Press, 1998.

28 Yuen Foong Khong, 'ASEAN and the Southeast Asian Security Complex', in David A. Lake and Patrick M. Morgan (eds) *Regional Orders: Building Security in a New World*, University Park: Pennsylvania State University Press, 1997, pp. 318–39. Nikolas Busse, 'Constructivism and Southeast Asian Security', *The Pacific Review*, vol. 12, no. 1, 1999, pp. 39–60. Amitav Acharya, *Constructing a Security Community in Southeast Asia: ASEAN and the Problem of Regional Order*, London: Routledge, 2001. Amitav Acharya, 'Regional Institutions and Asian Security Order: Norms, Power, and Prospects for Peaceful Change', in Muthiah Alagappa (ed.) *Asian Security Order: Instrumental and Normative Features*, Stanford, California: Stanford University Press, 2003, pp. 210–40. Alastair I. Johnston, 'Socialization in International Institutions: The ASEAN Way and International Relations Theory', in John G. Ikenberry and Michael Mastanduno (eds) *International Relations Theory and the Asia-Pacific*, New York: Columbia University Press, 2003, pp. 107–62.

29 Acharya, *Constructing a Security Community in Southeast Asia*, p. 202.

30 Ibid, p. 184.

31 Johnston, 'Socialization in International Institutions', pp. 107–62.

32 Sorpong Peou, 'Realism and Constructivism in Southeast Asian Security Studies Today: A Review Essay', *The Pacific Review*, vol. 15, no. 1, 2002, pp. 119–38.

33 See, for instance, Robert Jervis, *Perception and Misperception in International Politics*, Princeton, NJ, and Guildford: Princeton University Press, 1976. Alexander George, 'The Causal Nexus Between Cognitive Beliefs and Decision-Making Behaviour: The Operational Code Belief System', in Lawrence S. Falkowski (ed.) *Psychological Models in International Politics*, Boulder, Co.: Westview Press, 1979, pp. 95–124.

34 For details of Japan's foreign and security policy making institutions, see, *inter alia*, Peter J. Katzenstein and Nobuo Okawara, *Japan's National Security: Structures, Norms, and Policy Responses in a Changing World*, Ithaca, NY: Cornell University, 1993, pp. 21–56. Kent E. Calder, 'The Institutions of Japanese Foreign Policy', in Richard L. Grant (ed.) *The Process of Japanese Foreign Policy: Focus on Asia*, London: Royal Institute of International Affairs, 1997, pp. 1–24. Hook, Gilson, Hughes and Dobson, *Japan's International Relations*, pp. 42–50. Green, *Japan's Reluctant Realism*, pp. 35–64.

35 Green, *Japan's Reluctant Realism*, pp. 62–64.

36 For discussions on the impact of bureaucratic politics on the foreign policy process, see, *inter alia*, Steve Smith, 'Perspectives on the Foreign Policy System: Bureaucratic Politics Approaches', in Clarke and White, *Understanding Foreign Policy: The Foreign Policy Systems Approach*, Aldershot: Edward Elgar, 1989, pp. 109–34. Graham T. Allison and Philip Zelikow, *Essence of Decision: Explaining the Cuban Missile Crisis*, 2nd ed, New York: Harlow: Longman, 1999, pp. 255–313. For discussions on the problems of implementation, see Michael Clarke and Steve Smith, 'Perspectives on the Foreign Policy System: Implementation Approaches', in Michael Clarke and Brian White, *Understanding Foreign Policy*, pp. 163–84. Hill, *The Changing Politics of Foreign Policy*, pp. 127–55.

37 For discussions on the advantages of analytic eclecticism or cross-paradigmatic approaches to International Relations, see Katzenstein and Okawara, 'Japan, Asian Pacific Security, and the Case for Analytical Eclecticism', pp. 53–85.

38 For discussions on the advantages of a narrative approach to IR, see John Lewis Gaddis, 'History, Science, and the Study of International Relations', in Ngaire Woods (ed.) *Explaining International Relations since 1945*, Oxford: Oxford University Press, 1996, pp. 32–48. Andrew Bennett and Alexander. L George, 'Case Studies and Process Tracing in History and Political Science: Similar Strokes for Different Foci', in Colin Elman and Miriam Fendius Elman (eds) *Bridges and Boundaries: Historians, Political Scientists, and the Study of International Relations*, Cambridge, Mass.: MIT Press, 2001, pp. 137–66.

Chapter 1

1 The Yoshida Doctrine was predicated on the assumption that the advent of the Cold War would force the US to maintain its military presence in Japan and that this would effectively function as a major deterrent against the direct threat of invasion by the Soviet Union. In short, it was expected that the security umbrella provided by the US would allow Japan to avoid the huge cost of rearmament and to abstain from involving itself directly in regional security, thus enabling Japan to concentrate on economic recovery. Kenneth B. Pyle, *The Japanese Question: Power and Purpose in a New Era*, Washington DC: AEI Press, 1996, p. 26–27.

2 Glenn D. Hook, Julie Gilson, Christopher W. Hughes, and Hugo Dobson, *Japan's International Relations: Politics, Economics and Security*, London: Routledge, 2001, p. 124.

3 In 1950, under orders from the US occupation administration, the Japanese government established the National Police Reserve with 75,000 personnel in order to maintain domestic order as the bulk of US military was sent out to Korean Peninsula. After the Korean War, Washington further pushed Tokyo to take more responsibility for its national security, requesting the Japanese government to sign the Mutual Security Act (MSA), which would provide Japan with military aid for developing its defence capabilities, and to set up its own ground force consisting of 325,000 personnel in 1952. For more details, see Shinkichi Etō and Yoshinobu Yamamoto, *Sōgō Anpo to Mirai no Sentaku*, Tokyo: Kodansha, 1991, pp. 107–17. Akihiko Tanaka, *Anzenhoshō: Sengo Gojunen no Mosaku*, Tokyo: Yomiuri Shinbunsha, 1997, pp. 122–27.

4 The BPND consists of the following four principles: (1) to support UN activities and promote international cooperation for contributing to world peace; (2) to promote the public welfare and enhance patriotism in order to establish the foundation of domestic order; (3) to develop effective defence capabilities necessary for self-defence with due regard to national resources and the prevailing domestic situation; and (4) to deal with external aggression based on the Japan-US security arrangements until the time when UN grows mature enough to effectively deter and repel such aggression. Joseph P. Keddell, *The Politics of Defense in Japan: Managing Internal and External Pressures*, Armonk, NY: M. E. Sharpe, 1993, p. 38.

5 For an analysis of post war debate on Article 9 in Japan, see Glenn D. Hook and Gavan McCormack. *Japan's Contested Constitution: Documents and Analysis*, London: Routledge, 2001.

6 The Cabinet Legal Affairs Bureau established in 1983 proclaimed that SDF may support the US force resisting an attack on Japan but may not support it if the US force is engaged in offensive military operations which are not related to the defence of Japan. This delicate line between 'collective' and 'individual' self-defence has complicated the debate on the expansion of Japan's military role in the Japan-US alliance. Michael J. Green, 'State of the Filed Report: Research

on Japanese Security Policy', *Access Asia Review*, vol. 2, no. 1, September 1998, p. 19, available at: http://accessasia.nbr.org/ (accessed 15/09/06).

7 Christopher W. Hughes, *Japan's Security Agenda: Military, Economic and Environmental Dimensions*, Boulder and London: Lynne Rienner Publishers, 2004, pp. 136–37.

8 Peter J. Katzenstein and Nobuo Okawara, *Japan's National Security: Structures, Norms, and Policy Responses in a Changing World*, Ithaca, NY: Cornell University, 1993, pp. 108–13.

9 Hook, Gilson, Hughes, and Dobson, *Japan's international relations*, pp. 128–29.

10 Akihiko Tanaka, 'Japan's Security Policy in 1990s', in Yoichi Funabashi (ed.) *Japan's International Agenda*, New York: New York University Press, 1994, pp. 31–32.

11 Hiroshi Nakanishi, 'Redefining Comprehensive Security in Japan', in Ryōsei Kokubun (ed.) *Challenges for China-Japan-U.S. Cooperation*, Tokyo and New York: Japan Center for International Exchange, 1998, p. 78.

12 Shelia A. Smith, 'The Evolution of Military Cooperation in the U.S.-Japan Alliance', in Michael J. Green and Patrick M. Cronin (eds) *The U.S.-Japan Alliance: Past, Present, and Future*, New York: Council on Foreign Relations Press, 1999, p. 77. For the details of the NDPO, see Yoshimasa Muroyama, *Nichibei Anpo Taisei: Reisengo no Anzenhoshō Senryaku o Kōsōsuru*, vol. 2, Tokyo: Yuhikaku, 1992, pp. 329–67.

13 Koji Murata, 'Bōei Seisaku no Tenkai: Guideline no Sakutei wo Chushin ni', in Nihon Seiji Gakkai (ed.) *Nenpō Seijigaku, 1997*, Tokyo: Iwanami Shoten, 1997, pp. 79–95. In particular, joint military exercises were significantly expanded over the course of the 1980s. For instance, Maritime Self-Defence Force (MSDF) began to participate in the US-led Rim of the Pacific (RIMPAC) exercise from 1979 with other US alliances. Ground Self-Defence Force (GSDF) and Air Self-Defence Force (ASDF) also began to conduct joint exercises with their US counterparts after 1978. Smith, 'The Evolution of Military Cooperation in the U.S.-Japan Alliance', pp. 82–83.

14 The Fukuda Doctrine stipulated three principles in Japan's Southeast Asian policy; 1) to reject the role of a military power, 2) to promote mutual confidence based on heart to heart understanding, and 3) to become an equal partner of ASEAN while aiming at fostering mutual understanding with the nations of Indochina. Sueo Sudō, *The Fukuda Doctrine and ASEAN: New Dimensions in Japanese Foreign Policy*, Singapore: Institute of Southeast Asian Studies, 1992, pp. 4–5.

15 For instance, Japan and ASEAN established the Japan-ASEAN Forum in 1979, Japan-ASEAN Foreign Ministers Conference in 1978 and Japan-ASEAN Economic Ministers Conference in 1979. See Sudo, *The Fukuda Doctrine and ASEAN*, pp. 206–18.

16 For details, see Sōgō Anzenhoshō Kenkyū Group, *Sōgō Anzenhoshō Senryaku*, Tokyo: Ōkurashō Insatsukyoku, 1980, pp. 42–45. J. W. M. Chapman, R. Drifte and I. T. M. Gow (eds) *Japan's Quest for Comprehensive Security: Defence, Diplomacy, Dependence*, London: Pinter, 1983. Robert W. Barnett, *Beyond War: Japan's Concept of Comprehensive National Security*, Washington: Pergamon-Brassey's, 1984.

17 Thomas U. Berger, 'Alliance Politics and Japan's Postwar Culture of Anti-militarism', in Green and Cronin, *The U.S.-Japan Alliance*, p. 198.

18 Sōgō Anzenhoshō Kenkyu Group, *Sōgō Anzenhoshō Senryaku*, pp. 39–40.

19 Smith, 'The Evolution of Military Cooperation in the U.S.-Japan Alliance', pp. 73–74.

20 Etō and Yamamoto, *Sōgō Anpo*, pp. 260–67.

21 Keddell, *The Politics of Defense in Japan*, p. 114.

22 Akiko Fukushima, *Japanese Foreign Policy: The Emerging Logic of Multi-lateralism*, Basingstoke: Macmillan, 1999, p. 139.
23 Andrew Mack and Pauline Kerr, 'The Evolving Security Discourse in the Asia-Pacific', *Washington Quarterly*, vol. 18, no. 1, Winter 1995, pp. 123–24.
24 Masashi Nishihara, 'Ajiataiheiyō Chiiki to Takokukan Anzenhoshō Kyōryoku no Wakugumi: ASEAN Chiiki Forum wo Chyushinni', *Kokusai Mondai*, no. 415, October 1994, p. 63.
25 Pauline Kerr, 'The Security Dialogue in the Asia-Pacific', *The Pacific Review*, vol. 7, no. 4, 1994, p. 402.
26 For details of the US reaction, see Desmond Ball and Pauline Kerr, *Presumptive Engagement: Australia's Asia-Pacific Security Policy in the 1990s*, St. Leonards, NSW: Allen & U. (Australia), 1996, pp. 20–21.
27 Reinhard Drifte, *Japan's Foreign Policy for the 21st Century: From Economic Superpower to What Power?*, New York: St. Martin's Press, 1998, p. 83. *Nihon Keizai Shinbun*, July 24 1990, p. 2.
28 'Japan negative on Asia-Pacific security forum', *Japan Economic Newswire,* July 30, 1990, LexisNexis.
29 Michael Leifer, 'The ASEAN Peace Process: A Category Mistake', *The Pacific Review*, vol. 12, no. 1, 1999, p. 28.
30 Rosemary Foot, 'China in the ASEAN Regional Forum: Organizational Processes and Domestic Modes of Thought', *Asian Survey*, vol. 38, no. 5, 1998, p. 426.
31 Personal interview, Tokyo, April 16 2003.
32 Ibid. 'Japan ready to discuss security with USSR', *Japan Economic Newswire*, February 13 1990, LexisNexis.
33 *Yomiuri Shinbun*, April 13 1990, p. 3.
34 Personal interview, Tokyo, April 16 2003.
35 *Asahi Shinbun*, September 6 1990, p. 1 and November 13 1990, p. 1.
36 Personal interview, Tokyo, April 16 2003. Paul Midford, 'Japan's Leadership Role in East Asian Security Multilateralism: The Nakayama Proposal and the Logic of Reassurance', *The Pacific Review*, vol. 13, no. 3, 2000, p. 377.
37 *Yomiuri Shinbun*, May 4 1989, cited in Hiroshi Kimura, 'Gorbachev's Japan Policy: The Northern Territories Issues', *Asian Survey*, vol. 31, no. 9, 1991, p. 801.
38 Personal interviews, Tokyo, April 16 and 22 2003. *Asahi Shinbun*, May 26 1990, p. 1 and September 5 1990, p. 2.
39 *Asahi Shinbun*, May 26 1990, p. 1 and September 5 1990, p. 2.
40 Ministry of Foreign Affairs of Japan (MOFA), *Diplomatic Bluebook 1991*, Tokyo: Ministry of Foreign Affairs, 1991, p. 206. *Nikkei Shinbun*, September 15 1990, p. 2.
41 Statement by Foreign Minister Taro Nakayama at the 45th Session of the General Assembly of the United Nations, United Nations, New York, September 25 1990.
42 Personal interview, Tokyo, April 16 2003.
43 Yukio Satō, 'Asian Pacific Process for Stability and Security', in Ministry of Foreign Affairs of Japan (ed.) *Japan's Post Gulf International Initiatives*, Tokyo: Ministry of Foreign Affairs, 1991, pp. 35–36. See also MOFA, *Diplomatic Bluebook 1991*, pp. 69–70.
44 Satō, 'Asian Pacific Process', p. 43.
45 Ibid, p. 45.
46 Personal interview, Tokyo, April 16 2003.
47 Satō, 'Asian Pacific Process', pp. 42–43. Yukio Satō, 'Emerging Trends in Asia-Pacific Security: The Role of Japan', *The Pacific Review*, vol. 8, no. 2, 1995, p. 270.

48 Foreign Policy Speech by Foreign Minister Taro Nakayama to the 120th Session of the National Diet, January 25 1991.
49 Yukio Satō, '1995 Nen no Fushime ni Mukaate: Ajiataiheiyō Chiki no Anzenhoshō', *Gaikō Forum*, vol. 64, 1994, p. 14.
50 Nishihara, 'Ajiataiheiyō Chiiki', p. 64.
51 ASEAN-ISIS, *ASEAN-Isis Memorandum No. 1: a Time for Initiative: Proposals for the Consideration of the Fourth ASEAN Summit*, ASEAN Institutes of Strategic and International Studies, June 4 1991.
52 Nishihara, 'Ajiataiheiyō Chiiki', p. 64. Tsutomu Kikuchi, *APEC: Ajiataiehiyō Shinchitsujo no Mosaku*, Tokyo: Nihon Kokusai Mondai Kenkyujo, 1995, p. 268.
53 Personal interviews, Tokyo, April 16 2003. Satō, 'Asian Pacific Process', pp. 36–39.
54 Ibid. Satō, 'Asian Pacific Process', p. 43.
55 Personal interviews, Tokyo, April 16 and 22 2003.
56 Personal interview, Tokyo, April 16 2003.
57 Statement by Foreign Minister Taro Nakayama to the General Session of the ASEAN Post Ministerial Conference, Kuala Lumpur, July 22 1991.
58 Personal interview, Tokyo, April 16 2003. Midford, 'Japan's Leadership Role', p. 385.
59 Personal interview,Tokyo, April 16 2003. Nishihara, 'Ajia Taiheiyo Chiiki', p. 64.
60 Satō was stunned by the US negative reaction to the Nakayama proposal because he had consulted with US officials on the idea of promoting multilateral security dialogue since one year before the Nakayama proposal, and they actually supported Satō's idea. Personal interview, Tokyo, April 16 2003.
61 Midford, 'Japan's Leadership Role', p. 385.
62 Personal interview, Tokyo, April 16 2003.
63 'Japan's Security Forum idea receives cautious response', *Japan Economic Newswire*, July 22 1991, LexisNexis.
64 'ASEAN basically accepts Nakayama proposal', *Jiji Press Ticker Service*, July 23 1991, LexisNexis.
65 Takashi Inoguchi, *Japan's Foreign Policy in an Era of Global Change*, London: Pinter, 1993, pp. 139–46. Richard D. Leitch, Akira Kato, and Martin E. Weinstein, *Japan's Role in the Post-Cold War World*, Westport, Conn: Greenwood Press, 1995, pp. 34–35.
66 Policy Speech by Prime Minister Toshiki Kaifu to the 118th Session of the National Diet, March 2 1990.
67 Takakazu Kuriyama, 'Gekidō no 90 nenndai to Nihon Gaikō no Shinntenkai: Atarashī Kokusai Chitsujyo Kenchiku eno Sekkyokutekikōken no Tameni', *Gaikō Forum*, vol. 20, May 1990, p. 16.
68 Policy Speech by Prime Minister Toshiki Kaifu to the 120th Session of the National Diet, Tokyo, January 25 1991.
69 See Yoichi Funabashi, *Asia Pacific Fusion: Japan's Role in APEC*, Washington DC: Institute for International Economics, 1995, pp. 226–30.
70 Mike Mochizuki, *Japan: Domestic Change and Foreign Policy*, Santa Monica, CA: Rand, 1995, pp. 54–55.
71 Funabashi, *Asia Pacific Fusion*, p. 208.
72 Shunji Yanai, 'Funsōyobō e Seiji Anpotaiwa wa Kakudai: Hokutō Ajia dewa Kitachōsen nimo Sankayobikake', vol. 75, no. 13, *Sekai Shuhō*, April 5 1994, p. 25.
73 Yoshide Soeya, 'The Evolution of Japanese Thinking and Politics on Cooperative Security in the 1980s and 1990s', *Australian Journal of International Affairs*, vol. 48, no. 1, May 1994, p. 94.
74 MOFA, *Diplomatic Bluebook 1991*, pp. 12–13.
75 Personal interviews, Tokyo, April 16 and 22 2003.
76 Satō, 'Asian Pacific Process', p. 35.

77 MOFA, *Diplomatic Bluebook 1990*, Tokyo: Ministry of Foreign Affairs, 1990, pp. 9–10.
78 MOFA, *Diplomatic Bluebook 1991*, pp. 15–16.
79 Ibid, pp. 67–68.
80 For instance, see Midford, 'Japan's Leadership Role', pp. 377–78. Ashizawa Kuniko, 'Japan's Approach toward Asian Regional Security: From "Hub-and-Spoke" Bilateralism to "Multi-Tiered"', *The Pacific Review*, vol. 16, no. 3, 2003, p. 375.
81 Personal interviews, Tokyo, April 4, 16 and 22 2003.
82 Norman D. Levin, 'Prospects for U.S.-Japanese Security Cooperation', in Danny Unger and Paul Blackburn (eds) *Japan's Emerging Global Role*, Boulder, Colo: Lynne Rienner Publishers, 1993, p. 78.
83 Douglas T. Stuart and William T. Tow, *A US Strategy for the Asia-Pacific*, Adelphi Papers, no. 299, Oxford: Oxford University Press/IISS, 1995, pp. 7–10.
84 MOFA, *Diplomatic Bluebook 1990*, pp. 180–81.
85 MOFA, *Diplomatic Bluebook 1991*, p. 266.
86 Michael Leifer, *Singapore's Foreign Policy: Coping with Vulnerability*, London: Routledge, 2000, pp. 104–5.
87 See, for instance, Midford, 'Japan's Leadership Role', pp. 367–97.
88 Personal interviews, Tokyo, April 16 and 22 2003.
89 Yashuhiro Ueki, 'Japan's UN Diplomacy: Sources of Passivism and Activism', in Michael Blaker and Gerald L. Curtis (eds) *Japan's Foreign Policy after the Cold War : Coping with Change*, Armonk, NY: M. E. Sharpe, 1993, pp. 357–62. Courtney Purrington, 'Tokyo's Policy Responses during the Gulf War and the Impact of the "Iraqi Shock" on Japan', *Pacific Affairs*, vol. 65, no. 2, 1992, pp. 161–81.
90 Personal interviews, Tokyo, April 16 and 22 2003.
91 *Yomiuri Shinbun*, July 6 1991, p. 4.
92 *Yomiuri Shinbun*, October 27 1990, p. 2.
93 *Yomiuri Shinbun*, July 6 1991, p. 4.
94 Personal interviews, Tokyo, April 22 2003.

Chapter 2

1 Michael Leifer, *The ASEAN Regional Forum: Extending ASEAN's Model of Regional Security*, Adelphi Papers, no. 302, London: Oxford University Press, 1996, pp. 21–24.
2 Leszek Buszynski, 'Southeast Asia in the Post Cold War Era: Regionalism and Security', *Asian Survey*, vol. 32, no. 9, September 1992, pp. 834–38.
3 Leifer, *The ASEAN Regional Forum*, p. 19.
4 Michael Leifer, *Singapore's Foreign Policy: Coping with Vulnerability*, London: Routledge, 2000, pp. 126–35. Also based on a discussion with Michael Leifer. November 27 2000.
5 *Asahi Shinbun*, July 29 1992, p. 2. Paul Midford, 'Japan's Leadership Role in East Asian Security Multilateralism: The Nakayama Proposal and the Logic of Reassurance', *The Pacific Review*, vol. 13, no. 3, 2000, p. 387.
6 'Miyazawa's Speech on Asia-Pacific Policy', *The Daily Yomiuri*, January 17 1993, p. 2, LexisNexis.
7 *Asahi Shinbun*, February 18 1993, p. 3.
8 Leifer, *The ASEAN Regional Forum*, pp. 21–22.
9 Personal interview, Tokyo, April 16 2003. Toyoo Gyōten, Yukio Satō, and Takeshi Igarashi. 'Tōron: Clinton Seiken no Kadai to Nichibeikankei', *Kokusai Mondai*, no. 395, February 1993, pp. 7–8.

10 James Baker, The US and Japan Global Partners in a Pacific Community, Tokyo, September 11 1991.

11 *Yomiuri Shinbun*, January 10 1992, p. 6.

12 'Text of Prime Minister Miyazawa's Speech', *Japan's Economic Newswire*, July 3 1992, LexisNexis. Yukio Satō, '1995 nen no Fushime ni Mukatte: Ajiataiheyō Chiki no Anzenhoshyō', *Gaikō Forum*, no. 64, January 1994, pp. 15–16.

13 Personal interview, Tokyo, April 16 2003. Satō, '1995 nen no Fushime', p. 16.

14 Cited in Midford, 'Japan's Leadership Role', p. 387.

15 'Lord lays out 10 goals for US policy in East Asia', United States Information Service, Canberra, April 5 1993, p. 10, cited in Pauline Kerr, 'The Security Dialogue in the Asia-Pacific', *The Pacific Review*, vol. 7, no. 4, 1994, p. 402.

16 Leifer, *Singapore's Foreign Policy*, p. 135.

17 'Remarks by the President in Address to the National Assembly of the Republic of Korea', *U. S. Newswire*, July 10 1993, LexisNexis.

18 According to a retired MOFA official who led a series of these MOFA's initiatives, Anthony Lake, who was then Clinton's National Security Advisor and drafted Clinton's doctrine of the new pacific community, told him that the Clinton's doctrine was deeply influenced by Japan's concept of multifaceted approach. Personal interview, Tokyo, April 16 2003. This Japanese view was also implicitly expressed in the speech of Mutō Kabun delivered in the 1993 ASEAN-PMC. Muto stated that 'I welcome and commend the Clinton administration's attitude which attaches importance to the Asia-Pacific region. US ideas to employ multiple frameworks in an overlapping manner to meet with the diverse threats and take advantage of the opportunities in this region converge with what Japan has been advocating from the past. Japan thus welcomes that the US has adopted these ideas'. 'Statement By Foreign Minister Kabun Mutō, 26th ASEAN Post Ministerial Conference', Singapore, 26–28 July 1993.

19 Phillip C. Saunders, Roger Cliff and Daniel Byman, 'US Policy Options toward an Emerging China', *The Pacific Review*, vol. 12, no. 3, 1999, pp. 426–27.

20 'Remarks By the President in Address to the National Assembly of the Republic of Korea'.

21 'Chairman's Statement of the ASEAN Post-Ministerial Conferences Senior Official Meeting', Singapore, May 20–21 1993.

22 'Officials in ASEAN talks agree on need to include China in future meetings', *The Strait Times*, May 22 1993, LexisNexis. See also, Tsutomu Kikuchi, *APEC: Ajiataiehiyō Shinchitsujo no Mosaku*, Tokyo: Nihon Kokusai Mondai Kenkyujo, 1995, p. 273.

23 *Yomiuri Shinbun*, July 25 1993, p. 2.

24 Satō Yukio, for instance, argued that 'Soviet and Chinese participation in multilateral political dialogue should be realised gradually as they come to meet the conditions required'. Yukio Satō, 'Asian Pacific Process for Stability and Security', in Ministry of Foreign Affairs of Japan (MOFA) (ed.) *Japan's Post Gulf International Initiatives*, Tokyo: Ministry of Foreign Affairs of Japan, 1991, p. 43.

25 For the details of Chinese view of regional security multilateralism during the early 1990s, see Banning Garrett and Bonnie Glaser, 'Multilateral Security in the Asia-Pacific Region and Its Impact on Chinese Interests: Views from Beijing', *Contemporary Southeast Asia*, vol. 16, no. 1, June 1994, pp. 14–25.

26 Leifer, *The ASEAN Regional Forum*, pp. 28–29.

27 Ibid, p. 22.

28 *Yomiuri Shinbun*, December 25, 1992, p. 2, (evening edition).

29 Jiyuminshutō Anzenhoshō Kondankai, 'Reisengo no Anzenhoshō: 10 Kōmoku Teigen', *Kokubō*, no. 42, March 1993, pp. 18–27.

30 Bōei Mondai Kondankai, *Nihon no Anzenhoshō to Bōeiryoku no Arikata :Nijūisseiki e Mukete no Tenbō*, Tokyo: Ōkurashō Insatsukyoku, 1994.

31 MOFA, *Diplomatic Bluebook 1994*, Tokyo: Ministry of Foreign Affairs, 1994, available at: http://www.mofa.go.jp/policy/other/bluebook/index.html (accessed 15/09/06).

32 Personal interviews, Tokyo, March 5 (no. 2), 7, April 4 and 22 2003.

33 Yuji Miyamoto, 'Ajiataiheiyō no Anzenhoshō no Wakugumi Kōchiku e Mukete', *Gaikō Forum*, no. 56, May 1993, pp. 13–21.

34 Personal interview, Tokyo, April 22 2003. Michael J. Green, *Japan's Reluctant Realism: Foreign Policy Challenges in an Era of Uncertain Power*, New York and Basingstoke: Palgrave, 2001, p. 194.

35 *Yomiuri Shinbun*, August 24 1993, p. 2.

36 Japan Defence Agency, *Defence of Japan 1997*, Tokyo: Japan Defence Agency, 1997, pp. 78–80.

37 Personal interviews, London, August 9 2002 and Tokyo, April 22 2003. Yoichi Funabashi, *Ajiataiheiyō Fyūjhon: APEC to Nihon*, Tokyo: Chuōkōronsha, 1995, p. 346.

38 For the detailed discussions of the origin, development and roles of CSCAP, see Paul M. Evans, 'Building Security: The Council for Security Cooperation in the Asia Pacific (CSCAP)', *The Pacific Review*, vol. 7, no. 2, 1994, pp. 125–39. Sheldon W. Simon, 'Evaluating Track II Approaches to Security Diplomacy in the Asia-Pacific: The CSCAP Experience', *The Pacific Review*, vol. 15, no. 2, 2002, pp. 167–200. CSCAP has organised four working groups, such as maritime cooperation, security cooperation in North Pacific, CBMs and transparency. China has entered to CSCAP as a full member since 1996. Taiwan and North Korea have participated in some of those working group meetings since 1997.

39 For details, see Akiko Fukushima, 'Multilateral Confidence Building Measures in Northeast Asia: Receding or Emerging', The Henry L. Stimson Center, 2000, pp. 50–52, available at: http://www.stimson.org/about/pubs.cfm (accessed 15/09/06).

40 Ibid, p. 51.

41 Michael Leifer, 'The ASEAN Peace Process: A Category Mistake', *The Pacific Review*, vol. 12, no. 1, 1999, pp. 27–28. For a detailed discussion on the concept of cooperative security, see David Dewitt, 'Common, Comprehensive, and Cooperative Security', *The Pacific Review*, vol. 7, no. 1, 1994, pp. 1–15.

42 For instance, see Takako Ueda, 'Ōshu Anzenhoshō no Hendō to Kyōchoteki Anzenhoshō Kōzō: Ōshu Anzenhoshō Kyōryoku Kaigi Kitataiseiyō Kyōryoku Rijikai (Reisen to Sonogo)', *Kokusai Seiji*, no. 100, August 1992, pp. 126–51. Hiroshi Momose and Takako Ueda, *Ōshu Anzenhoshō Kyōryoku Kaigi CSCE: 1975–92*, Tokyo: Nihon Kokusai Mondai Kenkyujo, 1992. Bōei Mondai Kondankai, *Nihon no Anzenhoshō*. Shunji Yanai, 'Reisengo no Wakugumi no Anzenhoshō seisaku: Kokusaikankyō no Henka to Sono Eikyō', *Gaikō Forum*, July 1995, pp. 44–50. Yoshinobu Yamamoto, 'Kyōchoteki Anzenhoshō no Kanōsei', *Kokusai Mondai*, no. 425, August 1995, pp. 2–20. Takako Ueda, 'Kyōchoteki Anzenhoshō towa Nanika: Posuto Reisenki Ōshu no Mosaku', *Sekai*, no. 611, August 1995, pp. 257–66.

43 Glenn D. Hook, Julie Gilson, Christopher W. Hughes, and Hugo Dobson, *Japan's International Relations: Politics, Economics and Security*, London: Routledge, 2001, pp. 168–70.

44 Yoshihide Soeya, 'Japan: Normative Constraints versus Structural Imperatives', in Muthiah Alagappa (ed.) *Asian Security Practice: Material and Ideational Influences*, Stanford, Ca.:Stanford University Press, 1998, p. 204.

45 Between 1988 and 1994, for instance, China's official defence budget more than doubled, and total expenditure between 1993 and 1994 was estimated at $21.76 billion according to the International Institute for Strategic Studies (IISS).

Cited in David L. Shambaugh, 'Growing Strong: China's Challenge to Asian Security', *Survival*, vol. 36, no. 2, Summer 1994, p. 54.

46 Nicholas D. Kristof, 'The Rise of China', *Foreign Affairs*, vol. 72, no. 5, November/December 1993, p. 66.

47 *Yomiuri Shinbun*, July 22 1992, p. 2 and May 23 1993, p. 1. Satoshi Morimoto, 'Roshia, Chūgoku tono Anpotaiwa wa Kōsusumeyo', *Sekai Shūhō*, April 5 1994, vol. 75, no. 13, p. 28. The 1993 Japan Defence White Paper also mentioned the trend of the build up of China's military capability. Japan Defence Agency, *Defence of Japan 1993*, Tokyo: Japan Defence Agency, 1993, pp. 50–51.

48 'Japan Warns China Against Aircraft Carrier Purchase', *Japan's Economic Newswire*, September 7 1992, LexisNexis.

49 *Yomiuri Shinbun*, June 1 1993, p. 1, (evening edition)

50 Denny Roy, 'Hegemon on the Horizon? China's Threat to East Asian Security', *International Security*, vol. 19, no. 1, summer 1994, p. 162.

51 Soeya, 'Japan', p. 204.

52 *Asahi Shinbun*, August 3, 1992.

53 Desmond Ball, 'Arms and Affluence: Military Acquisitions in the Asia-Pacific Region', *International Security*, vol. 18, no. 3, Winter 1993/94, pp. 78–112.

54 'Arms build up in Southeast Asia not a race', *The Strait Times*, March 20 1993, LexisNexis.

55 Ball, 'Arms and Affluence', pp. 80–81.

56 Ibid, pp. 86–87. Malcom Chalmers, 'Openness and Security Policy in South-East Asia', *Survival*, vol. 38, no. 3, Autumn 1998, pp. 82–83.

57 Personal interviews, Tokyo, February 8 2002 (no. 1) and April 22 2003. Shige-katsu Kondō, 'Reisengo no Ajiataiheiyō Chiiki no Anzenhoshō wo Ikani Kakuho Suruka', *Shin-Bōeironshū*, vol. 20, no. 1, June 1992, pp. 65–66. Satoshi Morimoto, 'Ajiataiheiyō no Anzenhoshō to sono Wakugumi', *Gaikō Jihō*, no. 1302, October 1993. pp. 9–10. Yutaka Kawashima, *Ajiataihiyō no Anzenhoshō Taiwa: ARF no Kaishi to Kongo no Tenbō*, 1994, unpublished paper.

58 See, MOFA, *Diplomatic Bluebook 1993*, Tokyo: Ministry of Foreign Affairs of Japan, 1993, pp. 11–12.

59 Paul Bracken, 'Nuclear Weapons and State Survival in North Korea', *Survival*, vol. 35, no. 3, Autumn 1993, pp. 139–40.

60 Christopher W. Hughes, *Japan's Economic Power and Security: Japan and North Korea*, New York: Routledge, 1999, pp. 61–65.

61 Christopher W. Hughes, 'The North Korean Nuclear Crisis and Japanese Security', *Survival*, vol. 38, no. 2, Summer 1996, pp. 83–84.

62 Bōeicho, *Heisei 7 nendoban Bōeihakusho*, Tokyo: Okurasho Insatsukyoku, 1995, p. 43.

63 Personal interviews, Tokyo, April 16 and 22 2003.

64 Personal interviews, Tokyo, March 17, April 16 and 22 2003. See also Satō, '1995 nen no Fushime', p. 20. Shunji Yanai, 'Funsō Yobō e Seiji Anpo Taiwa wo Kakudai', *Sekai Shuhō*, vol. 75, no. 13, 1994, pp. 24–25.

65 *Asahi Shinbun*, August 3 1992, p. 1, (evening edition). Morimoto, 'Ajiataiheiyō', pp. 9–10. Nihon Kokusai Forum, *Seisaku Teigen: Chūgoku no Shōrai to Ajia no Anzenhoshō Atarashii Nitchū Kankei o Mezashite*, Tokyo: Nihon Kokusai Forum, 1995, pp. 31–32.

66 *Yomiuri Shinbun*, Decemeber 3 1992, p. 1, (evening edition).

67 *Asahi Shinbun*, May 26 1993, p. 1.

68 Thomas J. Christensen, 'China, the U.S.-Japan Alliance, and the Security Dilemma in East Asia', *International Security*, vol. 23, no. 4, Spring 1999, p. 71.

69 Tsuyoshi Kawasaki, 'Between Realism and Idealism in Japanese Security Policy: The Case of the ASEAN Regional Forum', *The Pacific Review*, vol. 10, no. 4, 1997, pp. 493–94.

70 Satō, '1995 nen no Fushime', p. 20.
71 Michael J. Green and Benjamin L. Self, 'Japan's Changing China Policy: From Commercial Liberalism to Reluctant Realism', *Survival*, vol. 38, no. 2, pp. 35–36.
72 *Nihon Keizai Shinbun*, August 8 1995, p. 8.
73 Personal interviews, London, August 9 2002 and Tokyo, April 16 2003.
74 Masaharu Kōnō, 'In Search for Proactive Diplomacy: Increasing Japan's Diplomacy Role in the 1990's: With Cambodia and the ASEAN Regional Forum(ARF) as Case Studies', *CNAPs Working Paper*, The Brookings Institution, Fall 1999, available at: http://www.brookings.edu/fp/cnaps/papers/1999_kono.htm (accessed 15/09/06).
75 Personal interviews, Tokyo, December 13 2000 (no. 1) and April 22 2003. Miyamoto, 'Ajia Taiheiyo'. A similar expectation for the role of a region-wide security framework for addressing specific regional security disputes was also expressed by the report presented by Prime Minister Miyazawa's Advisory Committee in 1992. The report suggested that regional countries establish a multilateral security framework, which could play a conflict resolution role. *Yomiuri Shinbun*, November 25 1992, p. 2.
76 Kōnō, 'In Search for Proactive Diplomacy'.
77 MOFA, *Diplomatic Bluebook 1994*, available at: http://www.mofa.go.jp/policy/other/bluebook/1994/index.html (accessed 15/09/06).
78 Yanai, 'Reisengo no Wakugumi', pp. 48–49.
79 Ibid, pp. 45–46.
80 Matake Kamiya, 'Ajiataiehiyō ni Okeru Jyūsōteki Anzenhoshō Kōzō ni mukatte: Takokukan Kyōchō Taisei no Genkai to Nichibei Anpotaisei no Yakuwari', *Kokusai Seiji*, no. 115, May 1997, pp. 144–60.

Chapter 3

1 'ASEAN – Uncharted waters', *Far Eastern Economic Review*, August 5, 1993, p. 11, LexisNexis.
2 TAC was concluded by ASEAN states in 1976 to demonstrate a corporate political identity and to codify norms for managing regional order. It enunciated a number of principles, such as respect for independence and sovereignty, non-interference in domestic affairs of states, and renunciation of the threat or use of force in settling disputes. It originated from ASEAN's 1971 declaration of a Zone of Peace, Freedom and Neutrality (ZOFAN), which called for regional autonomy and responsibility for managing regional order with guarantees of non-intervention to be secured from outside powers. For details, Michael Leifer, *ASEAN and the Security of South-East Asia*, International Politics in Asia Series, London: Routledge, 1989, pp. 163–64.
3 'Chairman's Statement, 'ASEAN Post-Ministerial Conferences Senior Official Meeting', Singapore, May 20–21 1993.
4 'ASEAN – Uncharted waters'.
5 ASEAN Regional Forum (ARF), 'Chairman's Statement, the First Meeting of the ASEAN Regional Forum', Bangkok, July 25 1994.
6 Michael Leifer, *The ASEAN Regional Forum: Extending ASEAN's Model of Regional Security*, Adelphi Papers, no. 302, London: Oxford University Press, 1996, pp. 33–35.
7 Australian Paper on Practical Proposals for Security Cooperation in the Asia Pacific in the Asia-Pacific Region, commissioned by the 1993 ASEAN PMC SOM, Canberra, April 1994.
8 Canadian Papers on 'No. 1. Preventive Diplomacy and Conflict Management' and 'No. 2. Non Proliferation', paper presented to ARF SOM, May 23–25 1994, Bangkok.

9 Republic of Korea's Paper on Northeast Asia Security Cooperation, paper presented to ARF SOM.
10 Leifer, *The ASEAN Regional Forum*, p. 32.
11 'First ASEAN regional security forum ends with vague roadmap', *Deutsche Presse-Agentur*, July 25 1994, LexisNexis.
12 For further discussions on the ASEAN Way, see Amitav Acharya, 'Ideas, Identity and Institution-Building: From the "ASEAN Way" to the "Asia-Pacific Way"', *The Pacific Review*, vol. 10, no. 3, 1997, pp. 328–33. Shaun Narine, 'ASEAN and the ARF: The Limits of the ASEAN Way', *Asian Survey*, vol. 37, no. 10, 1997, pp. 964–65.
13 Leifer, *The ASEAN Regional Forum*, p. 25.
14 'Singapore proposes a gradual approach', *The Straits Times*, July 23 1994, p. 1, LexisNexis.
15 Amitav Acharya, 'Culture, Security, Multilateralism: The ASEAN Way and Regional Order', in Keith Krause (ed.) *Culture and Security: Multilateralism, Arms Control, and Security Building*, Portland, OR: Frank Cass, 1998, p. 74.
16 Masashi Nishihara, 'Ajiataiheiyō Chiiki to Takokukan Anzenhoshō Kyōryoku no Wakugumi: ASESN Chiiki Forum wo Chyushin ni', *Kokusai Mondai*, no. 415, October 1994, p. 66, personal interview, Tokyo, April 22 2003.
17 Gaimushō Ajia-Kyoku Chiiki Seisaku-Ka (Ministry of Foreign Affairs of Japan, Asian Bureau, Regional Policy Division), 'Dai 1-Kai ARF Kōkyū Jimu-level Kaigō, Gaiyō to Hyōka'. (First ARF SOM, Summary and Assessment), May 27 1994.
18 Leifer, *The ASEAN Regional Forum*, p. 31.
19 Ministry of Foreign Affairs of Japan (MOFA), 'Japan's Views Concerning the ASEAN Regional Forum (ARF)', paper presented to ARF SOM, May 23–25 1994, Bangkok.
20 Japan Defense Agency, *Defense of Japan 1995*, Tokyo: Japan Defense Agency, 1995, p. 30.
21 MOFA, 'Japan's Views Concerning the ASEAN Regional Forum'.
22 Ibid.
23 Personal interviews, Tokyo, March 5 (no. 1) and 17 2003.
24 ARF, 'Chairman's Statement, the First Meeting of the ASEAN Regional Forum'.
25 For instance, Australia convened a workshop on 'the Building of Confidence and Trust' in Canberra in November 1994 while South Korea held an ARF workshop on PD in Seoul in early May 1995.
26 Gaimushō Ajia-Kyoku Chiki Seisaku-Ka, 'Dai 1-Kai ASEAN Chiiki Forum, Gaiyō to Hyōka' (First ARF Ministerial Meeting, Summary and Assessment), July 27 1994.
27 'Japan hopes to play visible but modest role in ARF', *Japan Economic Newswire*, July 29 1995, LexisNexis.
28 ARF, 'Chairman's Statement, The Second ASEAN Regional Forum, Bandar Seri Begawan, Brunei Darussalam', August 1 1995.
29 Gaimushō, 'Dai 2-Kai ASEAN Chiiki Forum no Gaiyō to Hyōka' (Second ARF Ministerial Meeting, Summary and Assessment), August 4 1995, *Asahi Shinbun*, August 1 1995, p. 2.
30 Leifer, *The ASEAN Regional Forum*, p. 42.
31 Personal interview, Tokyo, March 7 2003.
32 ARF, 'A Concept Paper', Bandar Seri Begawan, Brunei Darussalam, August 1 1995.
33 Ibid. The term 'immediate future' and 'medium and long term' written in the Concept Paper were not defined, but according to ARF senior officials Annex A should be achieved within one to two years whereas some of the measures in

Annex B could take from three to five years. Some preventive diplomacy measures would be put into place within about five years and some conflict resolution mechanisms in about ten years. See Desmond Ball, 'Multilateral Security Cooperation in the Asia-Pacific Region: Challenges in the Post-Cold War Era', in Hung-mao Tian and Tun-jen Cheng (eds) *The Security Environment in the Asia-Pacific*, Armonk, NY: M. E. Sharpe, 2000, pp. 139–40.

34 Leifer, *The ASEAN Regional Forum*, pp. 40–41.

35 'Canada Prepare for the ARF-SOM', *CANCAPS Bulletin*, no. 6, May 1995, p. 6.

36 *The Nikkei Weekly*, May 29 1995, p. 29, LexisNexis.

37 'ASEAN Regional Forum reaches agreement on group's role', *Japan Economic Newswire*, May 24 1995, LexisNexis.

38 'ARF officials disagree over forum's future role', *Japan Economic Newswire*, May 23 1995, LexisNexis.

39 Leifer, *The ASEAN Regional Forum*, p. 41.

40 Gaimushō, *Gaikō Seisho 1995*, p. 195.

41 Personal interview, Tokyo, Dec 13 2000 (no. 2) and April 22 2003. Michael Leifer, *The ASEAN Regional Forum. A Model for Cooperative Security in the Middle East?*, Canberra: Research School of Pacific and Asian Studies, Australian National University, 1998, p. 8.

42 Rosemary Foot, 'China's Role and Attitude', in Khoo How San (ed.) *The Future of the ARF*, Singapore: Institute of Defence and Strategic Studies, 1999, p. 121.

43 Leifer, *The ASEAN Regional Forum*, p. 55.

44 Gaimushō, 'Dai 2-Kai ASEAN Chiki Forum no Gaiyō to Hyōka' (Second ARF Ministerial Meeting, Summary and Assessment), August 4 1995.

45 Gaimusho Anzenhosho Seisaku-Ka (MOFA, National Security Policy Division), 'Shinrai Jyōsei ni Kansuru ARF Inter-Sessional Shien Kaigō, Gaiyō oyobi Hyōka' (ARF ISG on CBMs, Summary and Assessment), January 25 1996.

46 Ibid.

47 ARF, 'Summary report of the ARF Inter-Sessional Meeting on Confidence Building Measures', January 18–19 1996, Tokyo, Japan and April 15–16, Jakarta, 1996, Indonesia.

48 Gaimushō, 'ARF ISG Kisha Brief' (ARF ISG on CBMs, Transcripts of Press Conference), January 19 1996.

49 Jusuf Wanandi, 'ASEAN's China Strategy: Towards Deeper Engagement', *Survival*, vol. 38, no. 3, Autumn 1996, p. 124.

50 Gaimushō, 'ARF ISG Kisha Brief'.

51 'ARF hoping to craft registry to head off Asian arms race', *Japan Economic Newswire*, January 25 1996, LexisNexis.

52 Mitsuro Donowaki, 'Ajia ni Okeru Shinrai Jyōsei to Nichibei Dōmei, Sōgo-hokan Kankei ni Tatsu ASEAN Chiiki Forum to Shin Guideline', *Human Security*, no. 2, 1997, pp. 12–13.

53 Hiroshi Yasui, 'Ajiataiheiyō Chiiki ni okeru CBM no Shinten to Shomondai', in Nihon Kokusai Mondai Kenkyujo (ed.) *Ajiataiheiyō no Anzenhoshō (Chūkan Hōkoku)*, Nihon Kokusai Mondai Kenkyujo, March 1999, p. 134, unpublished paper.

54 Alastair Iain Johnston, 'The Myth of the ASEAN Way?: Explaining the Evolution of the ASEAN Regional Forum', in Helga Haftendorn, Robert O. Keohane and Celeste A. Wallander (eds) *Imperfect Unions :Security Institutions over Time and Space*, Oxford: Oxford University Press, 1999, p. 314.

55 ARF, 'Chairman's Statement, The Third Meeting of the ASEAN Regional Forum', Jakarta, July 23 1996.

56 Bōeicho Bōei Seisaku-Ka, 'Kāppatsuka suru Takokukan Anzenhoshō Taiwa', *Securitarian*, February 20–27 1997, p. 16.

57 Foot, 'China in the ASEAN Regional Forum', p. 426–29.
58 *Asahi Shinbun,* July 24 1996, p. 2.
59 Ibid, p. 3.
60 Makoto Matsuda, 'ARF no Chūchōkiteki Arikata', in Nihon Kokusai Mondai Kenkyujo (ed.) *Ajiataiheiyō no Anzenhoshō, Heisei 8-nendo Jishu Kenkyu Hōkoksho,* Nihon Kokusai Mondai Kenkyujo March 1997, pp. 30–45, unpublished paper. The aim of the workshop, involving security analyst and officials from MOFA and JDA, was to explore the initiatives and approaches that Japan should take for the ARF's future development. In March 1997, the first report of this workshop was issued, which consisted of a number of papers submitted by the participants. Although the report is not a kind of an official document, it is a useful reflection of how Japanese officials actually viewed the ARF three years after its formation.
61 Ibid, p. 33.
62 Ibid, pp. 33–34.
63 Ibid, pp. 35–36.
64 Gaimushō Anzenhoshō Seisaku-Ka, 'Dai 4-Kai ARF Kōkyū Jimu Level Kaigō (SOM) Hyōka to Gaiyō' (Fourth ARF SOM, Assessment and Summary), May 26 1997.
65 Gaimushō, Anzenhoshō Seisaku-Ka, 'Dai 4-Kai ASEAN Chiiki Forum Kakuryō Kaigō' (Fourth ARF Ministerial Meeting), July 27 1997.
66 ARF, 'Chairman's Statement, the Fourth Meeting of the ASEAN Regional Forum', Subang Jaya, Malaysia, July 27 1997.
67 'ARF cool to proposal to endorse S. China Sea declaration', *Japan Economic Newswire,* March 10 1997, LexisNexis.
68 Makoto Matsuda, 'Kokuren Gunbi Tōrokuseido', in Nihon Kokusai Mondai Kenkyujo, *Ajiataiheiyō no Anzenhoshō, Heisei 8-nendo Jishu Kenkyu Hōkokusho,* p. 103, unpublished paper.
69 The statement of Press Secretary of the Ministry of Foreign Affairs on Workshop on Transparency in Armaments, May 6 1997, available at: http://www.mofa.go.jp/announce/announce/archive_1/arma.html (accessed 15/09/06).
70 Gaimushō, 'Hōjin Kisha Brief'.
71 China was loath to support the inclusion of data for procurement through national production in the UNRCA since it would force Beijing to reveal information on its domestic arms industry. Malcom Chalmers, 'The debate on a regional arms register in Southeast Asia', *The Pacific Review,* vol. 10, no. 1, 1997, p. 120.
72 'ARF cool to proposal to endorse S. China Sea declaration'.
73 ARF, 'Summary Report of the ARF ISG on Confidence Building Measures', Beijing, March 6–8 1997.
74 Rosemary Greaves (Director, Regional Security Section, Department of Foreign Affairs and Trade), 'The Fourth Meeting of ASEAN Regional Forum', *Aus-CSCAP Newsletter,* no. 5, October 1997, p. 2.
75 ARF, 'Chairman's Statement, the Fifth ASEAN Regional Forum', Manila, July 27 1998.
76 ARF, 'Distillation of Agreed CBMs from the First up to the Fourth ARF', Annex E to the Chairman's Statement of the Fifth Meeting of the ASEAN Regional Forum.
77 Personal interview, February 28 2002.
78 ARF, 'List of new ARF CBMs', Annex F to the Chairman's Statement of the Fifth Meeting of the ASEAN Regional Forum.
79 Personal interviews, Tokyo, Dec 13 2000 (no. 2) and February 28 2002.
80 ARF, 'Co-Chairmen's summary report of the meetings of the ARF Intersessional Support Group on Confidence Building Measures held in Bandar Seri

Begawan, Brunei Darussalam on November 4–6 1997 and in Sydney, Australia on March 4–6 1998'.

81 ARF, 'Chairman's Statement, the Fifth ASEAN Regional Forum'.

82 Alan Dupont, 'An Australian Perspective', in Khoo How San, *The Future of the ARF*, pp. 40–43.

83 Personal interviews, Tokyo, December 13 2000 (no. 2) and February 28 2002. Yasui, 'Ajiataiheiyōchiiki ni okeru CBM', pp. 134–35.

84 ARF, 'Co-Chairmen's summary report of the meetings of the ARF Intersessional Support Group on Confidence Building Measures held in Brunei and Australia'.

85 'China Pulls out of U.N. Arms Register over Taiwan',*Inter Press Service*, November 11 1998, LexisNexis.

86 Personal interview, Tokyo, December 13 2000 (no. 2). Mibae, 'ARF no Genjō to Kadai', in Nihon Kokusai Mondai Kenkyujo, *Ajiataiheiyō no Anzenhoshō*, pp. 112–13.

87 Gaimushō, 'Yomiuri Shinbun, Tokyo Kaigi Shusai Kokusaientaku Kaigi ni okeru Kōmura Gaimu Daijin Kichōkouen, Ajia wo Anzen ni suru Hou' (speech delivered by Foreign Minister Masahiko Komura at Tokyo Colloquium 98 International Roundtable, an international forum on Asia), October 31 1998, available at: http://www.mofa.go.jp/mofaj/press/enzetsu/ (accessed 15/09/06).

88 ARF countries convened a first meeting of Maritime Specialist Officials (MSOM) in conjunction with the second ISG meeting held in Honolulu in November 1998.

89 ARF, 'Co-Chairmen's Summary Report of the Meetings of the ARF Intersessional Support Group On Confidence Building Measures held in Honolulu, USA, November 4–6 1998, and in Bangkok, Thailand, March 3–5 1999'.

90 Ibid.

91 'China publishes defence paper', *Financial Times*, July 28 1998, LexisNexis.

92 Gaimushō Anzenhoshō Seisaku-Ka, 'ARF SOM Gaiyou to Hyouka' (Sixth ARF SOM, Summary and Assessment), May 24 1999, personal interview, Tokyo, February 28 2002.

93 Gaimushō, 'Kōmura Daijin no ARF oyobi ASEAN PMC Shuseki, Kisha Brief' (Foreign Minister Komura in the Sixth ARF Ministerial Meeting and ASEAN PMC, Transcripts of Press Conference), July 27 1999. In the ASEAN+1 Summit Meeting held in Manila in November 1999, Japan's Prime Minister, Obuchi Keizō, proposed holding a conference of coast guard authorities to discuss how best regional countries can enhance coordination and cooperation among the countries concerned to tackle piracy. In April 2000, Japan hosted 'Regional Conference on Combating Piracy and Armed Robbery against Ships', *Yomiuri Shinbun*, November 29 1999, p. 2.

94 ARF, 'Chairman's Statement, the Sixth Meeting of the ASEAN Regional Forum', Singapore, 26 July 1999.

95 ARF, 'Chairman's Statement, the Seventh Meeting of the ASEAN Regional Forum', Bangkok, July 27 2000.

96 Gaimushō Anzenhoshō Seisaku-Ka, 'Dai 7-Kai ASEAN Chiiki Forum Kakuryō Kaigō, Gaiyō to Hyōka' (Seventh ARF Ministerial Meeting, Summery and Assesment), August 4 2000.

97 For details, see ARF, 'Future Direction of the ARF', adopted at the Ninth ASEAN Regional Forum, Bandar Seri Begawan, Brunei Darussalam, 31 July 2002.

98 Examples of proposed cooperation in this field, for instance, include: 1) providing technical assistance and capacity-building infrastructure to countries, 2) extending training and providing equipment to enhance the ability of ARF countries to share information, 3) instituting regional ARF cooperation and

training in anti-piracy and security, and 4) establishing a legal framework for regional cooperation in this field. For more details, see ARF, 'Statement on Cooperation Against Piracy and Other Threats to Maritime Security', June 18 2003.

99 Personal interviews, Tokyo, December 19 2002 and May 30 2003.

100 Gaimushō, 'ARF Kakuryō Kaigō, Kisha Brief' (Ninth AR Ministerial Meeting, Transcripts of Japanese Press Conference), August 1, 2002.

101 ARF, 'Chairman's Statement, the Ninth Meeting of the ASEAN Regional Forum', Bandar Seri Begwan, July 31 2002.

102 See ARF, 'ARF Security Policy Conference – an agreed concept paper', Jakarta, July 2 2004.

103 The First ASPC was held in Beijing November 2004 and the Second ASPC in Vientiane May 2005. See, ARF, 'Chairman Summery of the Second ASEAN Regional Forum Security Policy Conference', Vientiane, May 19 2005.

104 ARF, 'Chairman's Statement, the Twelfth Meeting of the ASEAN Regional Forum', Vientiane, July 29 2005.

Chapter 4

1 Boutros Boutros-Ghali, *An Agenda for Peace: Preventive Diplomacy, Peace-making and Peace-Keeping*, United Nations, New York, 1992, p. 11.

2 CSCAP Singapore, 'Review of Preventive Diplomacy Activities in the Asia-Pacific Region', in Desmond Ball and Amitav Acharya (eds) *The Next Stage: Preventive Diplomacy and Security Cooperation in the Asia-Pacific Region*, Canberra: Strategic and Defence Studies Centre Research School of Pacific and Asian Studies, The Australian National University, 1999, pp. 293–94.

3 Amitav Acharya, 'Preventive Diplomacy: Background and Application to the Asia-Pacific Region', in Ball and Acharya, *The Next Stage*, pp. 19–20.

4 ASEAN Regional Forum (ARF), 'Second ARF Seminar on Preventive Diplomacy: Chairman's Statement', Paris, 7–8 November 1996.

5 ARF, 'A Concept Paper', Bandar Seri Begawan, Brunei Darussalam, August 1 1995.

6 ARF, 'Second ARF Seminar on Preventive Diplomacy'.

7 Desmond Ball, 'Introduction', in Ball and Acharya, *The Next Stage*, p. 4.

8 Personal interviews, Tokyo, April 22 2003. Satoshi Morimoto, 'Ajiataiheiyō ni okeru Yobōgaikō to CBM', in Nihon Kokusai Mondai Kenkyujo (ed.) *Ajiataiheiyō no Anzenhoshō (Chūkan Hōkoku)*, Nihon Kokusai Mondai Kenkyujo, March 1999, p. 138, unpublished paper.

9 Mitsurō Dōnowaki, *Yobō Gaikō Nyūmon: Reisengo no Heiwa no Atarashii Kanūsei wo Saguru*, Tokyo: Nihon Kokusai Forum, 1999, p. 100.

10 Personal interviews, Tokyo, December 13 2000 (no. 1, 2, 3), February 28 2002, and May 30 2003. Taisuke Mibae, 'ARF no Genjō to Kadai', in Nihon Kokusai Mondai Kenkyujo, *Ajiataiheiyō no Anzenhoshō*, p. 117, unpublished paper.

11 Personal interviews, Tokyo, December 13 2000 (no. 1. 2. 3), February 28 2002, and May 30 2003.

12 Personal interviews, Tokyo, February 28 2002 and May 30 2003.

13 Alastair Iain Johnston and Paul Evans, 'China's Engagement with Multilateral Security Institutions', in Alastair I. Johnston and Robert S. Ross (eds) *Engaging China: The Management of an Emerging Power*, London: Routledge, 1999, p. 259.

14 Shi Chunlai, 'Preventive Diplomacy and the Asia-Pacific Region', in Ball *et al.*, *The Next Stage*, pp. 183–84.

15 'Chinese Foreign Minister urges ASEAN Forum to Focus on Confidence', *Xinhua News Service*, July 26, 1999, LexisNexis.

16 Makoto Matsuda, 'ARF no Chūchōkiteki Arikata', in Nihon Kokusai Mondai Kenkyujo (ed.) *Ajiataiheiyō no Anzenhoshō (Chūkan Hōkoku), Heisei 8 nendo Jishu Kenkyu Hōkoksho*, Nihon Kokusai Mondai Kenkyujo, March 1997, pp. 34–35, unpublished paper.

17 Gaimushō Anzenhoshō Seisaku-Ka (Ministry of Foreign Affairs of Japan, National Security Policy Division), 'Dai 4-Kai ARF Kōkyū Jimulevel Kaigō', Gaiyō to Hyōka' (Forth ARF SOM, Summery and Assessment), May 26 1997.

18 Ibid.

19 Personal interviews, Tokyo, December 13 2000 (no. 2 and 3) and February 28 2002.

20 Gaimushō, Anzenhoshō Seisaku-Ka, 'Dai 4-Kai ARF Kōkyu Jimulevel Kaigō, Gaiyō to Hyōka'.

21 *Nihon Keizai Shinbun*, July 28 1997, p. 8.

22 ARF, 'Chairman's statement, the Fourth ASEAN Regional Forum'.

23 'ARF ministers debate S. Asian nuclear tests, crisis', *Japan Economic Newswire*, July 27 1998, LexisNexis.

24 ARF, 'Chairman's Statement, The Fifth Meeting of the ASEAN Regional Forum,' Manila, July 27 1998.

25 See ARF, 'Chairman's report of Track Two Conference on Preventive Diplomacy', Singapore, September 9–11, 1997.

26 ARF, 'Co-chairmen's summary report of the Meetings of the ARF Inter-sessional Support Group on confidence building measures held in Honolulu, USA, November 4–6 1998, and in Bangkok, Thailand, March 3–5 1999'.

27 ARF, 'Chairman's Statement, the Sixth ASEAN Regional Forum', Singapore, July 26 1999.

28 Personal interview, Tokyo, February 28 2002. 'ASEAN-ARF members to move to conflict prevention – accord reached after three days of talks', *Bangkok Post*, March 5 1999, LexisNexis.

29 Mibae, 'ARF no Genjō to Kadai', p. 118. A similar view was also expressed by another MOFA official in charge of the ARF. See Takashi Okada, 'Ajiataiheiyō ni okeru Shinraijōseisochi (CBM)', in Nihon Kokusai Mondai Kenkyujo (ed.) *Ajiataiheiyō no Anzenhoshō, Heisei 8-nendo Jishu Kenkyu Houkoksho*, pp. 51–52, unpublished paper.

30 Simon S. C. Tay with Obood Talib, 'The ASEAN Regional Forum: Preparing for Preventive Diplomacy', *Contemporary Southeast Asia*, vol. 19, no.3, December 1997, p. 262.

31 Jusuf Wanandi, 'Boost ARF-and security', *Asiaweek*, 24, July 31 1998, p. 25.

32 Gaimushō Anzenhoshō Seisaku-Ka, 'ARF SOM Gaiyō to Hyōka' (Sixth ARF SOM, Summary and Assessment), May 24, 1999, personal interview, Tokyo, February 28 2002.

33 'ASEAN urged to defend stewardship of ARF process', *Japan Economic Newswire*, July 23, 1999. LexisNexis, personal interview, Tokyo, December 13 2000 (no. 2).

34 ASEAN, 'Joint Communiqué of the 32nd ASEAN Ministerial Meeting', Singapore, July 23–24 1999.

35 'Malaysia to chair meeting with Chinese officials', *New Straits Times* (Malaysia), July 27 1999, p. 8, LexisNexis.

36 Gaimushō Anzenhoshō Seisaku-Ka, 'ARF SOM Gaiyō to Hyōka'.

37 Email exchange with a participant in ARF meetings, December 2002.

38 Kenji Hiramatsu, 'Ajiataiheiyōgata no Anzenhoshōkikō wa Seiritsu Suruka', *Gaikō Forum* (special edition), 1999, pp. 120. *Yomiuri Shinbun*, September 1 1999, p. 2.

39 Personal interviews, February 28 2002 and May 30 2003.

40 Personal interviews, Tokyo, February 28, December 19 2002, and May 30 2003.

41 Ibid.

42 ARF, 'Co-chairmen's Summary Report on the Meetings of the ARF Intersessional Support Group on Confidence Building Measures held in Tokyo, Japan, on November 13–14 1999 and in Singapore, April 5–6 2000'.

43 Bruce Miller, (Director of the Asia-Pacific Section, Department of Foreign Affairs and Trade) 'Report on the Seventh ASEAN Regional Forum', Australia-CSCAP newsletter, no. 10, November 2000.

44 ARF, 'Chairman's Statement, the Seventh ARF Meeting of the ASEAN Regional Forum'.

45 ARF, 'Co-chairmen's Summary Report on the Meetings of the ARF Intersessional Support Group on Confidence Building Measures held in Tokyo and Singapore'.

46 Bruce Miller, 'Report on the First 1999–2000 Meeting of the ARF ISG on CBMs', *Australia-CSCAP newsletter*, no. 9, February 2000, p. 8.

47 Ken Jinbo, 'ASEAN Chiiki Forum to Yobō Gaikō: Tayōka Suru Yobōgaikō Gainen to Chiikiteki Tekiyō no Mosaku', *Shin-Bōeironshū*, vol. 27, no. 3, December 1999, p. 34.

48 CSCAP, 'Chairman Summary, CSCAP Workshop on Preventive Diplomacy', Bangkok, Thailand, February 28–March 2, 1999.

49 ASEAN Draft, ASEAN Regional Forum (ARF) Concept and Principles of Preventive Diplomacy, November 6 1999.

50 Alan Dupont, 'ASEAN's Response to the East Timor Crisis', *Australian Journal of International Affairs*, vol. 54, no. 2, 2000, p. 165.

51 *Mainichi Shinbun*, November 14 1999, p. 2.

52 Peter Oldham and Robin Wettlaufer, (Regional Security and Peacekeeping Division, Department of Foreign Affairs and International Trade) 'The Long Haul: Institution Building and the ASEAN Regional Forum', *CANCAPs Bulletin*, no. 27, November 2000, p. 21.

53 ARF, 'Chairman's Statement, the Seventh ARF Meeting of the ASEAN Regional Forum', Bangkok, July 27 2000.

54 Gaimushō Anzenhoshō Seisaku-Ka, 'Dai 2-Kai ARF Shinrai Jyōsei ni Kansuru ISG Kaigō, Gaiyō oyobi Toriaezu no Hyōka' (Second ISG on CBMs, Summary and Assessment), April 19 2001.

55 ARF, 'Concept and Principles of Preventive Diplomacy, Annex D to Chairman's Statement', the Eighth Meeting of the ASEAN Regional Forum, Hanoi, July 25 2001.

56 Personal interview, Tokyo, May 30 2003.

57 ARF, 'Enhanced Role of the ARF Chair', Annex B to Chairman's Statement, the Eighth Meeting of the ASEAN Regional Forum.

58 Ibid.

59 ARF, 'Co-Chairs' Paper on the Terms of Reference for the ARF Experts/Eminent Persons (EEPs)'. Annex C to Chairman's Statement, the Eighth meeting of the ASEAN Regional Forum.

60 ARF, 'Chairman's Statement, the Eighth Meeting of the ASEAN Regional Forum'.

61 *Mainichi Shinbun*, July 26, 2001, p. 2.

62 'Forum Treads Path Towards Preventive Diplomacy', *Australian Financial Review*, July 27 2001, LexisNexis.

63 ARF, 'Chairman's Statement, The Eighth Meeting of the ASEAN Regional Forum'.

64 *Asahi Shinbun*, July 26 2001, p. 7.

65 Gaimushō, 'ARF kakuryō kaigō hōjin kisha brief' (the Tenth ARF Ministerial Meeting, Transcripts of Press Conference), June 19, 2003.

66 ARF 'Chairman's Statement, the Ninth Meeting of the ASEAN Regional Forum', Bandar Seri Begawan, July 31 2002.

67 ARF 'Chairman's Statement, the Twelfth Meeting of the ASEAN Regional Forum', Vientiane, July 29 2005.
68 *Yomiuri Shinbun*, July 3 2004, p. 4.
69 ARF 'Chairman's Statement, the Eleventh Meeting of the ASEAN Regional Forum', Jakarta, July 2 2004,

Chapter 5

 1 Gaimushō Ajia-Kyoku Chiiki Seisaku-Ka (Ministry of Foreign Affairs of Japan, Asian Bureau, Regional Policy Division), 'Dai 1-Kai ASEAN Regional Forum Kōkyū Jimu Level Kaigō: Gaiyō to Hyōka' (First ARF SOM, Summary and Assessment), May 27 1994.
 2 Ibid.
 3 *Business Times*, July 23 1994, p. 3, LexisNexis.
 4 *Nihon Keizai Shinbun*, July 26 1994.
 5 Christopher W. Hughes, *Japan's Economic Power and Security: Japan and North Korea*, New York: Routledge, 1999, pp. 61–65.
 6 Gaimushō, 'ASEAN Chiiki Forum, ASEAN Kakudai Gaishō Kaigi no Gaiyō to Hyōka (First ARF Ministerial Meeting and ASEAN PMC, Summary and Assessment)', July 29 1994. *Yomiuri Shinbun*, July 26 1994, p. 4.
 7 Michael Leifer, *The ASEAN Regional Forum: Extending ASEAN's Model of Regional Security*, Adelphi Papers, no. 302, London: Oxford University Press, 1996, p. 34.
 8 Christopher R. Hughes, *Taiwan and Chinese Nationalism: National Identity and Status in International Society*, London: Routledge, 1997, pp. 91–92.
 9 Reinhard Drifte, *Japan's Foreign Policy in the 1990s: From Economic Superpower to What Power ?*, Basingstoke: Macmillan, 1996, p. 59.
10 Michael J. Green, *Japan's Reluctant Realism: Foreign Policy Challenges in an Era of Uncertain Power*, New York and Basingstoke: Palgrave, 2001, p. 80.
11 Amitav Acharya, *Constructing a Security Community in Southeast Asia: ASEAN and the Problem of Regional Order*, London: Routledge, 2001, p. 135.
12 *The Nation*, July 22 1996, cited in Sueo Sudo, *The International Relations of Japan and South East Asia: Forging a New Regionalism*, London: Routledge, 2001, p. 87.
13 *Asahi Shinbun*, October 27, 1995, (evening edition).
14 Boeicho, *Nihon no Bōei*, Tokyo, Okurasho Insatsukyoku, 1995, pp.70-74, available at: http://www.jda.go.jp/ (accessed 15/09/06).
15 Threatening language was deleted from the final draft of NDPO due to opposition from the Social Democratic Party of then Prime Minister Murayama. Michael Green and Benjamin Self, 'Japan's Changing China Policy: From Commercial Liberalism to Reluctant Realism', *Survival*, vol. 38, no. 2, summer 1996, p. 44.
16 *Nihon Keizai Shinbun*, August 3 1995, p. 8.
17 *Nihon Keizai Shinbun*, May 24 1995, p. 18.
18 *The Strait Times*, May 24 1995, LexisNexis.
19 *Business Times*, August 2, 1995, LexisNexis.
20 ASEAN Regional Forum (ARF) 'Chairman's Statement, the Second Meeting of the ASEAN Regional Forum', Bandar Seri Begawan, August 1 1995.
21 Gaimushō, 'ARF Kisha Brief' (Second ARF Ministerial Meeting, Transcripts of Press Conference), August 2 1995. 'Japan voices concern over planned nuclear tests', *Japan Economic Newswire*, August 1 1995, LexisNexis.
22 ARF, 'Chairman's Statement, the Second Meeting of the ASEAN Regional Forum'.
23 *Yomiuri Shinbun*, August 2 1995, p. 1.

24 Gaimushō, 'Dai 2-Kai ASEAN Chiiki Forum no Gaiyō to Hyōka' (Second ARF Ministerial Meeting, Summery and Assessment), August 4, 1995.
25 Yoichi Funabashi, *Dōmei Hyōryū*, Tokyo: Iwanami Shoten, 1997, pp. 403–8.
26 Ibid, pp. 385–88.
27 Yoshihide Soeya, 'Japan: Normative Constraints Versus Structural Imperatives', in Muthiah Alagappa (ed.) *Asian Security Practice: Material and Ideational Influences*, Stanford, CA: Stanford University Press, 1998, pp. 204–5.
28 *Far Eastern Economic Review*, August 15 1996, p. 28, cited in Ming Zhang and Ronald N. Montaperto, *A Triad of Another Kind: The United States, China, and Japan*, New York: St. Martin's Press, 1999, p. 71.
29 'Stop Search in Japan waters, Kono tells Qian', *Jiji Press Ticker Service*, December 19 1995, LexisNexis., *Yomiuri Shinbun*, December 19 1995, p. 27.
30 *Yomiuri Shinbun*, August 28 1996, p. 3.
31 'Japan not involved in Senkaku lighthouse', *Jiji Press Ticker Service*, July 17 1996, LexisNexis.
32 Gaikō Forum, 'Nichibei Anzenhoshō Kyōdō Sengen ni Tsuite no Kaisetsu', *Gaikō Forum*, vol. 94, 1996, pp. 156–60. Peter J. Katzenstein and Nobuo Okawara, 'Japan, Asian Pacific Security, and the Case for Analytical Eclecticism', *International Security*, vol. 26, no. 3, Winter 2001/2, pp. 158–59.
33 Akio Watanabe, 'Nichibei Anzenhoshō Kankei no Shintenkai', *Kokusai Mondai*, no. 456, March 1998, pp. 28–29.
34 *Yomiuri Shinbun*, April 15 1996, pp. 1–2, (evening edition).
35 Gaiko Forum, 'Nichibei Anzenhoshō Kyōdō Sengen', p. 160.
36 Akira Ogawa, 'Anzenhoshō Seisaku no Actor to Ishi Ketteikatei', in Gaikō Seisaku Kettei Yōin Kenkyukai (ed.) *Nihon no Gaikō Seisaku Kettei Yōin*, Tokyo: PHP Kenkyujo, 1999, pp. 152–56.
37 The issue of the declaration had been originally scheduled for November 1995, prior to the APEC summit in Osaka, but was postponed due to Clinton's cancellation due to a domestic budget crisis. Glenn D. Hook, Julie Gilson, Christopher W. Hughes and Hugo Dobson, *Japan's International Relations: Politics, Economics and Security*, London: Routledge, pp. 139.
38 For discussions on China's views of the redefinition of Japan-US alliance, see Banning N. Garrett and Bonnie S. Glaser, 'Chinese Apprehensions About Revitalisation of the US-Japan Alliance', *Asian Survey*, vol. 37, no. 4, April 1997, pp. 388–90. Thomas J. Christensen, 'China, the U. S.-Japan Alliance, and the Security Dilemma in East Asia', *International Security*, vol. 23, no. 4, Spring 1999, pp. 62–63.
39 *Wall Street Journal*, October 16. Cited in Ralph A. Cossa, 'Avoiding New Myths: US-Japan Security Relations', *Security Dialogue*, vol. 28, no. 2, 1997, p. 227.
40 *The Daily Yomiuri*, May 2 1996, p. 8, LexisNexis.
41 *Asahi Shinbun*, July 17 1996, p. 2.
42 Personal interview, Tokyo, February 28 2002. See also Hook, Gilson, Hughes and Dobson, *Japan's International Relations*, p. 221.
43 Michael Jonathan Green, 'Managing Chinese Power: The View from Japan', in Alastair I. Johnston and Robert S. Ross (eds) *Engaging China: The Management of an Emerging Power*, New York: Routledge, 1999, p. 161.
44 'Hashimoto designs a grander foreign policy: Changing balance of power in Asia has led to a more active development of regional links', *Financial Times*, January 14 1997, p. 6, LexisNexis.
45 Green, 'Managing Chinese Power', p. 163.
46 Ibid, pp. 162–63.
47 Gaimushō Anzenhoshō Seisaku-Ka (Ministry of Foreign Affairs of Japan, National Security Policy Division), 'ARF Kōkyū Jimu Level Kaigō, Gaiyō to Hyōka' (Third ARF SOM, Summary and Assessment), May 16 1996.
48 Personal interview, London, August 9 2002.

49 Gaimushō, 'ARF ASEAN PMC Kisha Brief' (Third ARF Ministerial Meeting and ASEAM PMC, Transcripts of press conference), July 24 1996, *Nihon Keizai Shinbun*, July 24 1996, p. 8.
50 'Ikeda sees security dialogue in Northeast Asia', *Jiji Press Ticker Service*, July 23 1996, LexisNexis.
51 Makoto Matsuda, 'ARF no Chūchōkiteki Arikata', in Nihon Kokusai Mondai Kenkyujo (ed.) *Ajiataiheiyō no Anzenhoshō, Heisei 8-nendo Jishu Kenkyu Hōkokusho*, Nihon Kokusai Mondai Kenkyujo, March 1997, pp. 37–38, unpublished paper.
52 Ralph A. Cossa, 'Northeast Asian Security Forum: Is such gathering possible?', *Pacnet Newsletter*, no. 19, May 14 1997. *Asahi Shinbun*, October 11 1997.
53 Green, *Japan's Reluctant Realism*, pp. 122–23.
54 Hughes, *Japan's Economic Power and Security*, p. 79.
55 *Nihon Keizai Shinbun*, July 23 1996, p. 1.
56 *The Daily Yomiuri*, June 26 1996, p. 10, LexisNexis.
57 'Russia, China urged to persuade Pyongyang to four-party talks', *Agence France Presse*, July 23 1996, LexisNexis.
58 Gaimushō Anzenhoshō Seisaku-Ka, 'ARF Kōkyū Jimu Level Kaigō'.
59 ARF, 'Chairman's Statement, the Third Meeting of the ASEAN Regional Forum', Jakarta, July 23 1996.
60 Michael Leifer, 'China in Southeast Asia: Interdependence and Accommodation', in David S. G. Goodman and Gerald Segal (eds) *China Rising: Nationalism and Interdependence*, London: Routledge, 1997, p. 168.
61 'China calms ASEAN fears over claims', *Business Times* (Malaysia), July 24 1996, p. 20, LexisNexis.
62 Richard L. Grant, 'China and Confidence Building in East Asia', in Tien and Cheng, *The Security Environment in the Asia-Pacific*, p. 310.
63 ARF, 'Chairman's Statement, the Third Meeting of the ASEAN Regional Forum'.
64 The final draft of the revised Japan-US Defence Guidelines was approved by the US-Japan Security Consultative Committee meeting in New York in September 1997.
65 *Yomiuri Shinbun*, June 6 1997, p. 1. For the details of the new defence guidelines, see 'Nichibei Bōei Kyōryoku no Tame no Shishin', *Gaikō Forum*, special edition, 1999, pp. 133–36.
66 Katzenstein and Okawara, 'Japan', p. 171.
67 *Yomiuri Shinbun*, June 6 1997, p. 2. Yoichi Funabashi, *Alliance Adrift*, New York: Council on Foreign Relations Press, 1999, pp. 422–23.
68 Rosemary Foot, 'China in the ASEAN Regional Forum: Organizational Processes and Domestic Modes of Thought', *Asian Survey*, vol. 38, no. 5, 1998, p. 435.
69 In the end, the language was not included in the Chairman's statement because of Chinese opposition. See, Jeffrey Winters, 'The Risks and Limits of a Corporate Foreign Policy', in Selig S. Harrison and Clyde V. Prestowitz, *Asia after the 'Miracle': Redefining U.S. Economic and Security Priorities*, Washington DC: Economic Strategy Institute, 1998, p. 228.
70 Funabashi, *Alliance drift*, pp. 469–71.
71 Gaimushō, 'Hōjin Kisha Brief: ARF Gozen Kaigō' (Fourth ARF Ministerial Meeting, Transcripts of Japanese Press Conference), July 27 1997.
72 'Opening Statement by H. E. Qian Qichen Vice Premier and Minister of Foreign Affairs, People's Republic of China', The Fourth Meeting of the ASEAN Regional Forum, July 27 1997.
73 Michael Yahuda, 'Chinese Dilemmas in Thinking about Regional Security Architecture', *The Pacific Review*, vol. 16, no. 2, 2003, p. 190. For discussions

on China's security concept, see Rosemary Foot, 'China's Role and Attitude', in Khoo How San (ed.) *The Future of the ARF*, Singapore: Institute of Defence and Strategic Studies, 1999, pp. 122–23. Alastair Iain Johnston and Paul Evans, 'China's Engagement with Multilateral Security Institutions', in Johnston and Ross, *Engaging China*, pp. 260–61.

74 Yahuda, 'Chinese Dilemmas', pp. 194–95.
75 Ibid, pp. 190–91. Avery Goldstein, 'The Diplomatic Face of China's Grand Strategy: A Rising Power's Emerging Choice', *The China Quarterly*, vol. 168, December 2001, pp. 836–37.
76 Foot, 'China's Role and Attitude', p. 124.
77 'Asia-Pacific security forum ends up in row over military alliances', *Agence France Presse*, March 8, 1997, LexisNexis.
78 Personal interview Tokyo, December 13 2000 (no. 2). *Asahi Shinbun*, July 24 1996, p. 3. Japanese and US hesitation to accept Indian participation in the ARF also reflected ASEAN's way of deciding it. Some ASEAN states contended that India's entry to the ARF should be endorsed automatically as long as ASEAN accepted India as an ASEAN dialogue partner. Japan and the US were highly dissatisfied with the way in which Indian participation in the ARF had been accepted by ASEAN alone without consulting non-ASEAN countries, seeing this as an unwanted extension of ASEAN's leading role. In particular, Japan was concerned that this would further increase the discontent of non-ASEAN participants over ASEAN's proprietary role, thus weakening their commitment to the ARF. Gaimushō Anzenhoshō Seisaku-Ka, 'ARF Kōkyū Jimu Level Kaigō'. Matsuda, 'ARF no Chūchōkiteki Arikata', pp. 38–39.
79 'Indonesia, China question U.S.-Japan defense changes', *Japan Economic Newswire*, July 27 1997, LexisNexis.
80 Ibid.
81 Ibid.
82 Personal interview, Tokyo, December 13 2000 (no. 2) and February 28 2002.
83 'US-China talks, Cambodian problem dominate ASEAN discussions', *Agence France Presse*, July 26 1997, LexisNexis.
84 Michael Leifer, *The ASEAN Regional Forum: A Model for Cooperative Security in the Middle East*, Canberra: Research School of Pacific and Asian Studies, Australian National University, 1998, p. 11.
85 'U.S. suspends aid to Cambodia for 30 days', *Japan Economic Newswire*, July 11 1997, LexisNexis.
86 *Yomiuri Shinbun*, July 28 1997, p. 8. 'US, China pressure Cambodians to end turmoil', *Agence France Presse*, July 26, 1997, LexisNexis.
87 Lam Peng Er, 'Japan's Diplomatic Initiatives in Southeast Asia', in Syed Javed Maswood (ed.) *Japan and East Asian Regionalism*, London: Routledge, 2001, pp. 123–25.
88 *Financial Times*, July 23 1997, p. 4, LexisNexis.
89 Green, *Japan's reluctant realism*, pp. 177–78.
90 'Japan, US insist they have unified approach on Cambodia', *Agence France Presse*, July 29 1997, LexisNexis. *Asahi Shinbun*, July 28 1997, p. 3.
91 ARF, 'Chairman's Statement, The Fourth Meeting of ASEAN Regional Forum, Subang Jaya Malaysia', July 27 1997.
92 'Cambodia, Burma and Korea top list of concerns at ASEAN forum', *Agence France Presse*, July 27 1997, LexisNexis.
93 Foot, 'China in the ASEAN Regional Forum', p. 435.
94 ARF, 'Chairman's Statement, the Fourth Meeting of ASEAN Regional Forum'.

95 Personal interviews, Tokyo, December 13 2000 (no. 1 and 2). Masashi Nishi-hara, 'Chiiki Anzenhoshō no Atarashī Chitsujo wo Mezashite: ARF no Genjō', *Gaikō Forum*, vol. 10, November 1997, pp. 35–40.

Chapter 6

1 National Institute for Defense Studies, *East Asian Strategic Review 1999*, Tokyo: National Institute for Defense Studies, pp. 49–62.
2 *Yomiuri Shinbun*, May 13, p. 1, July 1, p. 1, June 8, p. 1 and July 13. p. 1, 1998.
3 'Obuchi offers to mediate India-Pakistan talks', *Japan Economic Newswire*, July 27 1998, LexisNexis.
4 Satu P. Limaye, 'Tokyo's Dynamic Diplomacy: Japan and the Subcontinent's Nuclear Tests', *Contemporary Southeast Asia,* vol. 22, no. 2, August 2000, p. 327.
5 'Obuchi calls for Pakistan's attendance at ARF meeting', *Japan Economic Newswire*, June 13 1998, LexisNexis.
6 Gaimushō Anzenhoshō Seisaku-Ka (Ministry of Foreign Affairs of Japan, National Security Policy Division), 'Dai 5-Kai ARF SOM Gaiyō to Toriaezu no Hyōka' (Fifth ARF SOM, Summary and Assessment), May 27 1998.
7 'ASEAN officials fail to hammer out statement on Indian nuclear tests', *Agence France Presse*, July 19 1998.
8 Gaimushō Anzenhoshō Seisaku-Ka, 'Dai 5-Kai ARF SOM Gaiyō'.
9 ASEAN Regional Forum (ARF), 'Chairman's Statement, the Fifth Meeting of ASEAN Regional Forum', Manila, July 27 1998.
10 *Asahi Shinbun*, July 28 1998, p. 1.
11 Ministry of Foreign Affairs of Japan, *Diplomatic Bluebook 1999*, Tokyo, Ministry of Foreign Affairs of Japan, p. 64.
12 Cited in Limaye, 'Tokyo's Dynamic Diplomacy', pp. 326–27.
13 Sheldon W. Simon 'The Economic Crisis and Southeast Asian Security: Changing Priorities', *The NBR Analysis*, vol. 9, no. 5, December 1998, p. 7. Paul Dib, 'The Strategic Implications of Asia's Economic Crisis', *Survival*, vol. 40, no. 2, Summer 1998, pp. 13–17.
14 Amitav Acharya, *Constructing a Security Community in Southeast Asia: ASEAN and the Problem of Regional Order*, London: Routledge, 2001, p. 205.
15 Ibid, pp. 132–33. Jurgen Rutland, 'ASEAN and the Asian Crisis: Theoretical Implications and Practical Consequences for Southeast Asian Regionalism', *The Pacific Review*, vol. 13, no. 3, 2000, pp. 431–32.
16 For further details about ASEAN's intra disputes over the concept of the flex-ible engagement, see Jürgen Haacke, 'The Concept of Flexible Engagement and the Practice of Enhanced Interaction: Intramural Challenges to the ASEAN Way', *The Pacific Review*, vol. 12, no. 4, 1999, pp. 592–95.
17 Taisuke Mibae, 'ARF no Genjō to Kadai', in Nihon Kokusai Mondai Kenkyujo (ed.) *Ajiataiheiyō no Anzenhoshō (Chūkan Hōkoku)*, Nihon Kokusai Mondai Kenkyujo, March 1999, pp. 112–13, unpublished paper.
18 *The Nikkei Weekly*, July 29 1996, p. 24, LexisNexis.
19 'ARF ends without tension', *Business Times* (Singapore), July 24 1996, p. 6, LexisNexis.
20 'Albright scores deteriorating situation in Myanmar', *Japan Economic Newswire*, July 27 1998, LexisNexis.
21 *The Japan Times*, August 5 1998, LexisNexis.
22 Michael J. Green, *Japan's Reluctant Realism: Foreign Policy Challenges in an Era of Uncertain Power*, New York and Basingstoke: Palgrave, 2001, pp. 179–84.
23 'Japan urges Thailand to play mediating role in Myanmar', *Japan Economic Newswire*, August 7 1998, LexisNexis.

24 Christopher W. Hughes, 'Japan's "Strategy-Less" North Korea Strategy: Shifting Policies of Dialogue and Deterrence and Implications for Japan-US-South Korea Security Cooperation', *Korean Journal of Defense Analysis*, vol. 12, no. 2, 2000, pp. 169–72.

25 Robert M. Uriu, 'Japan in 1999: Ending the Century on an Uncertain Note', *Asian Survey*, vol. 40, no. 1, January/February 2000, pp. 39–41.

26 'Japanese Foreign Minister proposes new dialogue channels in Asia', *Japan Economic Newswire*, June 3 1999, LexisNexis.

27 For instance, in the Japan-US summit talks held in September 1998, Obuchi called for extending the four-way talks to the six-party talks with the participation of Japan and Russia. Foreign Minister Kōmura Masahiko also proposed the six-party talks in 'the Future of Asia forum' in Tokyo in June 1999. Ibid. 'Seoul to Pursue 6-Nation Talks Separately From 4-Party Talks', *Korea Times*, October 25, 1998, LexisNexis.

28 Personal interview, Tokyo, December 13 2000 (no. 2).

29 *Nihon Keizai Shinbun*, July 26 1999, p. 1.

30 Gaimushō, 'Kōmura Daijin no ARF oyobi ASEAN PMC Shusseki, Kisha Brief', ARF (Foreign Minister Kōmura in Sixth ARF Ministerial Meeting and ASEAN PMC, Transcripts of Press Conference), July 27 1999.

31 'US, Japan and South Korea issue stern warning to N Korea on missile test', *Agence France Presse*, July 27 1999, LexisNexis.

32 ARF, 'Chairman's Statement, the Sixth Meeting of the ASEAN Regional Forum', Singapore, July 26 1999.

33 Gaimushō Anzenhoshō Seisaku-Ka, 'Dai 6-Kai ARF Kakuryō Kaigō no Gaiyō to Hyōka' (Sixth ARF Ministerial Meeting, Summary and Assessment), July 26 1999.

34 Personal interviews, Tokyo, December 13 2000 (no. 2).

35 *Yomiuri Shinbun*, September 14 1999, p. 1.

36 Joseph Y. S. Cheng, 'China's ASEAN Policy in the 1990s: Pushing for Regional Multipolarity', *Contemporary Southeast Asia*, vol. 21, no. 2, August 1999, p. 193.

37 'Philippines orders probe of Chinese boat sinking', *Japan Economic Newswire*, July 20 1999. 'ASEAN considers draft code of conduct for S. China Sea', *Japan Economic Newswire*, July 20 1999, LexisNexis.

38 'Albright says good US-China ties a priority', *Agence France Presse*, July 26 1999, LexisNexis.

39 Wu Xinbo, 'U.S. Security Policy in Asia: Implications for China-U.S. Relations', *Contemporary Southeast Asia*, vol. 22, no. 3, December 2000, p. 486.

40 *Yomiuri Shinbun*, July 2 1999, p. 2.

41 Gaimushō, 'ARF Kakuryō Kaigō, Kisha Brief'(Sixth ARF Ministerial Meeting, Transcripts of Press Conference), July 27, 1999.

42 'US calls for early diplomatic solution to Spratlys dispute', *Agence France Presse*, July 26 1999, LexisNexis.

43 'ASEAN considers draft code of conduct for S. China Sea', *Japan Economic Newswire*, July 20 1999, LexisNexis. From the Chinese perspective, the main problem with ASEAN's code of conduct was that it was indented to freeze the status quo. Beijing was concerned that this would legitimise what it regards as the other claimants' illegal occupation of Chinese territory. China's position remains that China alone has indisputable sovereignty over the Spratly Islands. See 'A Code of Conduct for the South China Sea?', *Jane's Intelligence Review*, October 27 2000.

44 'Speaker condemns Chinese rejection of Spratly code', *BBC Summary of World Broadcasts*, December 1 1999, LexisNexis.

45 Jean-Pierre Cabestan, 'Taiwan in 1999: A Difficult Year for the Island and the Kuomintang', *Asian Survey*, vol. 40, no. 1, January/February2000, pp. 172.

46 *The Strait Times*, July 27 1999, p. 2, LexisNexis.
47 *Asahi Shinbun*, July 27 1999, p. 2.
48 *Yomiuri Shinbun*, July 26 1999, p. 8.
49 Angel Rabasa and Peter Chalk, *Indonesia's Transformation: And the Stability of Southeast Asia*, Santa Monica, CA: Rand, 2001, pp. 21–23, available at: http://www.rand.org/publications/MR/MR1344 (accessed 15/09/06).
50 Mary Caballero-Anthony, 'Partnership for Peace in Asia: ASEAN, the ARF, and the United Nations', *Contemporary Southeast Asia*, vol. 24, no. 3, December 2002, pp. 542–43. For a positive assessment of ASEAN's roles in the East Timor crisis, see Alan Dupont, 'ASEAN's Response to the East Timor Crisis', *Australian Journal of International Affairs*, vol. 54, no. 2, 2000, pp. 163–70.
51 Anthony, 'Partnership for Peace in Asia', p. 541.
52 G. V. C. Naidu, *Multilateralism and Regional Security: Can the ASEAN Regional Forum Really Make a Difference?*, Asia Pacific Issues, no. 45, Honolulu: East-West Center, August 2000, p. 7, available at: http://www.eastwestcenter.org// (accessed 15/09/06).
53 'Joint effort draws N Korea to forum', *The Nation*, July 27 2000, LexisNexis. *Nihon Keizai Shinbun*, April 29 2000, p. 6.
54 'Japan undecided on N. Korea's ARF bid', *Japan Economic Newswire*, May 11 2000, LexisNexis. Personal interview, Tokyo, December 13 2000 (no. 2).
55 Personal interviews, Tokyo, December 13 2000 (no. 2 and 3).
56 'N. Korean entry will let ARF deal with real issues', *The Strait Times*, July 13 2000, p. 22, LexisNexis.
57 *Asahi Shinbun*, July 27 2000, p. 1.
58 *Financial Times*, July 29 2000, p. 9.
59 ARF, 'Chairman's Statement, the Seventh Meeting of the ASEAN Regional Forum', Bangkok, July 27 2000.
60 For detailed discussions of Japan's approach to TMD, see Christopher W. Hughes, 'Sino-Japanese Relations and Ballistic Missile Defence (BMD)', in Marie Sóóderberg (ed.) *Chinese-Japanese Relations in the 21st Century Complementarity and Conflict*, London: Routledge, 2001, pp. 69–87. Michael J. Green and Toby F. Dalton, 'Asian Reactions to U.S. Missile Defence', *NBR Analysis*, vol. 11, no. 3, November 2000, pp. 15–20.
61 Hughes, 'Sino-Japanese Relations', p. 84. Green and Dalton, 'Asian Reactions to U.S. Missile Defence', p. 16.
62 'Cabinet ministers agree to join U.S. TMD research', *The Japan Times*, December 19 1998.
63 See, Kori J. Urayama, 'Chinese Perspectives on Theater Missile Defense', *Asian Survey*, vol. 40, no. 4, July/August 2000, pp. 600–7. Thomas J. Christensen, 'China, the U.S.-Japan Alliance, and the Security Dilemma in East Asia', *International Security*, vol. 23, no. 4, Spring 1999, pp. 75–77.
64 'China slams U.S. planned missile shield', *Japan Economic Newswire*, July 27, 2000, LexisNexis.
65 *Yomiuri Shinbun*, July 28 2000, p. 7.
66 Green and Dalton, 'Asian Reactions to U.S. Missile Defence', pp. 48–50.
67 'China, Russia take aim at US missile defence program', *Agence France Presse*, July 27, 2000, LexisNexis.
68 Gaimushō Anzenhoshō Seisaku-Ka, 'Dai 7-Kai ASEAN Chiiki Forum Kakuryō Kaigō, Gaiyō to Hyōka' (Seventh ARF Ministerial Meeting, Summary and Assessment), August 4 2000.
69 'ASEAN concerned with U.S. proposals on missile', *Japan Economic Newswire*, July 23 2000, LexisNexis.
70 *Asahi Shinbun*, July 28 2000, p. 7.

71 Gaye Christoffersen, 'The Role of East Asia in Sino-American Relations', *Asian Survey*, vol. 42, no. 3, May/June 2002, pp. 369–96.

72 'Chinese Foreign Minister Tang Jixan meets US counterpart Powell', *BBC Monitoring Asia Pacific*, July 25 2001, LexisNexis.

73 'China welcomes positive U.S. role in Asia-Pacific region', *Xinhua General News Service*, July 25 2001, LexisNexis.

74 *The New York Times*, July 17 2001, p. 1.

75 Gaimushō, 'ARF Kakuryō Kaigō Kisha Brief' (Eighth ARF Ministerial Meeting, Transcripts of Press Conference), July 25–26 2001.

76 National Institute for Defense Studies, *East Asian Strategic Review 2002*, Tokyo: National Institute for Defense Studies, pp. 155–58.

77 *Mainichi Shinbun*, July 28 2001, p. 6.

78 ARF, 'Chairman's Statement, The Eighth Meeting of the ASEAN Regional Forum'.

79 'South China Sea code still sailing in rough waters', *Agence France Presse*, July 25 2000, LexisNexis.

80 Ralf Emmers, *Cooperative Security and the Balance of Power in ASEAN and the ARF*, New York: RoutledgeCurzon, 2003, pp. 140–45. See also Declaration on the Conduct of Parties in the South China Sea, Phnom Penh, Cambodia, November 4 2002.

81 Gaimushō Anzenhoshō Seisaku-Ka, 'Dai 8-Kai ASEAN Chiiki Forum Kakuryō Kaigō no Gaiyō' (Eighth ARF Ministerial Meeting, Summary), July 25 2001.

82 *Yomiuri Shinbun*, July 26 2001, p. 2.

83 See, ARF, 'Chairman's Statement, the Ninth Meeting of ASEAN Regional Forum', Bandar Seri Begawan, 31 July 2002.

84 For details, see ARF, 'Statement on Measures Against Terrorist Financing', July 30 2002.

85 For a discussion on the US-ASEAN cooperation on counter-terrorism, see, David Capie, 'Between a hegemon and a hard place: the "war on terror" and Southeast Asian-US relations', *The Pacific Review*, vol. 17, no. 2, 2004, pp. 223–48.

86 Hideaki Mizukoshi, '9.11 Dōji Tahatsu Tero kara Ichinen: Nihon wa Nani wo Shitekitaka', in Akihiko Tanaka (ed.) *Atarashii Sensō Jidai no Anzenhoshō: Ima Nihon no Gaikōryoku ga Towareteiru*, Tokyo: Toshishuppan, 2002, pp. 165–66.

87 ARF, 'Chairman's Statement, the Ninth Meeting of ASEAN Regional Forum', Bandar Seri Begawan, June 18 2003.

88 For details, see 'Statement on Cooperative Counter-Terrorist Action on Border Security', July 18 2003.

89 For details, see ARF, 'Statement on Strengthening Transport Security Against International Terrorism', Jakarta, July 2 2004.

90 For details, see ARF, 'Statement on Information Sharing and Intelligence Exchange and Document Integrity and Security in Enhancing Cooperation to Combat Terrorism and Other Transnational Crimes', Vientiane, July 29 2005.

91 'Accord on measures to block terror funds', *The Strait Times*, August 1 2002, LexisNexis.

92 For a discussion on the evolution and problems of ASEAN's cooperation on counter-terrorism, see Jonathan T. Chow, 'ASEAN Counterterrorism cooperation since 9/11', *Asian Survey*, vol. 45, no. 2, March/April 2005, pp. 302–21.

93 Ibid, p. 319–21.

94 *Yomiuri Shinbun*, July 3 2004, p. 7.

95 Gaimushō, 'Dai 12-Kai ARF Kakuryō Kaigō, Kisha Brief'(Twelfth ARF Ministerial Meeting, Transcripts of Press Conference), July 30, 2005.

96 Christopher W. Hughes, Japan-North Korea Relations: From the North-South Summit to the Koizumi-Kim Summit, *Asia-Pacific Review*, vol. 9, no. 2, 2002, p. 62.

97 'Powell meets North Korean FM in highest-level contact in two years', *Agence France Presse*, July 31 2002, LexisNexis.

98 Robert Uriu, 'Japan in 2002: An Up-and-Down Year, but Mostly Down', *Asian Survey*, vol. 43, no. 1, January/February 2003, p. 86.

99 *Nihon Keizai Shinbun*, August 5 2002, p. 7.

100 *Yomiuri Shinbun*, September 18, p. 4.

101 Kyung-Ae Park, 'North Korea in 2003: Pendulum Swing between Crisis and Diplomacy', *Asian Survey*, vol. 44, no. 1, January/February 2004, pp. 141–42.

102 *Nihon Keizai Shinbun*, June 19 2003, p. 9. See also ARF, 'Chairman's Statement, the Tenth Meeting of the ASEAN Regional Forum', Phnom Penh, June 18 2003.

103 'US cool to Cambodian mediation offer in North Korean dispute', *Agence France Presse*, February 20 2003, LexisNexis. *Mainichi Shinbun*, March 5 2003.

104 *Asahi Shinbun*, June 19 2003, p. 2 and p. 3.

105 Kyung-Ae Park, 'North Korea in 2004: *Pendulum Swing between Crisis and Diplomacy*', *Asian Survey*, vol. 44, no. 1, January/February 2004, pp. 141–43.

106 *Yomiuri Shinbun*, June 25, 2004, p. 7.

107 'Powell says he restated views on arms with North Korean', *The New York Times*, July 2 2004, p. 4, LexisNexis.

108 'Japan, N. Korea agree on abductees family reunion in Indonesia', *JiJi Press Ticker Service*, July 1 2004, LexisNexis.

109 *Yomiuri Shinbun*, September 21, 2005, p. 7.

110 'ASEAN ministers disappointed at Japan, U.S. absence from coming forum', *Jiji Press Ticker Service*, July 27, 2005, LexisNexis.

Chapter 7

1 Personal interviews, London, August 9 2002, and Tokyo, December 13 (no. 2 and 3) 2000, and May 30 2003.

2 Rosemary Foot, 'China in the ASEAN Regional Forum: Organizational Processes and Domestic Modes of Thought', *Asian Survey*, vol. 38, no. 5, 1998, p. 439.

3 Personal interview, London, August 9 2002.

4 Personal interview, Tokyo, April 22 and May 30 2003.

5 Personal interviews, Tokyo, April 8 and 21 2003. Peter J. Katzenstein and Nobuo Okawara, 'Japan, Asian Pacific Security, and the Case for Analytical Eclecticism', *International Security*, vol. 26, no. 3, Winter 2001/2, pp. 174–75. Brian L. Job, 'Track 2 Diplomacy: Ideational Contribution to the Evolving Asia Security Order', in Muthiah Alagappa (ed.) *Asian Security Order: Instrumental and Normative Features*, Stanford, CA: Stanford University Press, 2003, p. 272.

6 Personal interview, Tokyo, May 30 2003.

7 Personal interviews, Tokyo, December 13 2000 (no. 2 and no. 3) and February 28 2002. See also, Hongying Wang, 'Multilateralism in Chinese Foreign Policy: The Limits of Socialisation', *Asian Survey*, vol. 40, no. 3, May/June, 2000, p. 484.

8 Satoshi Morimoto, *Anzenhoshōron: Nijūisseiki Sekai no Kiki Kanri*, Tokyo: PHP Kenkyujo, 2000, p. 323, (author's translation).

9 Personal interview, Tokyo, February 28 2002.

10 While the Asian and Oceanian Affairs bureau strongly supported Japan's accession to the TAC, the Foreign Policy bureau and the North American

Affairs bureau opposed it on the grounds that it would not only undermine Japan's relations with the US but also constrain Japan from levelling criticism at the internal affairs of ASEAN countries, such as human right issues in Myanmar. Yoichi Funabashi, 'TAC Ajia heno Kakugo', *Shūkan Asahi*, December 11, 2003, available at: http://www.asahi.com/column/funabashi/ja/ (accessed 15/09/06).

11 Personal interview, Tokyo March 17 2003. Hiroshi Yasui, 'Ajiataiheiyō Chiiki ni Okeru CBM no Shinten to Shomondai', in Nihon Kokusai Mondai Kenkyujo (ed.) *Ajiataiheiyō no Anzenhoshō (Chūkan Hōkoku)*, Nihon Kokusai Mondai Kenkyujo, March 1999, p. 135, unpublished paper. For details of Japan's policy toward CBMs at the bilateral level see Benjamin L. Self, 'Confidence-Building Measures and Japanese Security Policy', in Ranjeet KSingh (ed.) *Investigating Confidence-Building Measures in the Asia-Pacific Region*, Washington DC: The Henry L. Stimson Center, 1999, pp. 25–50.

12 Personal interviews, Tokyo, February 28 2002 and May 30 2003.

13 See, Bōei Mondai Kondankai, Nihon no Anzenhoshō to Bōeiryoku no Arikata: Nijūisseiki e mukete no Tenbō, Tokyo: Ōkurashō Insatsukyoku, 1994.

14 For details of American reaction to the Higuchi report, see Patrick M. Cronin and Michael J. Green, *Redefining the US-Japan Alliance :Tokyo's National Defense Program*, McNair Paper no. 31, Institute for National Strategic Studies, National Defense University, November 1994. Yoichi Funabashi, *Dōmei Hyōryū*, Tokyo: Iwanami Shoten, 1997. Masahiro Akiyama, *Nichibei no Senryaku Taiwa ga Hajimatta: Anpo Saiteigi no Butaiura*, Tokyo: Akishobō, 2002, pp. 44–56.

15 Michael J. Green, *Arming Japan: Defense Production, Alliance Politics, and the Postwar Search for Autonomy*, New York: Columbia University Press, 1995, p. 147.

16 Yoichi Funabashi, *Dōmei Hyōryū*, pp. 292–95. For details of Japan-US trade frictions during this period, see Kenichirō Sasae, *Rethinking Japan-US Relations: An Analysis of the Relationship between Japan and the US and Implications for the Future of Their Security Alliance*, Adelphi Papers, no. 292, London: IIS/Brasseys, 1994, pp. 32–46.

17 Funabashi, *Alliance adrift*, p. 266.

18 See, Bōeichō, *Heisei 8-nendoban Bōeihakusho 1996*, Tokyo: Ōkurashō Insatsukyoku, 1996, pp. 107–18.

19 Michael J. Green, 'Balance of Power', in Steven K. Vogel (ed.) *U.S.-Japan Relations in a Changing World*, Washington, DC: Brookings Institution Press, 2002, p. 27.

20 Personal interview, Tokyo, February 28 2002.

21 Mibae Taisuke, 'ARF no Genjō to Kadai', in Nihon Kokusai Mondai Kenkyujo, *Ajiataiheiyō no Anzenhoshō*, p. 119, unpublished paper.

22 Atsushi Kusano, 'Taigai Seisaku Kettei no Kikō to Katei', in Tadashi Aruga (ed.) *Kōza Kokusaiseiji: Nihon no Gaikō*, Tokyo: Tokyo Daigaku Shuppankai, 1989, pp. 62–63.

23 Gaimushō, *Gaikō Seiho 2003*, Tokyo, Gaimushō, available at: http://www.mofa.go.jp/mofaj/gaiko/bluebook/index.html (accessed 15/09/06).

24 Personal interviews, Tokyo, December 19 2002.

25 The same also applies to JDA. While a policy regarding the Japan-US security alliance is exclusively handled by the Defence Policy Division, which is the most powerful division in JDA, multilateral security activities are dealt by the International Planning Division, which holds relatively a weak position in JDA in the light of budget and human resources.

26 Personal interview, Tokyo, February 15 2002.

27 Peter J. Katzenstein and Nobuo Okawara, *Japan's National Security: Structures, Norms, and Policy Responses in a Changing World*, Ithaca, NY: Cornell University, 1993, pp. 27–29. MOFA consists of five regional (North American, Asia-Oceanian, Latin American and Caribbean, Middle Eastern and Africa, European affairs) and six functional bureaus (Foreign Policy, Intelligence and Analysis, Economic Affairs, Economic Cooperation, Treaty). Ministry of Foreign Affairs of Japan, *Diplomatic Bluebook 2000*, Tokyo, Ministry of Foreign Affairs of Japan, 2000, p. 195.

28 Personal interviews, Tokyo, December 13 2000 (nos 1. 2. 3), February 28, April 22 and December 19 2002, March 5 (no. 1), 7, May 30 2003 and London, August 9 2002.

29 The Foreign Policy Bureau was established in 1993 in response to a heavy criticism against MOFA for a poor diplomatic response to the Gulf Crisis. It was placed over other bureaus, including the powerful North American Bureau, to control Japan's overall foreign and security policy and to diminish the influence of the US factor in foreign policy decision making. Green, *Japan's Reluctant Realism*, p. 59.

30 For discussions on the role of politicians in Japan's foreign policy making, see Yasunori Sone, 'Nihon no Seiji to Gaikō', in Aruga, Uno, Kido, Yamamoto and Watanabe (eds) *Kōza Kokusaiseiji*, pp. 93–124. Kent E. Calder, 'The Institutions of Japanese Foreign Policy', in Richard L. Grant (ed.) *The Process of Japanese Foreign Policy: Focus on Asia*, London: Royal Institute of International Affairs, 1997, pp. 1–24. Kuniko Nakajima, 'Nihon no Gaikō Seisaku Kettei Katei ni Okeru Jiyūminsyutō Seimu Chōsakai no Yakuwari', in Gaikō Seisaku Kettei Yōin Kenkyukai (ed.) *Nihon no Gaikō Seisaku Kettei Yōin*, Tokyo: PHP Kenkyujo, 1999, pp. 70–105.

31 Green, *Japan's Reluctant Realism*, p. 46.

32 Katzenstein and Okawara, *Japan's National Security*, p. 45.

33 Reinhard Drifte, *Japan's Foreign Policy in the 1990s: From Economic Superpower to What Power?*, Basingstoke: Macmillan, 1996, p. 18.

34 For discussions on the impact of the domestic political realignment on Japan's foreign policy making, see Mike Mochizuki, *Japan: Domestic Change and Foreign Policy*, Santa Monica, CA: Rand, 1995, Green, *Japan's Reluctant Realism*, pp. 35–47.

35 Jiyūminshutō, Anzenhoshō Chōsakai, *Nichibeianpo Taisei no Kyōtekiigi*, Tokyo, April 9, 1996, available at: http://www.jimin.jp/jimin/index/seisaku.html (accessed 15/09/06). See also, Jiyūminshutō and Jiyūtō, *Anzenhoshō no Kihonteki na Kangae*, Tokyo, January 13 1999, available at: http://www.jimin.jp/jimin/index/seisaku.html (accessed 15/09/06).

36 Funabashi, *Dōmei Hyōryū*, pp. 324–25. Nakajima, 'Nihon no Gaikō Seisaku', pp. 86–87.

37 For details, see Jiyūminshutō, Gaikō Chōsakai, 'Jiyūminshutō Gaikō Seisaku no Shishin', *Gekkan Jiyūminshu*, no. 531, June 1997, pp. 94–112.

38 Jiyūminshutō Kokubō Bukai, *Waga Kuni no Anzenhoshō Seisaku to Nichibei Dōmei: Ajiataiheiyō Chiki no Heiwa to Hanei ni Mukete*, Tokyo, March 23, 2001, available at: http://www.jimin.jp/jimin/index/seisaku.html (accessed 15/09/06).

39 Thomas J. Christensen, 'China, the U.S.-Japan Alliance, and the Security Dilemma in East Asia', *International Security*, vol. 23, Spring 1999, pp. 64–65.

Conclusion

1 Ministry of Foreign Affairs of Japan (MOFA) 'Speech by Prime Minister of Japan Junichiro Koizumi: Japan and ASEAN in East Asia – A Sincere and

Open Partnership', Singapore, January 14 2002, available at: http://www.mofa.-go.jp/region/asia-paci/pmv0201/speech.html (accessed 15/09/06).

2 MOFA, *The Diplomatic Bluebook 2003*, Tokyo, Ministry of Foreign Affairs of Japan, available at: http://www.mofa.go.jp/policy/other/bluebook/index.html (accessed 15/09/06).

3 *Asahi Shinbun*, April 28 1998, (evening edition).

4 'Joint Statement, U. S. -Japan Security Consultative Comittee', Washington DC, May 1 2006.

5 *Yomiuri Shinbun*, December 19 2003, p. 1.

6 *Yomiuri Shinbun*, December 11 2004, p. 10.

7 'U.S. urges govt to rethink collective defense ban', *The Daily Yomiuri*, March 28 2004, LexisNexis.

8 For instance, in May 2003, Abe Shinzō, Deputy Chief Cabinet Secretary at that time, criticised the government interpretation of the Constitution, stating that 'in general, the possession of a right comes after the exercise of the right. The Cabinet Legislation Bureau has provided misleading explanations. This is a major issue that we must address'. Prime Minister Koizumi has also supported this, stating that 'it is desirable for Japan to be allowed to participate in collective defence activities and to help defend its allies in the event of regional crises'. 'Contingency laws – Overcoming the taboo; Diet lays groundwork for new defense policy', *The Dairy Yomiuri*, June 8 2003, LexisNexis. These voices have helped provide great momentum to a political debate on the revision of the Constitution focusing on Article 9 and the right of collective defence, and indeed the focus of Japanese constitutional debate has already moved from whether it should be revised to how it should be reformed. In September 2003, Prime Minister Koizumi assigned the LDP Research Commission on the Constitution to draw up the draft for the new Constitution by Fall 2005. The interim report of the research commission, released in February 2004, suggests that the Constitution stipulate the country's right to participate in collective security and defence. 'LDP panel: Call SDF a military', *The Daily Yomiuri*, April 15 2004, LexisNexis.

9 For instance, an opinion poll conducted by *Yomiuri Shinbun* in March 2004 indicates that a majority of respondents called for constitutional revisions for the sixth straight year. Of the respondents, 44 percent support the revision of Article 9. *Yomiuri Shinbun*, April 2 2004.

10 Robert Uriu, 'Japan in 2003', *Asian Survey*, vol. 44, no. 1, January/February 2004, p. 177.

11 The government's incremental approach to expanding the military dimension of Japan's security policy has increasingly come under attack from the new generation of politicians since, in their view, such an approach is no longer sufficient to cope with the rapidly changing regional security environment. In the face of North Korea's missile and nuclear threat, they have begun openly to question the country's exclusively defensive policy and to discuss the possibility of possessing offensive capabilities that would allow Japan to strike an enemy missile base. In 2003, the head of JDA, Ishiba Shigeru, for instance, argued in the Diet that 'it was worthwhile to consider launching a pre-emptive attack if it had evidence that North Korea was about to launch missiles aimed at Japan'. Ishiba's insistence represents not only his own personal view but also that of a group of younger legislators, known as 'the commission of young members of the Diet for the establishment of a national security framework for the new century', comprised of 167 Diet members from both the ruling JDP and the Democratic Party of Japan (DPJ), the largest opposition party. They call for a review of the nation's defence capabilities and more reciprocal relationship in the Japan-US security alliance in the view of the country's independence and its

national interest, See, *Yomiuri Shinbun*, August 14 2003, p. 1 and March 18 2004, p. 1. *Nikkei Shinbun*, February 23 2004, p. 1.

12 Liberal Democratic Party, Security Research Council, *The Current Importance of the Japan-U.S. Security Arrangement*, Tokyo, March 1996, available at: http://www.jimin.jp/jimin/index/seisaku.html (accessed 15/09/06).

13 Glenn D. Hook, Julie Gilson, Christopher W. Hughes and Hugo Dobson, *Japan's International Relations: Politics, Economics and Security*, London: Routledge, 2001, p. 224.

14 Katzenstein and Okawara, 'Japan', p. 174.

15 John Garofano, 'Power, Institutions, and the ASEAN Regional Forum: A Security Community for Asia?', *Asian Survey*, vol. 42, no. 3, May/June 2002, pp. 508–9.

16 Personal interviews, Tokyo, December 13 2000 (no. 2), February 28 and December 19 2002.

17 Ibid. *Business Day* (Thailand), November 4 1998, LexisNexis.

18 Amitav Acharya, 'Regional Institutions and Asia Security Order: Norms, Power, and Prospects for Peaceful Change', in Muthiah Alagappa (ed.) *Asian Security Order: Instrumental and Normative Features*, Stanford, Ca: Stanford University Press, 2003, p. 211.

19 Personal interview, Tokyo, December 19 2002.

20 For discussions on socialization in international instituions, see, *interalia*, Alastair Iain Johnston, 'Treating International Institutions as Social Environments', *International Studies Quarterly*, vol. 45, no. 3, 2001, pp. 487–515. Jeffrey T. Checkel, 'Why Comply? Social Learning and European Identity Change', *International Organization*, vol. 55, no. 3, 2001, pp. 553–88. Alexandra Gheciu, Security Institutions as Agents of Socialization? NATO and the New Europe , *International Organization*, vol. 59, no. 2, 2005, pp. 973–1012. Alastair Iain Johnston, 'Conclusions and Extensions: Toward Mid-Range Theorizing and Beyond Europe , *International Organization*, vol. 59, no. 2, 2005, pp. 1013–44.

Index

ABM (Anti-Ballistic Missile) treaty 138
Acharya, Amitav 9, 87–88
ACSA (Acquisition and Cross-Servicing Agreement) 112, 171
Afghanistan 21, 143, 144, 171
Agreed Framework accords 145
Aizawa Ichirō 144
Akiyama Masahiro 108
Alatas, Ali 32, 121, 128, 129
Albright, Madeleine 120, 121, 129, 132, 134, 136
al-Qaeda 143
AMM (ASEAN Ministerial Meeting) 44, 48, 97, 107, 127, 139
AMM SOM 132
Annual Security Outlook *see* ASO
Anti-Ballistic Missile treaty *see* ABM treaty
Anti-Terrorism Special Measures Law 171
APEC (Asia-Pacific Economic Cooperation) 3, 26, 28, 34, 46, 50, 57, 81, 118, 135, 140
ARF Ministerial Meeting 175; First (1994) 64–65, 69, 107–8; Second (1995) 69–70, 72, 88, 89, 109–10; Third (1996) 74–75, 114–16; Fourth (1997) 77–78, 79, 94, 117–18, 119–20, 121–22; Fifth (1998) 79, 80, 81, 94, 125, 126, 128, 129; Sixth (1999) 82, 95–96, 97, 131, 132, 134, 135; Seventh (2000) 83, 99, 101, 136, 137, 138–39, 152; Eighth (2001) 102–3, 140–41; Ninth (2002) 83, 84, 142, 144, 145; Tenth (2003) 84, 103, 143, 145, 146; Eleventh (2004) 84, 103–4, 143, 146; Twelfth (2005) 83, 84–85, 103, 143, 144, 147–48, 155

ARF-RMIC (ARF Regional Maritime Information Center) 83
ARF SOM 70, 74–75, 80, 89, 175; First (1994) 65–66, 67, 68, 107; Second (1995) 69, 71, 72, 109; Third (1996) 114; Fourth (1997) 78–79, 93, 128–29; Fifth (1998) 125–26; Sixth (1999) 82, 97; Seventh (2000) 96; Eighth (2001) 102; Eleventh (2004) 146
ARF Track Two Conference on Preventive Diplomacy 95
ARF Troika 99
ASEAN (Association of Southeast Asian Nations) and constructivist theory, 9; in relation to Japan's growing interest in security multilateralism 20, 23, 26, 28–29, 31–32, 34, 39, 41; in relation to security multilateralism 1992–93, 44, 45, 47, 53–54, 56; in relation to Japan's policy on evolution of CBMs in ARF 64–65, 66, 67, 68, 70, 71, 72, 73, 74, 75, 77, 78, 81, 85; in relation to Japan's challenges for promoting PD in ARF 87, 89, 91, 92, 94, 95–96, 96–97, 98, 99–101, 102, 103, 104; in relation to Japan and multicultural dialogue in ARF 1994–97 107, 108, 110, 113, 114, 116, 117, 118, 119, 120, 121; in relation to Japan and multilateral security dialogue in ARF 1998–2005 126, 127–28, 128–29, 132–33, 134, 135, 136, 137, 139, 141, 142, 143, 144, 145, 148; in relation to Japan's changing conception of ARF 151, 152, 153, 154, 156, 157; in relation to future direction of Japan's security policy 173–74
ASEAN + 1 133